Urban Transportation Policy
and Management

Urban Transportation Policy and Management

Milton Pikarsky
Regional Transportation Authority
of Northeastern Illinois

Daphne Christensen
Chicago Transit Authority

Lexington Books
D.C. Heath and Company
Lexington, Massachusetts
Toronto

Library of Congress Cataloging in Publication Data
Pikarsky, Milton.
  Urban transportation policy and management.

  Includes bibliographies and index.
  1. Urban transportation policy—United States. 2. Transportation—United States—Passenger traffic. I. Christensen, Daphne,
joint author. II. Title.
HE308.P44   388.4'0973   76-21933
ISBN 0-669-00955-5

Published simultaneously in Canada

Printed in the United States of America

International Standard Book Number: 0-669-00955-5

Library of Congress Catalog Card Number: 76-21933

Contents

List of Figures

List of Tables

Preface

Transportation management is just now beginning to come into its own. While there are those who would have us believe that in the "good old days before the automobile," well managed transit organizations were an accomplished fact, it is important to realize that in reality, the tools of good management were never employed.

It is true, of course, that public transportation in the 19th century was characterized by constantly increasing patronage and relatively stable costs, a milieu where one might assume good management practices existed, especially considering the monopoly position enjoyed by individual firms.

However, the transportation environment that then existed obscures the fundamental flaws incorporated in the public transit systems structure by the lack of real management. The fact is that by the time most transportation organizations were merged under more centralized control, they were burdened by overwhelming debt and there existed a situation where there was little relationship between the capitalization, the real value of the assets, and the earning power of the enterprise. Their monopoly position allowed these organizations to meet their debt service responsibilities but did not permit modernization and expansion typical of a well-managed growth industry.

The cause is obvious from a brief review of the origin and early development of the transportation organizations. At the time of the Civil War, most cities were small and many different companies operated within limited areas, using horse-drawn vehicles. The invention of the electric car, which could travel longer distances at greater speeds, together with the tremendous growth in population, resulted in the merger of smaller firms in order to link monopoly franchises in contiguous areas and to accommodate the financing of the more capital intensive electric systems. In larger mergers, all the previous debt was assumed by the newly formed company and this debt was usually "watered" to cover both capital investment and monopoly interests. Thus, the final merger of local firms was based on previous sublayers of incorporation and bore the compounded accumulated debt from preceding acquisitions.

Problems appeared at the turn of the century. Rising costs of labor, materials and equipment became perpetual concerns. This was especially the case when the operating franchises were controlled by municipal governments whose officials were reluctant to raise the fares of a public service and who were concerned for the public need. With overinflated capital structure, in order to keep operating, the only resort was often seriously deferred maintenance.

The development of the automobile, together with the increasing heavy federal expenditures which promoted automobile usage, soon began to erode public transportation ridership. Prior to 1926, transit ridership had increased yearly in direct proportion to the population increase, and the ratio of people to cars was 11 to 1. As this latter ratio of cars to people increased, transit ridership decreased and at the same time there occurred an increasing federal intervention in local affairs. The massive federal expenditures for automobile related improvements were matched by subtle, but just as important, local expenditures for traffic control, street lighting and other amenities and soon spelled the demise of public transportation systems everywhere.

Not until the 1960's when faced with the crisis of impending complete collapse, was federal action directed toward saving the threatened public transit systems. Only in recent times has it become clear that the private automobile, by itself, cannot provide the efficiency necessary to sustain a high level of mobility for Americans with varied travel needs and preferences. To finance an automobile fleet that would have the capacity to meet all our mobility demands would cost, in land use investment, pollution and congestion, far beyond what society can afford. Aside from economic considerations, there are life-style adjustments that would have to be made, dominated by waste and inconvenience, dependence on a complicated chain of material supplies and services, and loss of aesthetic values. The energy crisis is but one of a series of frightening specters of what can happen when fuel is no longer available to meet the demands of unlimited private transportation.

Today, reassessments of transportation priorities are taking place at all levels of government and important changes are occurring in the consciousness of responsible citizens. Public support is far from what will eventually be necessary, but the trend is clearly visible to those who would see.

The time is not far off when the challenge to management will be very clear: to reverse the deterioration process and produce an efficient, reliable, convenient and acceptable public transportation alternative for an affluent public, under circumstances which are financially feasible. There is no question that this must and can be accomplished. The task will require new management skills and techniques.

Understanding how a problem came about does not always aid in the solution but it does give clues as to where to look for better answers. The research and analysis presented here represent a first step toward understanding transit's dilemma from a policy/management viewpoint in order to meet the unique challenge of public transportation in today's complex, interdependent society.

1 Introduction

The upsurge of interest in urban transportation reflects the changing mood of the nation. After a decade of meager and grudging assistance, there is evidence of revitalized financial and ideological support to an extent that surprises those both inside and outside the transit community. It is one of the indicators of change within our society.

Evidence of change is everywhere [1]. The youth movement of the 1960s that rejected materialistic goals and startled the older generation seems to have taken root. The texture of national life that can be glimpsed through trips to the bookstore and through popular songs, television shows, and conversations in train stations reveals an increasing awareness of the need for a happier and more fulfilling existence and concern for the deeper meaning of life generally. There is less talk of larger automobiles and thinner television sets and more talk about where we are going, whether the endless quests for consumer goods is a satisfying goal, and of what makes a happy and good life. Thus, the trends of the times are marked by change and, almost before our eyes, new and different national attitudes develop.

Transportation reflects national attitudes in a curious way. In one sense, transportation is a powerful force, a basic kind of organizing force underlying all national activity. Much of the social, political, and economic well-being of the nation is dependent on the transportation system. Yet, transportation is a tenuous mechanism, perceived by the public only in a peripheral way. Perhaps this is the reason why it has been so easy to neglect certain aspects of transportation, such as urban transit, without realizing the ultimate impact on the hopes and aspirations of the nation's people.

Whatever the reason, our public transportation systems languished and nearly disappeared. Looking back over the deterioration of the transit systems, it seems more a case of piecemeal decisions based on expediency rather than on intent and purposeful action.

The history of transportation has frequently reflected misjudgments and careless decisions, based on the most narrow and immediate considerations, and has shown astonishing lack of awareness as to what the effects would be.

The perceptive critic Lewis Mumford saw what he termed "the fatal mistake" in sacrificing every form of transportation to the private auto-

1

mobile; he said the most charitable assumption was that Congress and the nation's people had not the faintest notion of what they were doing. He prophesied the damage to our cities and countryside, and the undermining of efficiency in this "ill-conceived, imbalancing of transportation." Considering that today transportation consumes 60 percent of the petroleum used in this country, and considering the relationship between energy and high rates of unemployment and inflation, the resulting inefficiencies appear to have surpassed anything Mumford projected.

Therefore, it is not surprising that today public transportation has been receiving increased attention from all sectors of society. Conservationists and economists, for example, worry about this nation's disproportionate use of energy and its relationship with the rest of the world. Within the past decade, polls show a striking reversal in public attitude indicating strong public support for a less wasteful life-style and a more responsible behavior.

The ranks of public transit supporters cover a wide social spectrum: environmentalists, sociologists, urbanologists, the elerly and the handicapped, downtown businessmen, bankers, realtors, and land-use planners all see potential benefits of urban transit to areas of their special interest. Although it would be an exaggeration to say that transit has become a focal point of the strongest forces operating within the society, it is surely true that transit is high among the primary interests of some of the most responsible groups in the nation today.

Yet, in spite of this encouraging support, transit remains in a greatly weakened condition. Although some face lifting is evident on most of the older capital facilities, many built in the last century, operation continues only with unreasonably high maintenance costs. Endless planning activities dominate considerations for new systems with little new construction underway. Ridership is generally holding its own after massive declines, but new services do not yield the hoped-for revenue. It is almost as if most people believe public transportation to be a wonderful thing, but for *other* persons, both to use and to finance.

Exasperating slowness characterized urban transit's reemergence into the mainstream of American life. Although a remarkable influx of federal funds shoring up transit has prevented collapse, there has been little progress in integrating transit into the budgetary and tax policies with the nation's other transportation systems. For example, the juxtaposition of revenues, biased in the direction of the private passenger car, is nearly imperceptible to the public. In vivid contrast, public transit is funded only through fare-box contributions or from direct subsidy. This subliminally biased bookkeeping remains a formidable obstacle and one receiving inadequate consideration.

Thus, although the upsurge of interest in urban transit is commendable, reflecting a change of mood within the nation, the lack of progress is disquieting. The elements of practical power still seem deeply rooted in automobile interests with transit receiving mostly rhetoric and minimal assistance. Because many of the complex issues involving transit management and policy are acknowledged only in the most simplistic terms, there is need to reconsider the choices and alternative and with greater care and conviction.

The Impact of History

A time perspective is crucial to achieving an understanding of the present dilemma of transportation. The sequence of historical circumstances has played an often dominant part in forming what has become a severely unbalanced transportation system. Embryonic developments often cast long shadows; they portend not only future events but can grow to become intertwined enigmas left for later generations to unravel and set right. This has been the case for transportation.

Not long ago, the benefits of American democracy, both material and spiritual, seemed to shower down almost as a matter of course. In every field, and transportation was no exception, technical advances brought new ways of doing things. These were incorporated by an eager people without concern for future difficulties. As a time when this nation was busy settling the West and building an industrial colossus, the emphasis was on fulfilling the American Dream, with little thought toward the consequences. The words of the poet Yeats, "In dreams begin responsibility," were not yet understood.

Reflecting the unperceptive nature of this period of rapid growth, the automobile is without equal. Invented in 1872, the auto was at first little more than a plaything of the rich. The organization of Ford Motor Company in 1903 changed that, and is generally considered the beginning of the automobile age. Initially Ford brought out an expensive Model K and found it did not sell well. The true market proved to be in the $500 "Workingman's Car," the Model T.

The nation was becoming obsessed with labor-saving machinery of all kinds and the automobile was perfect for the time. Labor rates and the standard of living were rising, people had more money and more time, and a pressing need for increased mobility permeated the country. Furthermore, the auto was hailed [1] as an environmental improvement, eliminating horses and their ubiquitous soilings of the streets. Had there been a technology assessment conducted that predicted the auto would become a major air pollutor, it would probably have been dismissed as incompetent.

Automobile sales rose steadily, discouraged only by the depression years. Yet in another sense, the depression actually stimulated auto-mobile production in future times through the entry of the federal government into the housing market.[a] Although the intent of the Federal Housing Authority and other similar agencies was to stimulate the building industry and provide jobs for the unemployed during the depression era, the net result was to encourage building on new land, farther from town, creating the so-called urban sprawl. Other massive federal investments followed, primarily in the form of highway construction, which in 1976 totaled over $76 billion for interstate construction alone.

The same historical events were to have a devastating effect on public transportation. Before the automobile, federal road programs, and the Federal Housing Authority, public transit was the crucial catalyst of expansion for cities. As the population began to grow at the end of the last century, special pressures were placed on transit services to offer service over greater distances; until then most transit companies had been small, independent organizations serving but a limited area. The potential profits from the growing ridership resulted in high prices being paid for new franchises and for mergers of existing smaller firms, often with little relationship between capitalization and the real value of the assets and the earning power. Through the monopoly franchise, the companies could usually pay their debt service and maintain their equipment as long as ridership increased rapidly and the costs of labor and material remained stable.

Several things happened over a period of years. Wages and materials increased in price beyond anything that had been projected previously. Further, the population surge expected for large cities having transit did not materialize. Although the population for the nation as a whole continued at a steady pace, the growth of the major cities slowed from the earlier exponential rises. The encroachment of the automobile, as a distinct effect separate from the slower population rise, did not begin until the mid-1920s. For example, at the start of World War I, there were about 2 million cars in the country but only 1 in 60 persons owned one. By 1920, 1 in every 13 owned a car, and by 1926 the ratio dropped to 1 out of 11. Until 1926 transit riders had increased in direct proportion to the population increase of the area served, but after 1926 transit ridership declined. (The single exception was during World War II when gasoline was rationed and automobiles curtailed.) Transit companies began having a hard time making ends meet.

---

[a] The Federal Housing Authority (FHA) was founded June 27, 1934, for the purpose of guaranteeing mortgages. Until this time, owning a house was difficult since nearly 50 percent was required as down payment, with loans paid typically in three to five years at painfully high interest rates. In the first 40 years of its existence, the FHA was to insure over $182 billion aiding over 50 million households and families. This federal investment in turn encouraged large private investments, leading to the vast urban sprawl landscapes surrounding most metropolitan regions.

Not all of the problems were related to ridership decline. A study of the economic commitments, laws, administrative actions, and legislative and political decisions of the first half of this century shows a growing trend to actions of all kinds that were contrary to the interests of transit. In some cases, transit was hurt by the often punitive legislation against rails. These resulted in part from certain excesses of the railroads especially in selective, preferential fare structure in freight handling. In the early part of this century, transporting of passengers was especially lucrative. (The term "commuter" in fact comes from the practice of reducing or commuting fares for patrons.) Yet, the legal and legislative rulings against the railroads was to hurt many commuter rail operations as well.

In other cases, decisions were unrelated to service practices. For example, one congressional act, the Holding Company Act of 1935, made it mandatory that all utility companies divest themselves of interest in transit, in the belief that transit received unfair advantage. The history of rapid transit service and of the nation's progress as a whole would most likely be quite different today had transit ownership been permitted by the utility companies.

There are also documented instances where automobile companies bought up rapid transit lines for the purpose of reducing the competition of the rapid rail service, forcing the use of motor buses or private automobiles. In one such instance, General Motors was found in violation of antitrust laws. Yet, there is little history of public protest. When fares were raised to cover increasing costs, ridership declined. It was not until 1961 that the federal government acknowledged public transportation to be an important entity essential to the well-being of the nation and action was initiated to prevent total collapse of public systems.

Clearly, the dimensions of the urban transportation problem are so enormous and the potential input for federal funds so great as to foster an extremely cautious attitude regarding transit management. It was realized at the outset that strong transit management had to be developed first. This was proven to be among the most challenging of tasks since public management is constrained in ways that private management is not.

Public Management Constraints

In comparing public with private management, three distinctive methods of practice stand out:

1. Public management must be concerned with the public good first and budget matters second, as opposed to private management where the profit is considered the guiding yardstick for performance.
2. Public transportation management is subject to constraints not placed

on private management and these restrictions prevent cost-saving actions that might normally be practiced by private management. The labor protection agreement under Section 13C of the Urban Mass Transportation Act is the key source of these differences.

3. Public management is directly involved with policy formation and interaction with the government bureaucracy to a greater degree than is private management. This calls for special skills in dealing with the governmental influence structure and legislative processes.

Public management is concerned with what might be called total benefit bookkeeping for the society as a whole. Almost any public transit system could operate at a profit if it functioned only at rush hour. However, some people work at night and could not continue employment if transportation were not available. Operating the transit system at night therefore may increase the deficit but at the same time keep people employed and off public welfare roles so that the total benefit to the community is increased.

Private industry may also engage in profit-losing campaigns but for a purpose. An airline, for example, may choose to take a losing service to a small, isolated community in order to obtain the franchise for a major, profit-generating run. A manufacturing firm may sell an item below cost to stimulate customer interest and build later profits. A public transportation organization, however, often takes on services that do not pay their entire expense and may never do so in terms of the transit bookkeeping. For example, a Sunday fare may be cut in half to build ridership, get people out who normally would not go, which in turn acts as a public service, benefiting business and improving the quality of life of the people. A reduction in fare of 50 percent, for example, would require a 100 percent increase in ridership to make up the difference. Most transit organizations would be satisfied with an increase more of the order of 50 percent in terms of public service needs. These kinds of judgment decisions do not arise in private industry.

This difference between goals and objectives of the public versus private organization manifests itself in other aspects. For example, the goal of an automobile manufacturer is to put out a good product that is marketable and profitable. But defining the goals of good public service is more difficult, and hence not easily evaluated or appreciated.

Transportation goals are closely interlinked and interdependent on other national goals. Although these other general goals are not yet clearly articulated, most people have certain images of a "good life" and a pleasing environment even though all of the details are not mapped out [2]. It is probably fair to say that there is a growing national awareness for greater economic stability, a need for a generally improved quality of life in terms of freedom from congestion, inconvenience, and pollution, for a more efficient use of resources, for a general reduction in national anxieties, and for an improved relationship between man and his environ-

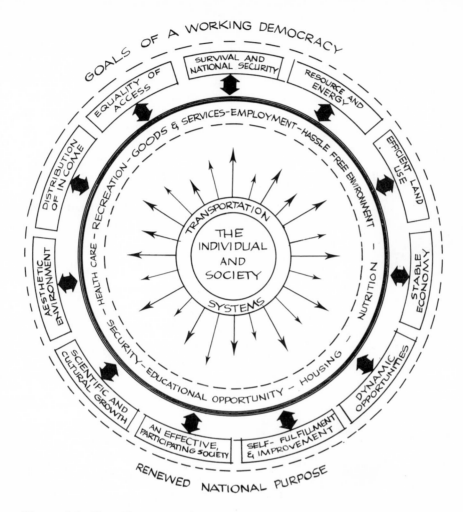

Figure 1-1. How Transportation Affects the World of the Individual and the Nation.

ment. Transportation objectives must therefore be constructed in such a way as to relate to these ideas and needs.

Transportation systems permeate the world of the individual and affect areas vital to individual needs and aspirations. These quests for a better life in turn interact with the major responsibilities and goals of the democratic structure eventually leading to readjustments and a renewed national purpose. In statistical terms, transportation accounts for 20 percent of all national expenditures (GNP), 16 percent of federal taxes collected, 10 percent of civilian investment, and 12 percent of total employment. (See figure 1-1.)

Another important difference between private and public management is in the area of labor protection agreements, which in this country apply generally to public but not private organizations. This is not the case in Europe, for example, where most manufacturers are prevented from reducing their work force even though it means losing profits. There private firms, such as Volkswagen, when overstaffed for the market, resort to such enticements as early retirement schemes to induce workers to leave. In England, when the financial reserves of Chrysler did not permit maintaining operation with the existing labor force, the government gave direct cash subsidies to maintain plant operation rather than face the welfare costs that would accompany unemployment with a plant shut down. In this country, such things are rare occurrences with only the financial assistance of the Lockheed Aircraft Corporation and certain railroads coming to mind.

The pattern of free enterprise as it is practiced here in fact is characterized by seasonal and recession-type unemployment. Of course, the threat of large labor layoffs can affect governmental policy with striking force.[b] These observations notwithstanding, a new professional manager, coming into a firm that has low profit for investment or red ink on the ledgers, is praised for "turning around" the organization even though this may mean reductions in the work force, or use of scarce resources, or other actions that reflect on the nation's balance sheets but not on those of the individual company. This narrow view of corporate behavior, so successful in building the nation's economy in the past, is now coming under closer scrutiny.[c]

Public management, however, does not have this kind of flexibility because of labor-protection agreements. In transportation, the so-called Section 13C agreement specifies that no action can be taken by public management that works to the disadvantage of existing labor practices, and that proposed changes must have the consent of organized labor.

The point is most vividly illustrated in studying what happens when a

---

[b] An interesting example of how this threat works is shown by the objection of the automobile manufacturers to the federal tax considered for discouraging purchase of large cars as a means of energy conservation. On April 29, 1975, T. A. Murphy, chairman of General Motors, wrote to Congressman Al Ullman (who in January 1975 succeeded Wilbur Mills as chairman of the House Ways and Means Committee) that of the 100,000 employees working on large-car production, a $3 billion investment, "many would be out of work immediately, and intense hardship could fall on them and the communities in which they reside." Consideration of a big car company energy tax was subsequently dropped.

[c] Biting insight was shown in a *Saturday Review* magazine cartoon by James Stevensen: at a board of directors meeting the chairman is shown saying: "I'm pleased to tell you, gentlemen, that in addition to serving the public, helping find answers to some of the world's problems, improving the quality of life in America and providing new and better products for the consumer, this quarter we made a *bundle*." (Copyright © 1976 by permission of *Saturday Review* and James Stevensen.)

public authority takes a failing, privately operated transit company. Under normal circumstances, new management might try to close out losing operations and build potentially profitable ones, and would try to eliminate excessive costs and needless expense. The classic case is of the railroads not being able to lay off firemen even though diesel or electrically operated engines no longer require firemen. Public management simply does not have the authority to impose cost-conserving measures at the expense of labor. Management of a new bus company would be frustrated in several ways. It is not free to devise more efficient routes, for example, since this might result in a reduced work force and loss of jobs. Management cannot seek to employ new technology that would reduce the work force. New controls that would permit a rapid transit train to be operated by a single individual, eliminating the conductor, could not be employed unless organized labor agreed. Similarly, a bus company cannot purchase new *articulated buses* (that is, oversized buses having a flexible accordion-like structure midbody for easy maneuverability) for the purpose of carrying more passengers per driver and thus reducing the number of drivers required. Before such equipment could be purchased, agreement with a relevant labor union is required.

In managing a bus company, a private firm will, of necessity, deal with regulatory agencies when applicable, and, in some cases, unions; they may also seek and receive grants. Public management is however subject to labor-protection agreements and in addition, must work together with citizen groups, such as the elderly and the handicapped, to develop new legislation and improved guidelines for administering existing legislation as well as seek a broader base of revenues from within the benefited sectors of society to obviate the need, eventually, for direct governmental subsidy. (See figure 1-2.)

Even simple rearrangements of operating personnel require consideration of the labor-protection agreements. For example, a public transit firm may find that during the off-peak service, a station may no longer be serving patrons in sufficient numbers to justify presence of a ticket agent. In such cases the passengers can simply "pay on train," to the conductor. Yet, such practices reduce the number of employees required and cannot be done without union negotiation. No action of any kind can be taken in the interests of efficiency without labor agreement.

These labor-protection agreements force the development of two types of special managerial skills that have been slow in coming into being. First, it is necessary to develop a body of techniques and a literature designed to eliminate obsolete or damaging work rules that hinder both management and labor. In many cases, because of the separation of work functions and the divisions in management responsibilities, there is difficulty in identifying long practiced rules that need revision. There is also a

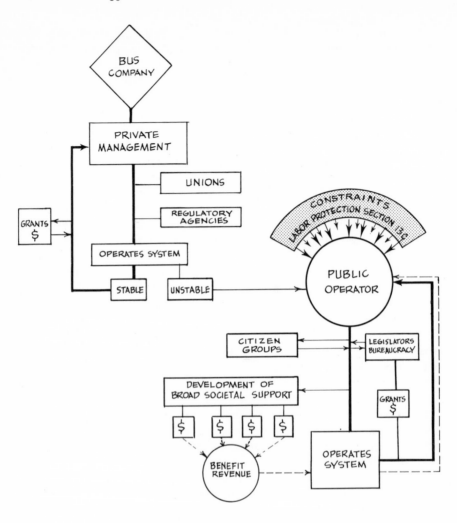

Figure 1-2. Private Management Compared with Public Management Functions.

practical public relations problem in advertising the gains made by management since many union members, not understanding all of the factors involved, might look on such concessions as weakness in their leadership and withdraw support.

This nation has adopted a national policy of full employment and it is from this policy that these labor-protection agreements arise. Although the implementation of this policy often makes the unions sound like villains, and there may be cases in which this is true,[d] the policy itself and the problems that arise are part of the continuing effort of the federal government to bring about full employment. It happens, that because of past circumstances, the transit industry feels this full employment policy more than most others.

Consequently, it is necessary for public management to find useful work for those job categories no longer required. Organized labor is in general interested in total number of jobs and pay scales, rather than in preserving specific job assignments. It becomes an essential part of a well-run function, presumably where the new job categories would provide useful service and be a part of an improved financial condition. Creative activities such as this are, however, slow to become a part of normal operation of large bureaucracies that characterize major transit organizations.

Such constraints do not apply at all to private management, whether in public transportation or any other concern although private firms often find themselves in similar situations with individual union agreements. Generally, these Section 13C agreements all comprise actions that free enterprise would consider an invasion of corporate rights. The net effect of such agreements is to further unbalance the nation's ground transportation system in favor of the private automobile, since privately owned automobile companies are not subject to these restraints, as is clear from the unemployment problems of this industry.[e] The foregoing is not meant to imply either that private ground transportation organizations should be subject to Section 13c-type agreements or that such agreements should be removed from public organizations. The point is that statements that automobile companies have good management and that public transit does not is to ignore the difference in the constraints imposed on public organizations.

A different kind of distinction between private and public management occurs with regard to policy. It is generally recognized [2] that profession-

---

[d] For example, in March 1976 an agreement to have Southern Railway take over 460 miles of Penn Central track to prevent abandonment of service was blocked by the Brotherhood of Railway Clerks even though 12 other unions had agreed, including the nation's biggest, the United Transportation Union. The dispute arose over the fact that Penn Central wage rates were higher. Southern agreed to pay the increased rates for all current employees but said future employees would be paid at Southern's regular scale, in a compromise worked out by Secretary of Transportation William T. Coleman, Jr.; he later said the union's refusal was an "exercise in unreasonableness and irresponsibility." This comment quoted nationwide in the media, referred to only one small union. The responsible behavior of the majority of unions was usually not mentioned.

[e] As an example of how recession hurts employment, at the end of 1974, more than 25 percent of the automobile industry's 700,000 hourly workers had been laid off. Automobile sales were 23 percent below what they had been the year before.

al managers in private enterprise do not make policy in the same sense that public management does. The basic guiding policy for a corporate entity is already understood to be that of maximizing profits in some sense. Private management, therefore, seeks to make qualitative judgments and decisions that best carry out this policy. In this broad spectrum of activities, successful private managers become adept at giving their organization a sense of direction and frequently become masters at developing opportunities in the marketplace. It is always a process that at least in principle depends on the "facts" of the matter.

By contrast, public management works in an area dominated by federal legislative-making procedures and must interface with the vast federal bureaucracy in what is said to be an environment where "the facts don't matter." Actually it is more a case of politicians and members of the bureaucracy often being more concerned as to how actions are perceived rather than the exact nature of what is being done. In this sense, "facts" are changeable, and can be viewed in different ways. Unlike private industry, where profits and losses are quantified and relatively fixed, in spite of possible bookkeeping adjustments, the benefits and success of most bureaucratic undertaking is less identifiable, and costs and expenditures are subject to greater variation in shifting and categorizing.

The approach of the political world differs in other ways as well. Unlike the executive boardroom, the political arena is one in which too careful or precise a description of any issue is not favored, and "facts" of the political world, can change abruptly.[f]

A wise legislator, for example, favors less distinct shaping of the issues than a businessman or engineer might prefer, and for a very good reason: any subject not now in debate may suddenly be up for negotiation. It is wise to keep as many options and alternatives open as possible to enhance bargaining power. Yet, it is scarcely an atmosphere that would feel familiar to the professional corporate manager.

The practice of circumlocution to obscure the endorsing of an idea is another method of practice common to the political world but foreign to most managers and professionals. In transportation especially, many of the principal participants, skilled in negotiation, may well be more interested in developing compromising language than in the technical facts that transportation planners and engineers may feel of paramount importance.

---

[f]One interesting illustration of this occurrence was the enactment of the National Traffic and Motor Vehicle Act of 1966. In spite of several years of persuasive technical arguments, the Senate was not convinced. It was not until the president of General Motors, James Roche, admitted on March 22, 1966, that his organization had been deliberately harassing Ralph Nader, the leading proponent for safety regulation, that the Senate reacted, passing the legislation unanimously.

Again, the facts of the situation do not carry the same weight as other considerations.[g]

Comprehending the rules and nature of the bureaucratic world is another skill to be learned by the public manager. Indeed, the bureaucratic decision-making process may at first glance not even appear rational to the professional private enterprise manager.

It might be assumed, for example, that since the governmental bureaucracy seeks the same goals and is motivated toward the same accomplishments as is the most thoughtful citizen, its decisions supposedly would reflect this shared concern. Actions might be presumed to flow directly and unambiguously from these decisions, but the reality of the situation is much more complicated.

The participants in federal level national policy resolution, although sharing some of the same images and goals as most concern citizens, often find it difficult to agree on a problem solution. Clearly any decision will affect their own careers, and the goals and missions of their organizations, as well as the positions and prestige these organizations have within the government hierachy. Objective attitudes are bound to suffer when so closely interlinked with personal gain.

Different individuals, depending on their relative level and position, may sense different personal dangers or opportunities, different ways to manifest old grievances, and different ways to aid an ally when presented with a new activity. However, it is the combination of individuals acting together in the various organizational structures that determines what can be accomplished on local levels. What such an organization does or does not do is crucial to present concerns.

Any organization within a bureaucracy necessarily favors policies and strategies that its members believe will make the organization (as they define it) more important. Each organization tries to protect its essential functions by taking on additional responsibilities if it believes that failure to do so would jeopardize sole control of its essential activities. It also will reject new functions that tend to lead to joint control operations with another involved organization. Therefore, an organization may accept a function initially to keep others from having it, but then reject that same function if it grows successfully in spite of tacit internal pressures to the

[g]The first documented use of the term "operating assistance" rather than the more descriptive "operating subsidy" was in 1956 by Hollman D. Pettibone, chairman of the Mayor's Central Area Committee. Pettibone had a talent for finding terms on which conflicting interests could agree. He managed to draft a statement that all members of the committee found acceptable, including Wayne A. Johnston, president of Illinois Central Railroad; he had emphatically opposed subsidies for the Chicago Transit Authority, saying, "I don't get one. Why should they?"

contrary. The organization also will tend to deprive funds and key personnel from functions viewed as peripheral.

Thus, many of the activities of the bureaucracy may have little relation to the technical problems for which local governments seek assistance. Yet, these are the practical aspects of the situation and ways and means must be found by urban transit management, or any other public management doing business with the government, to deal with the bureaucracy as it exists, there being no other alternative.

Since the history of the growth of government is a continued and expanding involvement of private business, all members of management, not just public management, find themselves at one time or another involved with the federal bureaucracy. The question is one of degree. For urban transportation, it is an essential aspect of doing business. Having access, and the "proper doors opened" is crucial to getting things done and relates directly to the issue of being able to function effectively within the bureaucracy and the various elements of the structure of influence.

Long-range Challenges

Today, managers of both private and public organizations often resort to short-term, incremental directives and policies, hoping for an immediate, measurable achievement. For example, a public official, someone associated with a strongly regulated industry, may wish to stop certain impending legislation or technical development that in the short term could be perceived as detrimental to his organization's immediate interests without consideration for the long term. Similarly, the manager of a private firm seeks to increase significantly the value of the firm's stock as a measurable and visible accomplishment without thinking of long-range consequences. The advantages to long-term research investments and similar risks are increasingly not considered in the types of decisions and choices currently pursued in all levels of much of the nation. One reason sometimes given is that with the nation's goals and obectives unclear, and in the face of dramatic change, incremental, short-range actions are perceived as being safe.

Not long ago the nation was viewed in a different light, as a more stable society, so that a Ford, a Firestone, or a Rockefeller could look into the future and undertake long-range technological development with confidence as to the affect on the total economy, and in terms of building a family dynasty and personal monuments. Under conditions of rapid change, this type of activity is less frequent than before. It is considered natural that professional managers plan to stay in a given organization only about five years before moving upward, usually in another firm.

Thus, a manager in the petroleum industry may see the best approach for his personal interests as investing less in research, in order to build profits and stock dividends, or to promote petroleum use, rather than build meaningful conservation policies and alternatives. These later considerations, crucial though they may be in the long run, do not contain specific, identifiable, and measurable events within a short-time frame, corresponding to the individual's perception of how long the job position will be occupied. Yet, the ultimate success of the organization may depend much more on these long-range strategies and goals rather than on short-range, highly visible, apparent achievements, which in the long range may be detrimental.

The true challenge to management is, therefore, not in increasing obvious short-range measurable performances based on immediate, apparent concepts of success—nor in engaging in activities to stop certain technologies or policies from being adopted that might have a short-term negative influence in spite of long-term advantages. Rather, it is in developing a broader perception of what needs to be done and undertaking appropriate investments and actions even though the measurable time frame of these activities may be longer than the anticipated employment span of the administrator or manager. These factors, so important in public transportation management, are little recognized by other spheres of management nor appreciated by the general public, which is evidence as to how widespread short-term performance criteria have become.

The challenge is, therefore, one of changing perceptions in a society where accomplishments are evaluated on a short-term basis. Short-range, limited-risk investments found in today's industrial and business communities produce gains too small to satisfy needs of a resource-constrained society. Increased perception and insight can lead to an action level closer to the investment-accomplishment arena of the entrepreneurs of an earlier era. (See figure 1-3.) An added complication is that all areas of activity impinge on every other area of activity; not only are there strong domestic level interactions, but international connotations as well, as responsible management becomes increasingly complex.

Management of Crises

Because of the multiplicity of pressures within a democratic system, and the tendency of democracies to operate solely on the principle of advocacy rather than on anticipatory principles, it has often been said that "the management of crises" is the customary response of government. This is especially true of transportation where virtually every change in policy followed some type of national crisis. It must now be observed that this

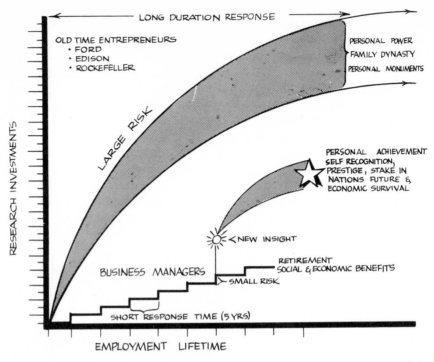

Figure 1-3. Increased Perception Needed to Alter Investment-Risk Choices.

habitual reliance on crisis management and the repeated failure to act on forecasts and projections of the most obvious nature in itself constitutes a crisis of frightening proportions.

Consequently, one of the major goals of the present effort is to examine strategies and actions that can aid in shifting away from the crisis-response syndrome. The hope is that if some of the inner workings of urban transportation are put in clearer view, it ought to be possible to stimulate a variety of response mechanisms throughout the society to create a better climate for a more logical approach to existing problems.

Given the strong interdependency of transportation with other forces operating within the society, special goals and objectives are difficult to articulate in a specific sense [3]. It is more a question of what should be done, what kind of investment should be made and how progress can be evaluated; it involves knowing what the alternatives are, whether the long-range benefits are adequate for the needs, and how policies can be articulated to reflect these general conclusions; it involves knowing how to work within the political process; it means having patience and persistence. Specifically, it means:

1. To undertake sensible trade-offs in the face of resource depletion. To achieve the benefits of high mobility, but to avoid the expense and other environmental disadvantages of urban sprawl.

2. To find ways of living in harmony with the environment; to be less wasteful and more aware of the consequences of our actions. We cannot continue, with one-sixth of the world's population, to use 30 percent of the world's supply of energy. Urban transportation offers an efficient alternative to some of the present wasteful practices.

3. To become better match makers; to take what we have in the way of materials, energy, money (stored labor), manpower, and time to meet the needs. One example of this concept would be the deliberate transfer of federal funds to cities for construction of efficient urban transit systems to conserve oil resources for use in rural communities.

4. To modify institutional arrangements to improve efficiency and productivity. Regionalism in transportation is an example of this as is aggregation of productive farm land into larger production units.

5. To resist simplistic solution in the face of tremendously complex problems and to find ways of measuring progress and giving rewards consistent with broader, long-range goals. The nation cannot continue to fund endless highways and sociological experiments of marginal benefit at the expense, for instance, of reasonable transit systems for urban areas.

6. To understand better the consequences of our actions; to develop the power to see what our actions mean ultimately in terms of costs or benefits to individuals and organizations as well as to the nation as a whole. Because of the interdependency qualities of transportation, technical assessments are especially complex. Better forecasting methods are required.

7. To respond both to the basic needs of individuals (higher quality shelter, improved health care, job opportunities, and recreation), as well as to perceived needs such as the hunger to know and the wish to improve and be fulfilled and to decrease levels of anxiety and fear. Urban transportation is closely intertwined with human opportunity and aspirations in ways obvious for the poor and disadvantaged but applicable to all economic levels of society.

8. To encourage increased participation in policy development by scientists and engineers, the academic and business communities, industrialists, and professionals, so that resulting policy reflects a combination of scientific, technical, and political skills. Transportation has long suffered from attention only by those who have something to gain or lose.

9. To find useful and workable techniques for "getting things done," and for becoming part of the solution rather than part of the problem.

Major Themes

In synthesizing the major activities and directions in public transportation today, certain concepts appear throughout the analysis and constitute major themes that can be categorized as follows:

Underlying Forces in Transportation Policy: One of the major themes permeating this work is developing an awareness for basic policy questions and the question of what can be done to improve matters. To an overwhelming extent, we are crisis oriented. Comprehensive rational analysis plays only a small part and actions often reflect expediency rather than forethought and insight. As a consequence, crisis decisions may undermine the strength of the system, placing original goals and objectives out of reach. These considerations arise not only in such matters as balance between highway and public transit construction, but in such critical areas as municipal fiscal policy, and energy and resource management.

Regionalism: The basic concept of regionalism has been growing for several decades within all areas of governmental influence across the nation. The approach to regionalism here does not concentrate on searching for a uniform set of criteria to divide the nation into a set of mutually exclusive regions or in defining complex patterns of varying purposes and needs as regions superimpose and overlap each other. Rather this work emphasizes the advantages of modifying existing institutional arrangements as a major objective. The emphasis is on practical problems, such as the technical, political, and jurisdictional disputes that arise; of special interest are legislative and administrative changes in the federal government that are more complementary (or at least not destructive) to local political constraints.

Technical Rather Than Intuitive Analysis: It is an unfortunate reality of our time that important decisions and policy judgments have been based on comfortable intuitive arguments often later found to be invalid. Transportation literature abounds with erroneous conclusions based on incorrect data or data applied to inappropriate situations. This constitutes one of the most serious problems facing transportation management today.

Making Government Work Better: Government impinges on all sectors of the economy, the business community, and on industrial and academic communities. The problems of "getting things done" and in dealing with a growing bureaucracy pervade modern life. It is not enough to decide how things must be done in principal; it is also a matter of making them happen if objectives are to be realized. Some urban centers have found ingenious ways of achieving at least moderate success in the face of all kinds of barriers. Although their performance is admirable, they illustrate the need to reduce common barriers.

Legislative Choices: Legislators are very much concerned about deciding what is worth doing, about what is really happening with ongoing programs, whether the people are getting their money's worth, how things are known, what kind of evidence exists, and how reasonable progress can be measured. Effective management responds to these needs at all levels. Public transit especially faces a difficult task in providing better quantitative description of cost-benefit performance to provide Congress with the necessary data and insight to make better choices.

Budgetary Information and the Bureaucracy: Public officials and government always need two kinds of information; namely, they want to know what is being accomplished and what the objectives are. This differs in some respects from the orderly analysis found in most company board rooms. Congressional hearings ring with the questions: What have you accomplished and what purpose did it serve? Government is always deeply involved in trying to find out how much it costs to achieve a given objective, and whether appropriate funds exist. This is often an exasperating task, since budgetary information is not always presented in useful ways, and because public issues are complex and subject to varying analysis and interpretation so it is frequently difficult to determine just what is being received for the money spent. These questions permeate every level of public transportation today; the federal budgetary process is the most powerful tool of the bureaucracy and easily the most dominant factor in public transit development.

To Remedy and Not Just Manage: And to recognize the difference.

Commentary: Urban Transportation Policy and Management

This nation has a tremendous capacity for accomplishment. The capacity, however, for taking responsibility for accomplishments with long-range views is less than adequate. It involves, among other things, balancing individual welfare against community welfare. In terms of transportation, this means balancing the individual's preferences in terms of mobility, as exemplified by the automobile, against community welfare, as exemplified by the use of public transportation in combination with and complementary to the personal automobile.

2 Urgent Issues in Public Transportation

One of the most striking aspects of urban transportation is how little the crucial issues have changed in this decade of federal assistance. Although urban transit has survived and not disappeared from the scene, the issues of greatest concern remain largely as they were when the Urban Mass Transportation Act of 1964 was passed. It is well to take a hard look at what these issues are.

Most of the urgent problems of public transportation are of two basic types: One is associated with increasing costs; the other is associated with human perceptions. Rising costs affect transit, first, through construction of system and purchase of capital investments and, second, through the rapid escalation of operating expense. Something in the way of perceptions is involved here, too, since how much of a rise in cost and how seriously it is viewed are tied to how one perceives the outcome. In this country, very large cost increases in airport or highway construction are accepted as a matter of course but relatively small increases in costs associated with public transit are frequently viewed as devastating.

The second type of issue, that of perceptions, is broadly of two kinds: first, there is the question of improving ways in which the public perceives transit as a mechanism for generating advocacy support for legislation and financial support and, second, there is question of how transit operators perceive the needs of the public as expressed in strategies to increase ridership, reduce crime, improve routes and schedules and other ridership-oriented services.

Rising Capital Costs

This country has never invested in public transportation to the extent that foreign nations have. It is interesting that following World War II, one of the first activities of most European nations was to make their systems operational, using Marshall Plan funding, while this country chose to dismantle most of the systems in existence in favor of the automobile. It was clearly a case of priorities and we chose not to invest in transit systems. At present there are less than 10,000 transit cars and under 50,000 buses in the entire country.

Consequently, we are faced with constructing major systems at a time of rapidly rising costs. Because of the scarcity of funds for all expenditures, both the federal and local governments hesitate to undertake new construction, an action that has caused a virtual paralysis of new activity. Since World War II, only the San Francisco BART system has been completed;[a] the Washington, D.C. Metro is just partly operational and will not be completed until 1982. Several other systems are in embryonic stages of developments, such as the Atlanta and Miami systems, and face the dilemma of explaining why costs, computed in years previous to the inflation spiral, will exceed those of earlier estimates.

Washington's Metro, for example, originally estimated to cost $2.5 billion for approximately 100 miles of track, will probably cost twice this figure to complete, owing to the effects of inflation, strikes, increased government red tape, and even Hurricane Agnes. Because of this cost overrun, the Department of Transportation began telling other cities that the federal government would not pay for cost overruns, even though they themselves, through delays and red tape, may have been the cause of some of the increase. Consequently, Baltimore began to shy away from construction of proposed new systems since it, like most local governments, is hard pressed for funds, and fears excessive delays and costs.

Yet, the costs involved are not that much when compared with other transportation investments. Certainly, the record of public investment in highways and aviation has risen so sharply in the last 50 years as to dwarf the effort of other transportation endeavors. For example, in highways, the federal government has spent over $73 billion in less than 20 years, between 1957 and the end of 1975, and by 1990 plans to spend [1] $592 billion, more than ten times that planned for transit. One might logically ask, what kinds of waste, inefficiency, overrun, and inflation costs are involved in a half-trillion-dollar program, and whether just the overrun will not exceed the entire funding of transit.

The question of costs is, therefore, related to the question of perceptions. The nation has come to accept massive highway expenditures but questions even small (by comparison) transit expenditures. No doubt these views will alter with time, but the transitional period is long and exasperating for those who would build better public systems.

Operating deficits are another kind of cost problem and the approach to solving this fund shortage has required adoption of an entirely different federal policy. It was not long ago that federal policy dictated transit operation to be paid out of the fare box. As late as 1974, federal administrators were saying that federal subsidies for operating assistance would never be given. Within a few months, the policy was reversed through congressional action and legislation enacted to provide federal assistance up to 50 percent of operating losses. With local regions having to provide the

---

[a] The Bay Area Rapid Transit System of San Francisco and surrounding areas was the largest public works program ever financed by a local government: a $1 billion bond issue.

remaining funds, local interest in voting for new systems there is compromised. Although transit operators succeeded in convincing their audience that it was unrealistic to support transit entirely from fare box collections, this has not produced an entirely workable policy. The 50 percent subsidy must be viewed more as a stopgap measure, as are so many other transit actions. There are really three different factors involved: (1) Most national and local leaders readily acknowledge transit to be essential in meeting the social and economic needs of the nation, but have not provided a way for the financial benefits received to be redistributed to transit operations;[b] (2) fares are largely set for the journey to work and favor long-distance commuters rather than short-distance travelers, who presumably should have reduced rates especially in midday; and (3) direct increases in tax revenues from transit improvements go to general funds and not to transit.

The whole question is one of having to do things differently. This is very difficult for a bureaucracy, which tends always to keep on doing those things it always has done. Once some steps are taken to correct one or more of these financial dilemmas (and there are a great many things that no doubt can be done, once they are brought to light), many of the current financial impasses can be ameliorated. Perhaps the most urgent task of all is to build a national purpose in solving these problems, with what might be called a national persistence and national patience, qualities never much in evidence as part of our national character.

The Importance of Advocacy

Our nation has become a government that runs primarily on the process of advocacy. When priorities and carefully defined commitments are not fully spelled out, an indecisive drift may set in and accomplishments decline.

Yet, as the problems of modern society multiply in number and complexity, the individual finds it increasingly difficult to know or understand the decisions and solutions proposed. Further, without public support, the elected legislator often cannot generate the political momentum necessary to enact desired legislation, particularly if the short-term consequences are unpleasant or displeasing to some segment of the electorate. Awareness of the nature of the problem, proposals for its solution, and laws aimed at implementing these solutions are to no avail if public will to resolve the problem is lacking.

Public transportation occupies a curious position relative to these ob-

---

[b] Robert E. Patricelli, UMTA Administrator, said in January 1976: "We're not interested in any kind of single-minded transportation experiment that doesn't take into account the broader social and economic impact." This excellent statement of goals does not indicate how the financial benefits of these social and economic impacts can be redistributed to transit, or even if the UMTA Administrator feels they should be.

servations. On the one hand, there has been enough support so it cannot be said the public has not shown interest. In fact, the amount of legislative support has increased at a surprising rate.[c] Yet, even in cases where the public has shown strong support, there has not been a general willingness to give up automobiles in any number sufficient to indicate a general kind of advocacy.

One of the most urgent needs, therefore, is to discover what types of inducements would lure individuals from their automobiles for at least a portion of their travel, for those systems that have capacity available, and to discover what visions of opportunity are necessary to create a strong citizen advocacy movement for the nationwide construction of new and advanced transit systems.

Operation Issues

In any issue as sensitive, as complex, and as insolvent as public transportation, there are bound to be disputes as to what needs doing first. Some emphasize the need for improved capital equipment; others point to the need for better maintenance, or improved quality of service, extended routes, better public relations and advertising, adjustments in fare structure, and so on. A public transit service is never short of critics.

Crime

One dominating issue, and possibly the least tractable, is that of crime, an issue that is not discussed much in the literature. Among transit operators, it is considered to be the most important factor in preventing increased ridership during the off-peak service hours on older systems.

Curiously, crime [2] is not as serious as it is perceived to be in the mind of the public. Prior to 1968, robberies of bus drivers (who normally carried $100 in change) increased dramatically and transit operators were forced to use exact-fare collection. Then the passengers became the victim of the attack. Even so, the crime rate is always markedly less, typically one-third to one-fifth less than for the rest of the community, so it is statistically safer to be on the subway than on the street. One reason the public may be confused is the unfortunate practice of newspapers to report criminal activities using subway stations or rapid transit terminals as

[c] Professor Alan Altshuler, of the Massachusetts Institute of Technology, in October 1975, observed that in view of the efforts required in 1963 and 1964 to secure passage of a transit capital investment act, "the rapid growth in aid over the past eleven years could not have been imagined."

Table 2-1
Comparison of Major Subway Systems

City	Hours of Operation
Chicago	24
Cleveland	24
New York	24
Philadelphia	24
Boston	20 : 5:00 A.M. - 1:00 A.M.
San Francisco (BART)	14 : 6:00 A.M. - 8:00 P.M.
Toronto	20 : 6:00 A.M. - 2:00 A.M.
Montreal	20 : 5:00 A.M. - 1:00 A.M.
Mexico City	16 : 6:00 A.M. - midnight
Paris	20 : 5:00 A.M. - 1:00 A.M.
London	20 : 5:00 A.M. - 1:00 A.M.
Moscow	19 : 6:00 A.M. - 1:00 A.M.
Tokyo	19 : 5:00 A.M. - midnight
Hamburg	21 : 4:00 A.M. - 1:00 A.M.
Stockholm	21 : 5:00 A.M. - 2:00 A.M.

landmarks to identify locations of crimes. Thus, a crime reported in the press may have nothing to do with the transit system but is nevertheless identified with it.

Another frustrating problem for transit organizations concerns the fact that most crimes are committed by the same individuals known to the transit personnel.[d] Because of the way the criminal justice system works, it is difficult to restrict these persons from using transit services, since sentencing is light and legal experts maintain that to refuse these persons use of the systems is to abuse their civil rights. This is an example of the interdependent quality of transit and of a situation where the solution to the transit problem lies outside the influence of the transit field.

Transit organizations have done what they can to improve matters. In addition to having special patrols, closed circuit TV, public address systems, alarm bars, and emergency telephones, it has been found helpful to reduce the length of trains to just two cars at night after rush hour, so each of two remaining cars carries a transit employee, either the conductor or motorman [3]. However, surveys show declines in ridership are heaviest where criminal activity is the highest, creating a cyclical spiral of decreasing revenue and increasing crime. Many systems have, therefore, discontinued night service after midnight. (See table 2-1.)

Increased published crime rates can reflect changes in bookkeeping or

[d] Most crime is committed by young males under 21. Victims are typically lone males between 21 and 50. New York officials report an average of 14 robberies per 24-hour period on their system, and Chicago reports about half of that number on a system about half as large, indicating a similar rate. In 1975 Chicago had but one single serious crime.

Table 2-2
Comparison of Rapid Transid Fares

City	Fare
Boston	25¢
Chicago	45¢ (10¢ transfer)
Cleveland	35¢
New York	50¢
Philadelphia	35¢
San Francisco	25¢ (first zone; $1.25 maximum)
Washington, D.C.	55¢ (40¢ off peak)

accounting procedures and annexation of surrounding territory. In most cases, transit crime has been reduced through better law enforcement procedures, although street crime may have increased. (See table 2-3.)

Transit crime is symptomatic of the location and conditions and reflects the poverty of certain inner-city areas. It is possible that in the long run, by improving the stricken regions, the increased prosperity will have a direct impact on reducing the crime rate, saving not only the transit system but society as a whole.

Fares and Deficits

Although most public transportation operators have succeeded in stabilizing fares, the operating deficits continue to grow at a rapid rate. (See figure 2-1.) Critics complain that transit is poorly managed, and maintains an obsolete fare structure.

Rising deficits occur primarily because of rising wage rates, which reflect the nation's economic index of inflation rate. Under normal circumstances of operation, most businesses would simply raise the price of their product to cover the increased costs inflation brings. In transit operations, this is not advisable for several reasons.

Transit ridership is composed essentially of three different groups: (1) the elderly and poor for whom an increase in fare would represent a real hardship, perhaps cutting off their access to opportunities that hold the only hope for improving their lot and for reducing the societal welfare burden; (2) a middle income group who have automobiles but use transit service because it represents a substantial cost savings, but who, under a fare increase, revert to their automobiles for all trips; and (3) the affluent suburban commuter who is less affected by fare increases.

It would make no sense in terms of national policy to increase fares for the elderly and handicapped since existing federal policy calls for mandatory 50 percent fare reductions of current fares. Otherwise transit operators could not participate in federal programs, which means the transit op-

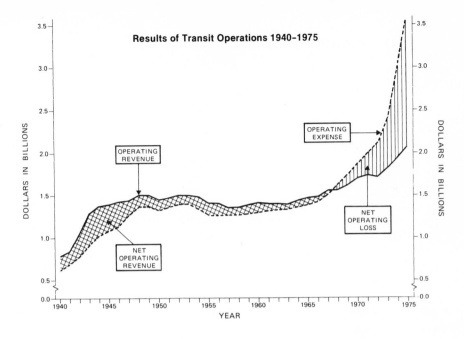

Figure 2-1. Results of Transit Operations, 1940-75.

erator would be out of business. This more or less prevents transit operators from increasing fares; however, it should be recognized that there is a
significant fare differential throughout the nation. An affluent suburban
community may have free bus service, for example, completely subsidized by the local government. The Atlanta and Salt Lake City fares are
only 15¢ and Los Angeles offers service over a wide area for 25¢. Cities
having rapid transit tend to have higher fares so as to have the same fare
on both the rapid transit and bus system for easy transferring. There is
also a wide variation nationwide over basic rapid services. (See table 2-2.)

The lack of zoning is one of the greatest deterents to fare adjustment.
At present, the poorer, inter-city riders are in a sense subsidizing the long-
distance commuters who are also the most affluent. Although raising fares
for the longer distance commuters would probably not significantly influence ridership and would result in a net increase in revenue, the increase
in fare for the short, inner-city rides always causes significant ridership
and revenue losses.

The question is whether zoning should be considered seriously for the
first time in this country, with the attendant increased collection costs, or
whether it is preferable to be patient until a more equitable bookkeeping
system for transit is developed providing other sources of revenue.

One characteristic of American public transportation that distin-

Table 2-3
Increased Crime in Major Cities, 1970-74

City	Change
Atlanta	Up 78%
Baltimore	Up 22%
Chicago	Up 90%
Cincinnati	Up 70%
Cleveland	Up 17%
Dallas	Up 63%
Denver	Up 26%
Los Angeles	Up 23%
New York	Up 0.4%
Philadelphia	Up 79%
Portland, Oregon	Up 80%
San Francisco	Down 2%
Seattle	Up 48%
Washington, D.C.	Down 8%

guishes it from foreign services is that foreign countries almost always use some type of fare structure that is a function of distance but Americans do not. This distinguishing characteristic, which has existed for more than 100 years, reflects differences in societal values. In America, efficiency has always been rated higher than expensive distribution equality perhaps because equality is in principle guaranteed by the basic political system. By contrast, other countries, such as England, France, Russia, Japan, Germany, and Sweden, have long incorporated zoning systems into their service networks and so have absorbed increased cost incrementally over the years.

Consequently, American transit organizations find themselves in the situation of not being able to raise fares for the small distances traveled, and not wanting to incorporate expensive zoning systems so fares could be increased for longer distances, while costs continue to rise. Until other supplementary sources of revenue can be provided, transit must depend on direct operating assistance from the federal and local governments.

Systems Design

Any community contemplating construction of a major transportation system is confronted with a number of possible alternatives. Because the nation's cities differ markedly with each other in every respect as to geography, demography, growth prospects, and so on, it is difficult to identify common denominators of service needs. This has so far prevented a national focusing of identifiable needs and solution.

For example, it is clear that only large cities having reasonable densities can efficiently use heavy rapid rail service. It is by no means clear what these guiding values should be. Generally, designers require a population density of at least 15,000 per square mile to justify rail service. Los Angeles, for example, with only an average population density of 7,000 per square mile would not qualify. However, Los Angeles has a physical barrier in the way of a mountain range within the city, which contains essentially no population. Eliminating this unused space, and examining high-density corridors, Los Angeles has a population density of 14,000 per square mile or enough to justify a rapid rail system over significant parts of the city. Thus, each community must be studied individually with respect to optimum design.

Whether a community needs heavy rail, light rail (trolley), exclusive bus service or conventional bus operation, or some kind of paratransit such as dial-a-ride or subscription, door-to-door service is dependent on the particular circumstances of the community. Subways, because of the large capital outlay required, have been discouraged by federal agencies. Similarly, there has been a reluctance to fund the once popular Personal Rapid Transit (PRT) systems because of high cost per rider in many cases. Exclusive bus systems have been found to be advantageous where lanes are available on existing highways, such as the Shirley Highway near Washington, D.C., and where the streets at destination can carry the added bus traffic. The so-called light rail, or trolley, is currently favored in many areas although the reduced cost, over grade-level heavy rail, does not always seem to justify the loss in passenger capacity. Almost every major system, of course, needs some conventional, on-the-street buses; experience with most paratransit services are too limited to make definite judgments.

Generally, federal authorities prefer funding bus systems; such systems are highly visible, with the vehicles on the street showing the progress being made. Rail systems, in contrast, take years to design and build, and are usually the source of various kinds of setbacks involving strikes and equipment failures and, most important, take a large capital outlay that may only be visible and useful years hence, possibly in another party's administration. Most city planners and transit operators favor rail where justified, because of the lessening of congestion on city streets, the more stable patronage[e] over a period of years, the greater po-

[e] Since 1963 rapid transit has maintained steady ridership even in the face of large fare increase. For example, in Chicago, ridership remained at 111 million between 1963 and 1968 in spite of a 24 percent increase in fare; Philadelphia carried 62 million, increasing to 70 million over the same period, with a 20 percent fare increase; in New York, the rapid system carried 1,356 million, declining slightly to 1,306 million by 1968, with a 33 percent fare increase. Overall, the subway and elevated subway nationwide carried 1.7 billion passengers in 1960 and 1.6 billion in 1970, representing only a slight decline of about 6 percent in spite of large fare increases, general declines in service, and deterioration of equipment and massive highway construction.

tential for scaling capacity up to as much as 100,000 persons per hour (something no other design can promise), and the tendency of business to invest when it knows that transit is permanent, as is rail, and not subject to capricious change, as is a bus route.

The main issue is the low funding level. Too often either no systems at all are funded or at a level too small to meet the eventual need. As a result, many systems have remained in advanced planning stages for years, even through periods of peak unemployment that in earlier times spurred transit construction. Obvious additions to existing services such as the rapid transit extension to O'Hare Airport in Chicago are not yet underway either. Even though federal authorities have done a reasonable job in holding existing systems together to prevent total collapse, have added some much-needed face lifting, and have scattered a generous supply of buses around the country, it must nevertheless be stated that the nation as a whole has not turned seriously to the task of building serviceable and endurable transit systems. Admittedly, the ground work has been good, especially considering the short time involved. However, if transit is to become viable, the time has come for deliberate and comprehensive action. Serious conflicts impede this action.

Unresolved Conflicts

Transportation is said to provide the basic mechanism for integrating and maintaining society. Unfortunately, in attempting to carry out this important and responsible role, transportation is confronted with other forces within society that act as negative elements in preventing positive accomplishments. Whether urban transportation can become an effective force in meeting naional needs depends on whether these detrimental elements can be circumvented.

Urban-Rural Polarization

The growing polarization between rural and urban interests is one of the most detrimental processes taking place in this nation today. It is an element of our society that has always existed, and that at one time or another has caused grievous harm. Public transportation, being associated exclusively with urban interests, is a victim of this polarization. It is, therefore, instructive to consider the polarization phenomena in some detail.

The increased intensity of this rural-urban polarization today no doubt relates in part to the much publicized financial difficulties many cities are experiencing, and how rural interests interpret these difficulties. In recent years, the growth of municipal spending has been far more rapid than either that of the federal government or private industry; the spending itself is cause for concern with highly conservative sectors. Cities have been called upon to provide more services but many question whether the funds are always used wisely. The problem is complicated by the fact that productivity in public service areas is difficult to measure and cities have not always been as responsive as might be desired in recognizing that some disturbing financial trends require better efforts at relating cost-benefit information to the public. This is typical of the new generation of activities being pressed on government generally.

The increased reliance[f] of city governments on federal and state aid is another source of general revenue and is another cause for concern among rural conservatives. Two aspects of this trend cause concern:

1. As cities depend more on external funds for support, they inevitably lose their independence. Efficiency is bound to decline and criticism from external sources increase, intensifying the polarization between cities and suburbs.

2. There is no assurance that the growth of federal and state support will continue. Municipal debt is reaching a limit, and represents the largest single indebtedness in the nation, far surpassing federal, private, and corporate debt in growth rate. This is a frightening aspect of city life to more conservative rural interests and indicates a lack of control, especially with regard to New York, where borrowed funds have been used in part for operating expenses.

Consequently, to many who live outside the great cities, it seems that cities may become too expensive to maintain, especially since the automobile appears to have made cities obsolete in many ways. Financial problems are therefore translated into questions about the value of urban centers and many begin to question the central city's "raison d'être."

Clearly, such views are simplistic. In spite of the apocalyptic press concerning the fate of large cities, they still have tremendous force and the bulk of the nation's industry and financial power.

Cities appear less well off than they are because of the large federal tax drain from city sources. If cities were allowed to keep the federal income tax, for example, they would be rich and the rest of the nation poor. It is

---

[f]Between 1959 and 1972, general municipal revenue quadrupled from $30 billion to almost $120 billion. During this same period, fiscal aid for other governmental sources rose from about 30 percent to 40 percent. As a consequence, property tax revenue dropped from about 50 percent to 37 percent and sales tax sources remained relatively static. These shifts increase the dependency of cities on state and federal funds. Nationwide, over 60 percent of city spending within the past five years has been financed with federal aid. In major cities, this effect is even larger.

only the strange mechanism of the federal tax bookkeeping system that makes it appear otherwise. This realization makes it all the more difficult to understand why congressional action is so often contrary to the interests of cities, since it amounts to an attempt to "Kill the Goose that Lays the Golden Eggs."

Admittedly, the cycle for cities has been as depressingly vicious as it is familiar. Business, the well educated, and the affluent leave; the tax base erodes. Taxes are then forced higher and more of those who can leave, do. However, it is erroneous to assume that because inner cities have been repositories for the poor that the cities themselves are without resources. It is more a situation of the resources being drained by the federal government for use in rural areas.

Taxation bookkeeping is just one of the factors involved; another is that of the traditional immigration patterns of a basically immigrant culture that believes things will be better if you move. Settling the West was never a problem although it well might have been; it was something the people wanted and hardships did not seriously impede the process. America built magnificent cities because it was expedient to do so, not because of natural desires to live in a more efficient and convenient surrounding. Because of the strong tradition in migration away from cities, there is no doubt a tendency among many to consider the rebuilding of cities as unnatural, no matter how convincing the technical assessments to the contrary.

In a sense, this tradition of migration belongs to a now closing era of open land resources, similar to disappearance of once considered unlimited oil reserves. It identifies with a kind of expansionist privilege that suggests all mistakes are canceled by the new horizon, suggesting unlimited opportunity. Declining natural resources, whether petroleum or open land, demand greater responsibility in actions and choices. To many, the city is symbolic of restricted opportunity, representing the loss of the wide open spaces.

Another factor in polarized attitude probably stems from confusion that accompanies any problem not understood. Cities were built largely on immigrant populations, the poor who sought opportunity and found it in the large factories of the industrial revolution. Today the central cities have lost much of the manual labor the poor can do, and have built instead large office and service complexes requiring a type of educated and knowledgeable employee not found in poorer communities of people in transition. As a consequence, welfare costs have increased beyond all projections. Solutions have been elusive; it is a new kind of problem not understood with no one quite knowing what to do.

Urban transportation can be an important part of the solution. The polarization factor perceives transit as part of the problem and consequently

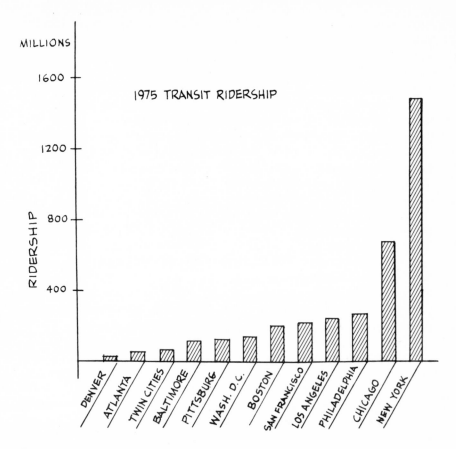

MILLIONS

1975 TRANSIT RIDERSHIP

Figure 2-2. Urban Transit Ridership by City for 1975. New York dominates national ridership having nearly as much (43% of total) as all other cities combined.

acts to constrain funding. This misunderstanding is one of the chief weaknesses of transit today.

New York furnishes an interesting example. (See figure 2-2.) The New York transit system is not only the largest in the nation,[g] but as large as all

[g] New York also has the largest subway system in the world (137 miles), considerably larger than either the Paris or London systems, which have approximately 100 miles each, and the next two largest systems, Moscow and Tokyo, which have about 80 miles each. New York also has more stations (461) and more cars (6,681) than any other system. Both Moscow and Tokyo carried more passengers (1.8 billion and 1.6 billion, respectively) than New York (1.1 billion) in 1974. Including rapid transit at grade or elevated, New York ties with London for first place at over 230 miles. Chicago, at 110 miles, is just slightly larger than the Paris system. San Francisco BART has 75 miles.

other transit systems put together. This greatly unbalances any aggregate transit data since such data reflects primarily New York and not other cities. Consequently, feelings about New York's financial crisis tend to be directed against transit generally as well.

The narrow geographic base is another of the major weaknesses or urban transit. The majority of transportation dollars appropriated by Congress go to relatively few cities. In the decade following the Urban Mass Transportation Act of 1964, 80 percent of funds went to just ten cities, and surrounding regions. Thus, transit is in the position of not having a wide geographic support in Congress, plus receiving the negative impact of the urban-rural polarization effect.

Automotive Vulnerability

The health of the automobile industry is very closely tied to the health of the national economy. Consequently, any action that threatens to intrude even to a small degree on the automobile's position is in conflict with the needs of individuals employed or associated with the automobile industry. This amounts to one in every six persons employed.

Even a small decline in automobile production reverberates through hundreds of industries in every part of the country.[h] Much of the output of the nation's basic industries is for automobile use[i] and automobile manufacturers purchase $10 to $20 million worth of goods from over 50,000 companies in all parts of the country. Aside from the 1.3 million employed in manufacture of vehicles and parts, and another 3 million in sales and service, millions more work in insurance, banks, and related agencies directed toward automobile industry needs.

Although all of these factors indicate the vast power of the automobile industry—the strong leadership that success brings, equally strong labor unions, well financed lobbies—it is not this practical power that troubles urban transit proponents; it is the vulnerability of the automobile industry. With the automobile industry standing as it does close to the center of the American economy, great care must be exercised in taking any action—such as offering a suitable alternative to the automobile—since small sales losses and attendant job losses could depress the economy even more.

---

[h] The Nobel Prize economist, Wassily Leontief, estimated that a $1 billion decline in sales representing 250,000 fewer automobiles produced resulted in a loss of 57,900 jobs with 24,100 of these jobs being in industries not directly related to auto vehicle production but in associated industries.

[i] Sixty percent of synthetic rubber, 15 percent of all steel, 12 percent of aluminum, 63 percent of lead, and 47 percent of malleable iron is directed to automobile production, in addition to significant quantities of glass, copper, textiles, and plastics.

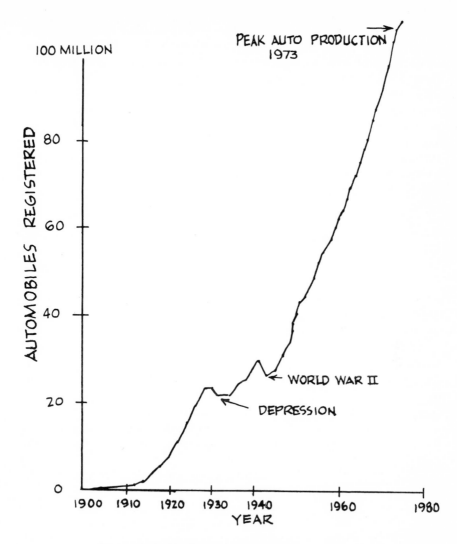

Figure 2-3. Registered Automobiles by Year.

Peak automobile production came in 1973 when 11.5 million cars were sold, 9.7 million manufactured here; in 1974 sales dropped to 8.9 million and domestic production to 7.5 million, down to 7 million in 1975. The growth in cars in use was about 42 percent between 1953 and 1963, and 3.7 percent until 1973. From then on, the rate is anticipated to slow to about 2.5 percent and perhaps to as low as 1 percent per year. (See figure 2-3.) Since that year of peak production in 1973, the automobile industry has

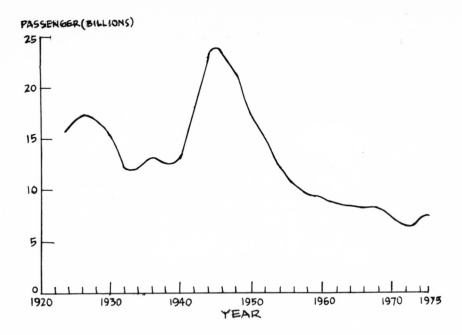

PASSENGER (BILLIONS)

YEAR

Figure 2-4. Total Transit Passengers, 1924-76.

faced hard times. Chrysler, for example, lost over $50 million in 1974 and over $200 million in 1975. This situation is due as much to the rising costs, partly associated with government-mandated equipment, as with the need to retool to produce smaller cars to meet emissions and fuel conservation requirements, as well as the lower sales. Although these firms recovered in 1976, the extent of the recession will continue to haunt legislators and influence transportation decisions.

The dilemma facing the federal government is one of cyclical conflicts: national survival and the inflation and general unemployment spiral dictate that gasoline consumption must be cut and alternatives found to the automobile; yet, any successful counter effort, such as a revitalized mass transit industry, could damage auto sales and hence bring on another, immediate recession, with attendant job losses.

The impact on urban transit is a destructive one. Transit is given a little encouragement and criticized for not being more successful, even though major funds are withheld so it cannot be too successful. In contrast, even during the 1960s many transit organizations were doing well financially. For example, in 1950 the Chicago Transit Authority carried over a billion passengers and revenue exceeded expenses by about $50 million, typical of the early to mid-1960s. (See figure 2-4.) The existing situation in the automobile industry has fostered an extremely cautious attitude on the part of the federal government and is typical of the new types of policy conflicts that confront federal policy makers with increasing frequency.

Commentary: Urgent Issues in Public Transportation

Conscience is said to pose problems, and power solves them. Many of the most critical issues facing urban transit stem from pressures and conflicts outside the transit community. Resolving such issues of interdependency requires a renewed effort on the part of transit advocates outside their immediate area of influence, and requires the support of others not directly associated with the transit industry to build coalitions with sufficient power to affect these crucial issues.

3 Regionalism

As the nation has grown in size and complexity, efficient and responsive management requires some type of decentralization in a process generally known as regionalization. Whether any organization having a budget with the dimensions of the federal budget, now approaching a trillion dollars, can hope to be efficient and responsive is obviously debatable because of the sheer magnitude of the various competing forces involved. It is clear also that the type and kind of information needed to sustain such an operation will rarely be available in a sufficiently complete form or as quickly as needed.

It is not surprising then that many federal policies enacted to relieve stress in one region of the country will actually create stress in another area where none existed previously. As one strategy to overcome this dilemma, the government has been in the process of developing various subregions for better administration of existing policies, and also a means of developing information exchange to stimulate policy development as a way of moving closer to the people.

Features of Regionalism

The special problems of urban areas in defining jurisdictional regions has existed since colonial days. What was a meaningful reference area when man's chief source of transit was walking was probably the distance that could be walked in an hour, about three miles. Better modes of transportation changed that; horse drawn vehicles could average about six miles an hour, or twice as fast a man could walk—enough to double the size of a community. Today it would be difficult to use this criteria to define a region in any working sense. The Census Bureau was one of the first agencies to encounter this general problem and as early as 1910 developed the statistical concept of an urban region through the concept of the metropolitan districts [1]. Today this has been extended to the definition of the standard metropolitan statistical area (SMSA), which continues to be the most useful reference area [2] in terms of daily commuter activity. There were 252 SMSAs in the 1970 census,[a] and an additional 22 SMSAs have been identified since 1970 with others pending.

---

[a] The highway planning program is the only federal planning funding that does not use the SMSA, but instead uses a specially defined urbanized area as a reference base. This testifies

The problem arises as how to define a meaningful area in terms of any given consideration, such as transportation. What kind of scale factor should be considered? Some of this generation's most astute planners have found it convenient to define four levels of transportation regions:

1. The smallest reference region has come to be called the *functional economic area (FEA)* and refers to that area normally covered by a working member of the labor force in the journey to work [3].
2. Local groups of FEAs called *national metropolitan regions (NMRs)* cover regions of about 200 miles radius at most.
3. National regions typically divide the nation in six or more major areas: the Northeast, oriented around New York; Southwest, oriented around Los Angeles; Midwest, around Chicago; the Dallas-Forth Worth, Atlanta and Pacific Northwest areas, depending somewhat on the parameters and functions considered.
4. The entire nation as an area, considering Washington as the political capital, New York as a communications or economic center, Chicago as a rail and commodities center.

These regions were defined as a convenience in technical understanding. Other kinds of regions must be defined for administration considerations. One of the principal purposes of federal government, for example, is to stabilize currency, and for this purpose the 12 major Federal Reserve Districts were created in the 1930s. Other kinds of regions were created to help improve coordination of programs of the federal government. One example of this is a loosely structured, politically responsive set of regions defined by the Economic Development Administration (EDA), which cover the traditionally broad, cultural areas: the Far East, Mountain, Southwest, Southeast, Great Lakes, Middle Atlantic, and New England areas. The EDA was developed in 1965 to coordinate various federal efforts directed at reviving stagnant regional economies both in areas of appreciable geographic size, such as Appalachia, and in urban areas. Certain distressed areas were defined as economic development regions (EDRs), which, except for New England, refer to areas having no central urban area large enough to sustain prolonged development and which gave the Commerce Department a way of dealing with these problems that had not existed previously. Most federal agencies use the standard ten administrative regional designations shown on figure 3-1. These regions correspond directly to the 10 major continental regions used as a standard in most government administrative work. The older Federal Reserve Districts, for example, have somewhat different boundaries, dividing the continent into 12 regions. The Federal Highway Administration

to both the universality of acceptance of the SMSA, and also to the power of the highway administration in setting a different standard.

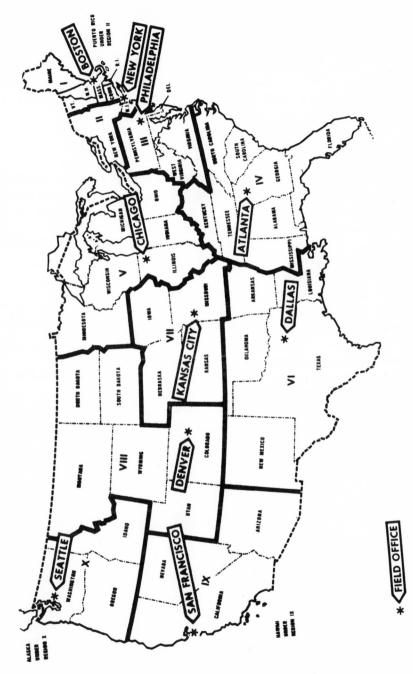

Figure 3-1. Urban Mass Transportation Administration (UMTA) Regions.

and Federal Aviation Administration use the same administrative region as above but not always the same field aviation office location.

Figure 3-2 shows the Federal Railroad Administrative Regions. These regions differ only slightly from the standard administrative regions, illustrating the common needs of the various modes. AMTRAK routes are given in figure 3-3. For some applications, the concept of treating the entire nation as a unified region is most appropriate.

Criteria for Local Regional Formation

Aside from the interests and problems of the federal government, an effective case for regionalism can be made based on the observation that existing boundaries, such as state of municipal boundaries, have little relevance to the problems of area economies. State and municipal borders present no special barrier to the commuter and very little inconvenience to the shipment of goods. If transportation is to relate to the needs of region, where a *region* is that area made up of common economic opportunities and shared problems, the attention must be directed to the political and organization characteristics internal to this area. Attempts [4] to formulate guiding principles for solving regional problems include the following criteria:

1. There should be a general, comprehensive understanding of the operating policies of the various governmental levels of a given area as to differences and similarities.
2. The federal government has a special responsibility to ensure coordination of its own agencies in dealing with various local governing strata.
3. A sharing and compromising of powers within the region's governments is essential.
4. Development must be decentralized to a level at which there can be a total review of problems of any given area by all agencies concerned.
5. The selection of an area and its operating subregions or centers should be made with reference to the general coincidence of major transportation problems.

Practical implementation of these concepts is almost always difficult, the type of difficulty depending on the location conditions. However, this kind of analytical activity [4] and the general tendency toward regionalism in all areas of government, and the experience gained in these endeavors, provided essential ground work for the creation of successful public transportation regions throughout the country.

43

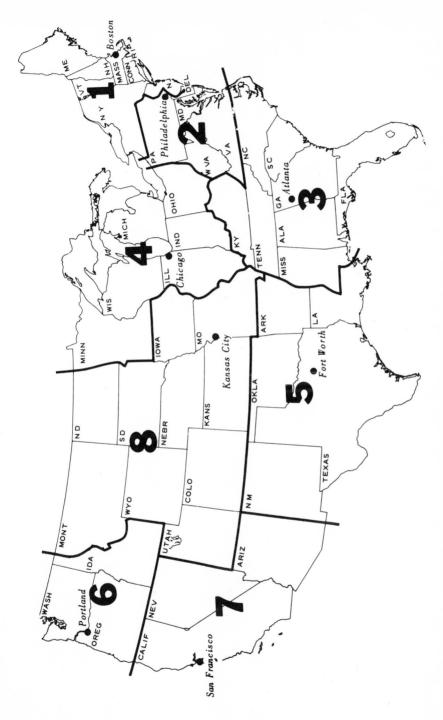

Figure 3-2. Federal Railroad Administration Regions.

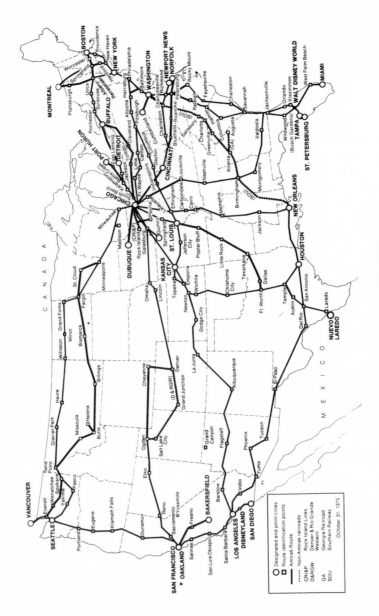

Figure 3-3. AMTRAK Routes.

Public Transportation Regions

The past 30 years have witnessed a progressive development in regional transportation, with some regions crossing state boundaries. At the present time, 15 major regional authorities have formed. (See table 3-1.) These 15 major transportation authorities differ markedly as to responsibility, taxing powers, method of formation, type of budget, and area of influence. Their development history is slow or rapid, simple or complex, depending on the local situation. All were formed under economic pressures and all are primarily directed toward achieving economic stability as a first goal.

Not all of these authorities have the power to tax: taxing powers have been prohibited in Baltimore, Atlanta, Bi-State (St. Louis), and SEPTA, although the others all have some form of taxing authority. BARTD, for example, has the most extensive, being able to levy both a property tax and a sales tax; Twin Cities uses both a motor vehicle tax and a property tax; New York, a mortgage recording tax; Seattle, a property tax. No authority other than the Northeastern Illinois RTA can impose a motor fuel tax.

Those authorities that are not allowed to tax in some instances do have taxes levied and set aside for their use by the state or municipality. An example in Atlanta's MARTA, which is supported by sales taxes issued by the constituent municipalities.

Almost all the authorities are empowered to accept and do depend on additional state, local, and federal appropriations. For some RTAs this is the only source of revenue, notably, Boston, which depends on a very complicated system of "assessed contributions" from constituent municipalities, as do Baltimore and St. Louis. All the RTAs except St. Louis have the power to issue bonds in some form.

In 1972 a Transportation Task Force was created in Illinois to examine the pending crisis in public transportation in the state and to recommend the best course of action for state and local governments toward revitalization and strengthening of the region's public transportation system. The findings of this study were presented in a technical report [5] and one of the technical appendixes presented, in matrix form, the summary of the characteristics of other transit authorities including information on pertinent aspects of regional formation as to:

1. Form and structure of governing bodies
2. Responsibilities and substantive powers
3. Form and structure of management and operations
4. Fiscal requirements and capabilities
5. Relationships with existing governmental and transportation entities
6. Other considerations (severability, repeal, limitations, etc.)

Selected portions of this material appear in table 3-2.

Table 3-1
Major Regional Transportation Authorities

Date	Symbol	Authority
1945	CTA[a]	Chicago Transit Authority[a]
1949	Bi-State	Bi-State Metropolitan Development District, St. Louis
1953	NYCTA	New York City Transit Authority[b]
1957	BARTD	San Francisco Bay Area Rapid Transit District
1957	MMC	Seattle Metropolitan Municipal Corporation
1960	TTC	Toronto Transit Commission
1960	WMATA	Washington, D.C. National Capital Region Transportation
1963	SEPTA	Southeastern Pennsylvania Metropolitan Transportation Authority
1964	MBTA	Massachusetts Bay Transportation Authority
1965	NYMTA	New York Metropolitan Transportation Authority
1965	MARTA	Metropolitan Atlanta Rapid Transit Authority
1967	TCAMTC	Twin Cities Area Metropolitan Transit Commission
1969	Rochester	Rochester-Genesee Regional Transportation Authority
1970	Baltimore	Mass Transit Administration/Metropolitan Transit District
1974	RTA	Regional Transportation Authority of Northeastern Illinois
1975	RTA	Greater Cleveland Regional Transit Authority

[a]The CTA, operating in Chicago and authorized to serve portions of Cook County outside Chicago, was incorporated into the Northeastern Illinois Regional Transportation Authority in 1974.
[b]New York has several regional-type authorities, each with special jurisdictions. In 1968 these various authorities were placed under a single umbrella authority called the Metropolitan Transportation Authority (MTA).

Management styles differ depending on the structure of the organization and its relationship to the other government units. A fairly common situation is that typified by the state of Georgia. (See figure 3-4.) Georgia authorized the local governments, in this case five counties plus the city of Atlanta, to form jointly a local transit authority, MARTA. The local units had the option of choosing whether or not to join. One county, Cobb County, did not join although it might do so later if it so wished. The control of the transit authority in this case is with the local government, as is the taxing power, although the tax support collected need not be a locally imposed tax. Through a joint venture agreement, the state of Georgia collects a 1 percent sales tax, which is delivered to MARTA; after ten years this tax is to be reduced to 0.5 percent.

For smaller states, a structure that has worked well is having the transit operation contained within a single state Department of Transportation (DOT). Maryland has this form wherein the entire public transit control falls under the state offices along with the Tunnel, Bridge, Airport, and Highway Divisions. (See figure 3-5.) The state collects a gas tax authorized by the legislature and supports the DOT operations and also pays the Maryland share of the Washington, D.C. rapid transit.

For large states having highly diversified economies such as California

Table 3-2
Comparison of Regional Authorities

Authority	Region Served	Board Structure	Funding
Baltimore	Baltimore + two counties	One administrator (part of state DOT)	Motor fuel tax collected by Maryland
BARTD	San Francisco + nine counties	By population	Direct property, transactions and use taxes
Bi-State	St. Louis, Mo. + three Missouri & three Illinois counties	Ten commissioners	Missouri earmarks tax support; Illinois contributes
NARTA	Atlanda + five counties	Eleven directors	1% sales tax collected by Georgia for transit
MBTA	Boston + 78 cities and towns	Five directors + 78 advisor members	Complex system of municipality support
MMC	Seattle area	Six regular members + ex officio members by population	One mill property by 3/5 voter approval; cities pay deficits on assessed property
NYCTA	New York City	Nine members of MTA board serve ex officio	City/state share costs
NYMTA	New York City + seven counties	Ten members + chairman	Mortgage recording tax
Rochester	Seven counties	Seven members	Mortgage recording tax
RTA	Chicago + six counties	Eight members + chairman; 26 suburban advisor members	3/32 sales tax, auto license fees (5% motor fuel tax and parking tax authorized also)
RTA	Cleveland area	Ten members	1% sales tax
SEPTA	Pennsylvania	Two from each county	No taxing power
TCAMTC	Minneapolis, St. Paul + seven counties	Nine commissioners	2.9 mills property tax (wheelage tax unconstitutional)
TTC	Toronto Metropolitan area	Five member commission	An integral part of the metropolitan government
WMATA	Washington, D.C. + two Virginia counties, three Virginia cities, & two Maryland counties	Six directors	An ad velorum tax pays for Virginia share; a portion of Maryland motor fuel tax for the Maryland share

(Illinois might be thought of as having these same features on a reduced scale), a different arrangement has been found effective. Here the state authorizes a local authority, such as BARTD or the RTA, to form a unit of

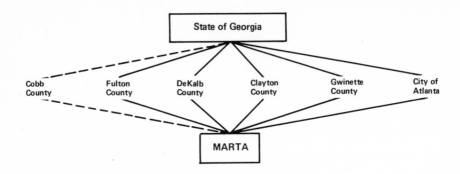

48

Figure 3-4. Regional Transit Authority Organization in Georgia.

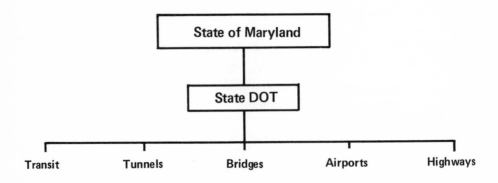

Figure 3-5. Transit Operation Structure in Maryland.

government that is also a taxing authority. BARTD has broad powers in terms of taxing and ownership of right-of-way. There are some restrictions: California, for example, has state restrictions on the amount of property tax that can be levied. There are also restrictions as to how the tax-raised funds can be used. The county boards are empowered to raise additional taxes, other than from the presently authorized property, sales (transaction), and use taxes (including tolls, certain auto fees etc.), but the proportion of county transportation funds contributed cannot exceed the proportion of the county's residents served. Originally BARTD served five counties and today it is nine, including San Francisco where the county and city governments have merged. (See figure 3-6.)

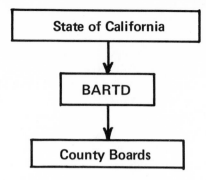

Figure 3-6. Transit Authority Arrangement in California.

As previously mentioned, the Illinois RTA is in many ways similar to BARTD and was partly formed on some of the positive results of the BARTD experience, but there are important differences. The RTA is empowered to tax, but only in specific and limited ways, as discussed below. However, nationwide, the RTA is considered to be the only agency with a "range of funding powers that give it effective clout" [6].

The RTA management approach is therefore substantially different from BARTD even though the basic structure is similar. This observation is true of any regional system. Looking at the structural arrangement is, therefore, a convenient way to classify certain constraints, to identify organizational patterns and styles of management behavior, and to define some kind of convenient yardstick for classifying the regional authority, but it is only part of the analysis. Consequently, it is worthwhile to study the elements of a particular system in some detail to gain a greater depth of understanding of the processes involved. The Chicago area RTA is the largest regional organization in the nation with 8 commuter railroads, 14 suburban bus companies, and the second largest mass transit system on continent—the Chicago Transit Authority. Many of the problems of formation, jurisdiction, financing, and authority exemplify those of other regions.

The Regional Transportation Authority of Northeastern Illinois

It is instructive to consider in some detail the formation of a complex regional organization, complex in terms of diversity of area, political characteristics, and economic pressures. The formation of the RTA represents the successful culmination of meticulous balancing of competing social and political forces in response to public needs.

Historical Background

As in other urban centers, Chicago's public transportation system suffered severe decline and financial difficulties beginning in the late 1920s. Repeated reorganization attempts failed, and eventually the private companies and crucial railroad right-of-way were purchased by the Chicago Transit Authority (CTA), a municipal corporation organized by the Illinois legislature in 1946 to operate throughout most of Cook County and empowered to issue revenue bonds. At first the CTA management coped with increasing cost by small but systematic fare increases. By 1971 CTA had purchased $250 million in capital improvements from the fare box. The first difficulties in meeting debt service did not occur until 1970 when the shortage was made up from the reserves. By this time it had become increasingly clear that increased revenue was urgently needed to offset rising costs, but that increased fares would only decrease ridership and not produce the needed, additional revenue. Similar situations existed with the suburban bus and commuter rail operations.

In February 1971, the governor, Richard B. Ogilvie, set up the Governor's Task Force on Transportation, a competent committee to study and propose solutions to the mass transit problems of northeastern Illinois. The present RTA is largely an outcome of that study.

Other forces were at work that would aid in the RTA formation. The 1970 Illinois Constitutional Convention gave the governor powers to effect, through executive order, the creation of an Office of Mass Transportation, which was to become the first recognition of public transportation at the state level in the executive branch. In 1971, with the strong backing of the governor, the legislature passed a $900 million bond issue that included $200 million for capital improvements in mass transit facilities and also recognized the need for debt service by transit operators.

As the task force was continuing its work to arrive at an equitable and acceptable solution to the transit problem, the incumbent governor was defeated in the general election of 1972, where one of the key issues of the election was spending and taxes. Although both governors, the defeated incumbent and the newly elected, strongly supported mass transit and the need for an effective regional authority, the resolving of the tax issue problem delayed enactment of regional legislation.

The close political balance in the legislature resulting from that election was another factor to complicate regional considerations. The House was almost evenly divided, 89 Republicans and 88 Democrats, as was the Senate, 30 to 29, with both having Republican leadership. Watergate was also a strong, negative factor, acting to restrict Republicans who otherwise would have been vigorous supporters of the RTA. Throughout the course of the protracted regional transit debate, a variety of shaky coalitions were formed, primarily in the House. The political situation was particularly delicate for those Republicans with political ambitions, who would need the support of the populous northeastern region, which was demanding an effective regional system but whose local constituencies feared the possible extension of influence from the strong central city that was largely Democratic.

Meanwhile, the transit situation in Illinois had worsened. Suburban railroads, which reported losses in excess of $6.7 million in 1971 and larger losses in 1972, were requesting the right to increase fares and abandon portions of their service. CTA fares had increased 400 percent in 25 years while ridership decreased 500 million. By early 1973 it was apparent that mass transit problems were reaching crisis proportions. Chicago's Mayor Daley conferred with the governor in February of 1973 to discuss the growing crisis. A Mass Transportation Crisis Conference was held March 3. The breadth of interest and scope of concern were evidenced by the speakers: a professional transportation planner, the former chairman of the Governor's Task Force on Transportation, a CTA board member, several state legislators (who explained their proposed legislation), the lieutenant governor, a representative from the U.S. Department of Transportation, and the mayor of Chicago, Richard J. Daley. Over 300 persons representing a cross section of public service-oriented organizations and others attended. The afternoon workshops reached "a clear consensus that the six counties must have a single Regional Mass Transit Authority in order to effectively solve the festering problem." It is interesting to note that the conference had difficulty resolving the same issues that would plague the legislature when detailed RTA legislation was considered, namely:

1. The size and makeup of the Board of Directors reflecting the concerns of the largely Democrat central city versus the largely Republican suburbs—that one would have control to the detriment of the other.
2. The funding: the conference did find that the state motor fuel tax was believed to be the most "popular" source of funding. A major confrontation was to arise between those fiscal policies of the governor and legislative leaders, and among the various pressure groups, namely, the oil lobbies.

The conference set the scene for the legislative process.

Legislative Compromise

In all, six different bills were introduced in the 78th session of the Illinois legislative in the spring of 1973. It is interesting to note the points of variation between them and the forces that eventually won. The bills introduced were:

The members of the original Governor's Task Force proposed a bill based primarily on the results of their study. Besides setting up an RTA for the six-county area, two operating agencies would be placed under it: the CTA and a new suburban organization. It would be financed by 1/2 of 1 percent sales tax and a motor vehicle parking tax, 2/3 of the revenue from the then proposed state lottery and $15 million annually from the city of Chicago. The nine member board would consist of four members appointed by the Chicago mayor, two by the Board of Commissioners of Cook County, and two by the chairmen of the five other county boards; the chairman of the board would be selected by the other eight members. This bill circumvented the issue of new taxes by providing a general 1/2¢ sales tax reduction to be effective throughout the state, thus providing a bonus to downstate legislators to support the legislation, and reimposing the tax in the six-county northeastern region. The fear was that such a maneuver would fail to provide sufficient support for the new RTA. Further, the separation of central city and suburban transit operation responsibility negates the advantages of a presumably unified system, one of the primary objectives.

Another bill represented essentially an extension of the existing CTA and was to be funded by a 5¢ motor fuel tax collected within the region. This bill did not receive strong support among suburban interests and the 5¢ tax was considered an unreasonable burden by oil lobbyists.

A package proposed originally by the commuter railroads favored railroad considerations and was never widely supported. It called for funding from several sources including motor fuel tax, 20 percent of the state federal revenue sharing, a parking tax, and increased toll road fees.

A bill based essentially on the Task Force program but calling for larger funding, which would include motor fuel tax, an extra nickel on tolls of the Illinois tollway system, aimed at providing a viable financial base.

A bill that included 1/2¢ per gallon motor fuel tax, up 1/3 of 1 percent income tax, a vehicle tax, a $50 per-person employment tax and a parking tax, all to be collected from within the region. The flexible funding of this bill was intended to broaden the financial base of the RTA to increase financial stability.

A bill introduced late in the session by the governor recommended a board composition to be based on population representation. It also recommended a variety of funding sources, such as increased utility tax but opposed the elimination of the downstate 1/2¢ sales tax in the interests of overall state fiscal responsibility.

The two issues of major concern were (1) funding and (2) board structure. It was generally recognized that the problem of board representation had no completely equitable solution that was still feasible in terms of efficient operation, since to have representation based on true population proportions, still including the least populous areas, governing units would require a board of unwieldy size. If each county were to be given at least one seat on the board, the city of Chicago would have to seat over 30 members on population distribution and the total board would be over 60 members. Clearly, compromises were essential both in terms of those densely populated areas that would receive slightly less than one man, one vote representation, and the outlying counties in terms of individual representation for all county units.

The funding issue was less clear-cut. All concerned believed that sufficient funds should be provided to eliminate the continual economic crisis of the public transit systems and also to provide a stable base to extend and improve public systems. Yet, one of the key issues in the recent election in which Governor Ogilvie had been defeated for reelection was the unpopular income tax associated with the governor, an event clear in the memory of all elected officials.

Another reality was the acknowledged impact of the highway lobby. In a February 17, 1973 *Chicago Daily News* article, Joe Harris, lobbyist for the Illinois Oil Producers Agency, was quoted as saying, with regard to a plan Governor Ogilvie had announced to collect a 1/2¢ a gallon tax to pay for mass transit:

We sent out news releases to every Downstate newspaper. The one we sent to Quincy for instance said 'Residents of Adams County will pay $325,000 a year to support the CTA.' You should have seen the response. We got stories with big headlines on page one of many newspapers, then front page editorials supporting our position. Some Downstate legislators wanted to support Ogilvie out of party loyalty but came under tremendous pressure.

The memory of how Governor Ogilvie's proposed tax was defeated within ten days after it was introduced—handing him one of the worst defeats of his term—was also fresh in the minds of the legislators.

The highway lobby used other pressures as well, including indicated actions regarding their campaign contributions, which were said to run "in the high five figures or the low six figures" for state offices according to the same *Daily News* article. The Chicago Motor Club also warned against having the motorist bear a "disproportionate and unfair share of the cost."

The Illinois State Chamber of Commerce lobbyist issued a position paper supporting mass transit but avoided the critical issues of structure and finance. The League of Women Voters also took a stand, generally supportive but advocating "continuous and wide-spread community participation." John Kearney of the Peoples' Policy Organization, speaking on a television editorial reply, said his organization "believes in, and is working for, 'no fare' mass transit," calling for complete, permanent mass transit subsidy. To illustrate the wide spectrum of opinion, an organization called Save our Suburbs (SOS) objected to the proposed hearings on the transit bills saying that such hearings "force the taxpayers to do what government officials have a duty to do: protect the taxpayers against substituting socialism for our Constitutional Representative Republic" and added: "We oppose the principle of subsidies because this is socialism."

Against this background, the legislative processes were taking place. The events were recorded in daily newspaper articles, with every edition counted on to carry some story on the RTA.

One of the key arguments centered on the funding. One problem with the favored approach of taking 1/2¢ of the existing sales tax and refunding the 1/2¢ to downstate areas was that it would not provide sufficient funds. It was favored by downstate representatives as it gave a financial refund but lacked financial responsibility as far as mass transit in the urban areas were concerned. As a May 23 *Chicago Tribune* editorial stated: "It is all too apparent that the leaders are far more interested in getting credit for a tax cut downstate than in providing safe, adequate and economical public transportation for the 6.4 million citizens of Northeastern Illinois."

As the legislative session wore on, all of the bills were sent from committee to the floor for debate. An amendment to add a 1.5¢ a gallon tax on gasoline eventually passed both houses. The governor made an unprecedented appearance at a closed party caucus to urge that the 1/2¢ sales tax reduction not be voted in, in the interests of state budget balancing; the House vote on this measure was then stalled by a shouting match on the House floor. Although this tax relief was later passed, clearing the way for the 1/2¢ replacement in the six-county regional area, in what some considered a defeat for the governor, a few days later the governor was able to win a 5 percent tax levy on utility bills by an 86-75 margin. This was opposed by some legislative leaders on the basis of regressive tax arguments.

The final days of the legislature saw a situation that sometimes occurs at session's end when two issues become entangled. In this case the issues were transportation policy and tax policy. As a *Chicago Today* editorial stated: "Some mechanisms have an infuriating way of going wrong— stripping a gear or just breaking a mainspring—when you need them the most. An automobile that acts this way is called a lemon. We are not sure what to call the Illinois Legislature."

The 78th General Assembly went home several days late having failed to pass an RTA.

Efforts continued throughout the summer and in a special session, following a series of summit meetings involving the governor, legislative leaders and the mayor of Chicago, the terms of a compromise bill were agreed upon. It passed both houses and was signed into law on December 12, 1973, based on the contingency of the bill's passing a special referendum election to be held March 19, 1974.

The compromise bill offered as a referendum created a single umbrella authority responsible for transportation needs throughout the six-county, northeastern Illinois region extending between the Wisconsin and Indiana borders. The RTA was provided with the option of (1) providing grants to carrier, (2) negotiating purchase of service agreements, or (3) acquiring and operating the services directly. In all cases, RTA would have the essential authority to request fares, routes and schedules, and power to implement. The key issues were in board structure and funding:

The Board of Directors consists of nine persons. Eight members are chosen by local governments with the chairman chosen by the board. Four of these members are appointed by the mayor of Chicago, two by the suburban commissioners of Cook County, and two appointed by the commissioners of the remaining five counties.

The funding[b] is provided from five sources: An authorized 5 percent sales tax on motor fuel and a public parking tax, at the discretion of the RTA board, to be levied only in the region; 3/32 of the state sales tax collected in the region; $14 per vehicle license fee collected only in the city of Chicago; and $5 million in direct contribution from Cook County and city of Chicago. The state lottery was enacted to offset the loss in revenue to the state from the transfer of 3/32 sales tax to the RTA.

The Referendum: Getting Out the Vote

Less than ten weeks elapsed between the enactment of the RTA law in December and the date of the primary election and referendum in March 1974. To help get out the vote and stimulate a positive response, an RTA Citizens Committee for Better Transportation[c] was formed to launch a public information campaign. The goals were:

1. To explain the present and future merits of the RTA legislation
2. To overcome the highly articulate opposition to the bill by primarily suburban interests who feared and distrusted the establishment of a superagency
3. To neutralize and correct the opposition's misrepresentation of the powers and authorities of the new RTA
4. To encourage the print and broadcast media to cover RTA issues thoroughly and to resolve complications arising from the fairness and equal time doctrine related to fact that many legislators who were running in the primary were often among the pro or anti-RTA spokesman

---

[b] The revenue collected in Chicago from the state imposed motor fuel tax would be sufficient to fund RTA needs. However, most of these funds have traditionally gone to suburban counties for road construction. Setting up the sales tax contribution would help rebalance the tax distribution by transferring some funds from suburbs to the center city. On a 5¢ gas tax, Chicago annually collects over $100 million but keeps $30 million with $70 million going for suburban road construction. Of the 15/32 percent of sales tax for the RTA about 70 percent is spent in Chicago although 50 percent comes from the suburbs.

[c] "Chicago's RTA: A Short Course in Getting Out the Vote," A.M. Gertler and R.E. Bouzek, *Public Relations Journal*, June 1975. The unintended but sometimes negative effect of the local newspapers is discussed in "Railroading the RTA," by Bill Nugut, *Chicago Journalism Review*, May 1974.

Unexpected issues arose. Opponents, for example, claimed incorrectly that the proposed tax on parking could be extended to taxing vehicles parked in a taxpayer's own driveway. Certain individuals with special interests managed to convince a limited number of black leaders that the RTA was, in a complicated way, a threat to undermine the black movement for equality. Highly articulate and hostile suburbanites saw the RTA as an opportunity to voice their dislike of central city politics, equating a vote for the RTA as a vote to extend the central city political power. One suburban political leader warned his primarily white constituents that this extension would lead eventually to domination by a black minority. Much of the rhetoric centered not on the merits of a unified transportation system as on disputes of various kinds, often unrelated to transportation issues.

In less than 10 weeks, 26 news conferences were held by the pro-transportation forces. These conferences were credited with generating approximately one-quarter of the 4,000 press clippings collected during this time. Specialized press sessions featured black, Spanish-speaking community leaders, city planners, transportation experts, teachers, suburban mayors, business and labor leaders, senior citizens, the handicapped, and environmentalists. Over 100 hours of radio and television time were supported by the pro-transit forces, covering the 70 stations in the six-county area. More than 150 press releases and feature stories and over 200 speaking engagements were arranged. The three major Chicago newspapers presented 19 favorable editorials and dozens of articles. Publication material included 200,000 lapel buttons, 1 million question and answer brochures, 10,000 posters and car cards, 500,000 sample ballots, 1 million flyers, 1.5 million bill stuffers, and 150,000 copies of a last-minute message from former Governor Richard B. Ogilvie, a Republican whose support was important to the suburban areas.

By election time, 32 community groups and public service organizations had endorsed the RTA, which had become a household word. The election was very close; the RTA won by a margin of approximately 1 percent of the 1,353,653 votes cast. The margin of victory was less than two votes per precinct of the six-county region's 6,797 precincts with all suburban counties voting against RTA. Figure 3-7 shows the representation on the RTA Board of Directors.

These figures reflect deep cultural and political differences within the RTA, a six-county area, which extends from the Wisconsin to the Indiana borders surrounding Chicago. Yet, looking at the growth patterns of the suburban areas, and the economic core represented by the central city, it is clear that the region is becoming more and more a unified region. The problems of energy scarcity will strike harder at the suburbs than the central city because suburban residents use more energy per capita. Thus,

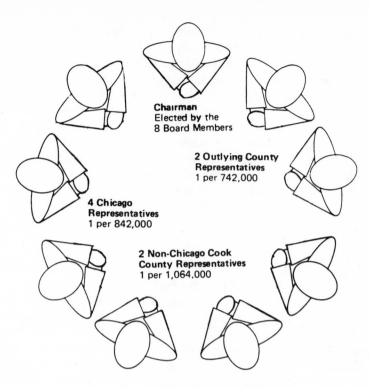

Chairman
Elected by the
8 Board Members

2 Outlying County
Representatives
1 per 742,000

4 Chicago
Representatives
1 per 842,000

2 Non-Chicago Cook
County Representatives
1 per 1,064,000

Figure 3-7. RTA Board of Directors.

the need for public transit will be greater in those areas, even though the concept is presently not well understood by many.

The statistics for McHenry County show both sides of the problem very well. McHenry is a predominantly rural area with all of the beauty and serentity that such areas offer. It is very far in thought and attitude from the bustling central city of Chicago. The median income is only $3,815. Yet, the 1970 census shows that 21 percent of the people of McHenry earn their living outside the county and that over 60 percent of those who work outside work in Chicago or suburbs close to Chicago. These people have a much higher income, almost three times that of other McHenry residents. Consequently, over 58 percent of the earned income of McHenry County is derived because of the close proximity of the Chicago metropolitan area. Thus, in economic terms, McHenry is very much a part of the Chicago region, although very far in other respects. This observation makes a special problem for the regionalization of transportation everywhere.

As a young and untried agency, the RTA is being put to the test. Suburban interests object to the disproportionate tax funds from suburban areas being spent in the central city to operate the existing transit system and the suburbs as yet have little transit. Arguments that this is only fair, since large portions of the motor fuel tax collected in Chicago by the state are spent on suburban roads, fail to satisfy objectors since they say that the city of Chicago benefits from the suburbs having better roads. It is evidently difficult for the suburbs to realize that the reverse is also true, namely, the suburbs benefit in many ways from a healthy central city. This unfortunate polarization between suburban and central city interest slows progress, tests the patience of all involved and is a common problem throughout the nation as a whole.

Transportation Planning

As the various levels of government react and adjust to the variety of societal processes impinging on it, needs develop faster than the levels of government can respond. Coordination becomes difficult and events change meaningful reference information before adjustment can be made within the system.

In an attempt to assess what is happening relative to what is wanted, and to evaluate how one set of events or actions affects other happenings, a variety of planning agencies have gradually come into being. The growth and development of the planning agency has been one of the essential elements of regionalism.

One unfortunate consequence of this rapid growth in which the nation is currently involved has been the appearance of a baffling array of groups and organizations, all having distinctive acronyms, so many as to almost form a special language, with an equally distinctive set of regional dialects.

To understand something of the complexity and variation of function that occur in any highly developed region, it is first necessary to have a glossary of terms. Table 3-3 provides a list of federal acronyms.

Planning Organizations

The evolution of planning agencies within any regional area is usually a case history of how these agencies grew in response to federal pressures. The federal influence is essentially of two kinds.

1. Federal agencies require a variety of actions to take place within a region before federal funding will be released for projects.
2. Federal agencies provide direct funds for supporting such agencies and

Table 3-3
Glossary of Federal Acronyms

A-95	A reveiw process established by OMB requiring that all federally funded programs be reviewed in compliance with regional plans
DOT	U.S. Department of Transportation
EPA	Environmental Protection Agency, a federal agency
FAA	Federal Aviation Administration, under DOT
FHWA	Federal Highway Administration, under DOT
HHFA	Housing and Home Financing Agency
HPR	Highway planning and research funds, established by the federal Hayden-Cartwright Act of 1934
HUD	U.S. Department of Housing and Urban Development
ICC	Interstate Commerce Commission, a federal regulatory agency
IPC	Interstate Planning Agency
IPG	Intermodel Planning Group, a federal advisory committee
MPO	Office of Management and Budget, a federal executive office
PL	Planning funds, established by federal highway legislation, 1973
UMTA	Urban Mass Transportation Administration, under DOT

analysis work and this support comes from a variety of sources within the federal level.

The great complexity of the federal bureaucracy then begins to impinge directly on local organizations that try to adjust to this maze of interests and demands and do so in a large variety of ways. In looking at the structures that exist in any local region, it is possible to present quite different histories depending on whether matters of policy are being examined, ways of responding to maximize federal funds, ways of responding to achieve special local goals and needs or ways of increasing efficiency of government and conserving local investment.

Problems that may seem small in principle often loom large in practice. As one small example, consider the difficulty of writing a grant application that meets both federal criteria and state criteria. It may seem that these criteria might be in some sense naturally complementary, one stressing one set of values, and the other a different set. In any region these kinds of problems are not simple and require sizable time investments and high level professional commitments to resolve. These are the types of activities that modern government produces and that are little understood or appreciated by the public.

Planning Background

Modern transportation planning is generally considered to have begun with the 1900 Burnham plan for Chicago; this plan was essentially a "city beautiful" plan incorporating the strong transportation needs of Chicago. Comprehensive planning, as it is known today was first practiced by another private group, the Regional Plan Association of New York City, about 1920.

Planning as a national activity was not incorporated in federal programs until the 1930s. It was of two kinds: (1) comprehensive planning and (2) highway planning. From the start, highway plans were separate and unrelated to comprehensive planning. Many of the current ills can be traced to this unfortunate beginning and are still unresolved.

The first attempts at comprehensive planning from a federal level were carried out by the federal transportation coordinator, a position established under the Emergency Transportation Act of 1933. This work was primarily with regard to railroad problems since at the time, railroads completely dominated the national transportation scene. He worked in conjunction with the National Resources Planning Board in assessing long-range results of certain practices and in developing better coordinating activities. About the same time the National Transportation Committee, formed by various investment firms and businessmen as well as by concerned philanthropic groups, began looking at various elements of comprehensive planning and the need to integrate these plans with other aspects of city planning.

By contrast, highway planning was limited to read construction considerations. It began as a 1-1/2 percent authorization from the Federal Aid Highway Act of 1934 specifically for planning purposes, where planning meant road surveys, engineering plans, and economic impact studies. At the time, there were few road systems in the nation.

During the late 1930s a number of presidential committees and studies looked into the planning process. The Committee of Three and the Committee of Six in addition to various highway studies resulted in so many studies that the term "studyities" came into use. One of these studies, the National Resources Planning Board, is outstanding for its work in comprehensive analysis of all national transportation systems.

The planning study committee concept[d] continued after World War II with the 1949 Hoover Commission, the Sawyer Report from the Department of Commerce, the Weeks Report resulting from a presidential advisory committee in 1955, the Mueller Report in 1960 and the Doyle Report in 1966, both for the U.S. Senate. All of these studies were important in organizing data in influencing federal comprehensive planning requirements that later found their way into legislation and the formation of the Department of Transportation.

Present-day urban transportation planning began first on the local lev-

[d] An excellent review of the work of these committees and other policy mechanisms is found in "Dimensions of National Transportation Policy Formation," a Ph.D. thesis by Herman Mertins, Jr., Syracuse University, 1954.

el. The Chicago Area Transportation Study (CATS),[e] formed in 1955, and Penn Jersey, formed at about the same time, were the first major such groups in the nation. CATS produced a series of documents that came to be considered as the definitive analysis for community transportation planning in its time. It was formed to analyze existing travel behavior, to forecast what the future requirements of the metropolitan region would be and to advise long-range plans for needed highways and mass transportation facilities. On the basis of this work, many other communities expressed interest and worked on developing similar plans although the activity was not well organized and progress was slow.

Urban transportation planning as a federal activity began with the Housing Act of 1961, which specifically provided funds for integrating transportation with general community planning. The following year, the Federal Aid Highway Act of 1962 also called for comprehensive planning between highway interests and the states and local communities. Note, however, that the two pieces of legislation stem from and were administered by different federal agencies, one by HUD and the other by the Department of Commerce initially and, later, after 1966, the Department of Transportation. Consequently, different sets of requirements and guidelines came from each department and each certified different local agencies. With the passage of the UMTA legislation and the attendant mass transit planning, a third set of guidelines and certified local agencies came into being. Thus, even without other types of planning agency involvement, transportation was handled in a disjointed fashion from the start of the early 1960s.

At the same time transportation planning was developing as a discipline, planning in other functional areas of government influence was growing at a rapid rate also. The federal government, for example, began favoring regions for grants that had overall planning councils, such as the regional council or "Council of Governments" (COG) and Regional Planning Commission (RPC). By 1970 there were 476 such organizations. Today every metropolitan area has at least one major planning body. Most of these were originally funded through the so-called "701" planning grants. Beginning in 1961, funding had increased from other agencies acting along functional lines and by 1973 some 17 different programs, in addition to the 701 work, were actively funding different types of planning activities including such programs as open space, water and sewer, new communi-

---

[e] CATS was established by executive order of the state, and agreement with the city of Chicago, Cook County, and the Bureau of Public Roads. In 1967 CATS was expanded to include the six counties in the Chicago SMSA (Cook, DuPage, Kane, Lake, McHenry, and Will), and also has an agreement with Indiana to perform certain planning functions in the bordering Indian region.

ties, aged and handicapped manpower, criminal justice and health planning, in addition to highway and transportation planning.

Sometimes the most important urban planning was done by community groups that were not recognized by the federal government and that were not involved with federal programs in any way. For example, 80 percent of regional planning councils adopted transportation policies and plans at a time when only 37 percent of the groups were officially designated as DOT planning organizations. Another distinction occurs in the transportation legislation that formally recognizes the differences between comprehensive planning and local transportation planning; sometimes both are carried out within a single local planning group and sometimes not. A special problem also arises with a planning group that may have an active voice in local planning but that is not recognized by the federal agencies as able to receive grants and administer implementation programs. It removes planning from implementation that is a serious but prevalent occurrence.

Implementation is seriously hindered, of course, by the division of transit planning even among the various recognized agencies. For example, a transit planning agency will tend to make plans for the kinds of transit improvements they have the power and financing to implement. If one of their plans involves highway funds, the transit agency must work jointly with a highway agency that has its own priorities for those funds.

Urban planning (as distinct from transportation planning) is often practiced outside the metropolitan planning process by virtue of the fact that highway groups have traditionally been state organizations. Thus, highway urban planning funds fall under state organizations as well. These state agencies, usually called Section 134 agencies after the section of the congressional acts allocating funding, often dominate in the planning process: 42 percent of the organizations recognized by DOT to do urban transit planning out of highway funds were still state agencies in 1973; 37 percent were councils directed by local elected officials; and 17 percent were miscellaneous city and county organizations. This situation changed dramatically with the 1973 highway legislation that specifically designated planning funds be passed through the states to local groups so as of 1974, 74 percent of metropolitan areas are officially recognized and funded by DOT. Prior to this, over half of the federally funded mass transportation planning was done by organizations other than those recognized by Section 134 as official comprehensive planning agencies.

The problems are more complex than simply being the result the planning groups that have grown rapidly without coordination. Deeply rooted reasons account for these differences and they are not easily rectified. Size of area is one consideration. Typically UMTA tends to recognize areas smaller than the highway Section 134 designated areas and HUD 701 funds tend to be given to organizations representing still larger areas. The reason is obvious: transit systems are highly localized to city areas, highways relate to state regions, and HUD is concerned with complete metropolitan areas. It is apparent from this that the general concept of regionalism is truly in its infancy as far as transportation planning is concerned: one cannot yet agree on what the size a transportation should be.

Another problem has to do with political expediency and tradition. State governments are naturally reluctant to give up power and influence and significant federal funds; for this reason about 17 percent of metropolitan planning is still done by state agencies.[f] The dilemma of the federal government is clearly that whatever guidelines are developed must apply uniformly to all of the states. Yet, the states differ tremendously not only in transportation needs, but in size and political structure: Alaska, the largest state, is 483 times the size of Rhode Island, the smallest state.

Yet, political pressures and American Federalists tradition demand local control over local affairs. Consequently, regional transportation groups are frequently organized with the responsibility in the hands of local, elected officials. However, some local governments may be mistrustful of such new and unproven groups and may prefer to continue working with state groups where prior relationship exists. This attitude makes difficult the effective development of new regional groups but by no means precludes success.

It should be added that not even state government is sufficient in size to include the geographical scope of many transit issues. There are 38 metropolitan areas, involving two-thirds of the states, that cross state boundaries. The additional burden of these so-called bistate agencies is then a significant factor in the multilayered planning jurisdiction. Although such groups remain largely advisory, complications can arise because of lack of clear specifications of functions and jurisdictions.[g] Bistate groups illustrate the administrative complexity involved in trying to meet regional needs when the traditional jurisdictions do not.

---

[f] In several small states, such as Maryland, Massachusetts, New Jersey, and Connecticut, states assume a dominant role in decision making for metropolitan areas. In both Baltimore and Boston, for example, Section 134 metropolitan transportation planning is carried out by state agencies.

[g] An example of well-intentioned interference occurred in 1975 in Chicago when the designated Bi-state Planning Commission took six months to review an application to the federal government for new equipment for the financially troubled Rock Island line. Since this railroad operates completely within the state of Illinois, it should not have been subject to this delay by a group formed specifically to handle Illinois-Indiana affairs. The fact that the bistate group chose to do this, in the absence of firm guidelines on the layered planning agencies, was highly criticized by other regional planning groups but such criticism did not serve to eliminate the problem.

Realizing that the fragmentation and overlapping of responsibility and authority made planning management difficult, several steps have been taken since 1961 to attempt to improve matters. The Urban Mass Transportation Act amendments of 1966 required that planning studies under this act fit into the coordinated urban transportation system comprehensive development plan of the area. The Demonstration Cities and Metropolitan Development Act of 1966 required that coordination of any transportation project be consistent with the official comprehensive plans. One of the most far-reaching guidelines was that defined by the Office of Management and Budget (OMB) in 1969, which requires that any request for federal funds be reviewed by a designated official comprehensive planning agency to verify that the proposed project is consistent with the nation's comprehensive plan, in a process called the A-95 review.

To enhance regional cooperation, OMB usually certified agencies for A-95 review that were HUD certified and receiving the "701" planning grants. These of course were typically metropolitan groups, the Councils of Governments (COGs) of the Regional Planning Commissions (RPCs) that generally had long-range planning capability. In 255 of the 263 metropolitan areas, both the HUD and OMB designated the same area for organization for certification. This was an important step in unifying and coordinating both planning and implementation activities.

The use of state agencies[h] for comprehensive planning under the highway acts, of course, does not relate to the A-95 designated agency or the HUD "701" agency selection. Further, the UMTA planning grants tend to be given to general, all-purpose planning groups rather than specifically to long-range planning groups, which in many cases is the A-95 agency.

Consequently, in 1975, in an action to promote better coordination, the Department of Transportation asked each governor of each state to designate a single, general-purpose metropolitan planning organization to act as the official Metropolitan Planning Organization (MPO) to perform the required planning for both the highway planning and UMTA planning. It was indicated that any nonprofit organization would be suitable as long as it had general-purpose planning capability. Critics objected because creating the MPO does not combine planning with implementation [7].

DOT did state that for obtaining UMTA certification for the new MPO, the agency previously having A-95 certification be designated. This

[h] Actions to enhance planning flexibility often magnify implementation complexities. The 1973 Highway Act specified that, for the first time, funds for highway planning could also be used for transit planning, provided that all the state, local, and regional bodies could agree, but none of the grant approval procedures was changed. Thus, there was no incentive for change. Few agencies would relinquish funds losing power and prestige and perhaps its very existence on the basis of some believed, federally inspired efficiency move.

did not work well in all cases, and in March 1976 a new regulation was passed stating that when the MPO agrees to projects and plans, the A-95 review is no longer necessary. Instead, if the project is part of the MPO approved Transportation Improvement Program (TIP)—a list of annually updated specific projects—A-95 review is no longer required. Some feel the MPO does little to improve matters.

The failure to combine planning with implementation is a common complaint especially in federal analysis reports. The thought is that if the two were combined, it would be possible for decisions to be made within a single agency regarding the regulation of street traffic (banning of automobiles) in favor of transit. This criticism fails to note that the real reason automobiles cannot be constrained from use of the street or expressway is that there is no real alternative at present. Some transportation agencies, such as the Regional Transportation Authority of Northeastern Illinois, do have the undisputed authority to block off automobile traffic from streets or expressways. They do not do so because it would result in chaos, except in a few instances where exclusive bus lanes are practical. Similarly, in other communities it is probably not the lack of control over implementation that prevents an agency from securing traffic control constraints, since it would be easy enough in most cases to work jointly with the traffic control groups, but rather that no responsible agency would take measures to "ban automobiles" with no suitable alternative available. Creating new and different agencies will not solve the problem of a society where over 90 percent of all trips are by the private automobile.

Another group formed to improve the planning process is the Intermodel Planning Group (IPG), a group of primarily senior planning representatives of the major planning disciplines. This group is an advisory council to DOT, having also important contacts with HUD and the EPA, and forms a stronger linkage among local, state, and federal governments. Aside from offering technical assistance and recommending actions to reduce fragmentation and duplication among competing agencies, the group specializes in eliminating red tape and unnecessary documentation, specifically with respect to ensuring more responsive and equitable funding.

The charge is frequently put forth that there are too many planning organizations, with overlapping and indistinct responsibilities, and that there is continual need for improving the planning process. *Although the process, especially that of complying with federal requirements for funds, may be awkward and clumsy, it does for the most part work.* In part this is because of a variety of practical working mechanisms that promote communication and understanding. On the local level, it is usually some type of ad hoc task force arranged by the lead agency in a specific need, and on the national level it is the technical conference or seminar.

Conferences and Seminars[i]

The increasing complexity of federal legislation and administrative guidelines has proven an increasing barrier in the nation's planning network. To overcome these obvious difficulties, a series of four conferences on highway-oriented issues, a series of planning seminars, and two conferences directed toward UMTA guidelines have been held in the last 20 years. They have been successful in bringing together diverse views and generally developing an effective planning consensus.

The first conference, at Sagamore Center, Syracuse University, was held in 1958 for the purpose of promoting highway and community development; it did not concern mass transit. The second conference, at Hershey, Pennsylvania in 1962, was held the first year that urban planning was required for federal grants; the emphasis was on urban values, land use, and esthetic values; it also did not include mass transit. The 1965 Williamsburg, Virginia conference stressed urban values. It was not until the Mt. Pocono, Pennsylvania conference in 1971 that the focus turned to mass transportation as an important part of transportation planning.

In a remarkable way, these conferences reflect the changing public advocacy in this nation. The first conference focused primarily on highway construction and considered highway planning as an activity separate from urban planning; the second combined land use values and highway construction, bringing together implementation and planning; the third recognized the growing interests of communities in becoming involved in the decision process, especially with regard to disruptive freeways, and the fourth recognized that public opposition to new urban highways was a stimulus to considerations for mass transit.

Important as these four conferences were, they did not provide the scope required for the newly emerging urban transit planning field. Consequently, a series of seminars were held by the American Institute of Planners during 1971 at the request of the U.S. Department of Transportation. The six conferences focused on means of improving transportation processes and involved planners and experts in the urban transit field. These conferences called for specific changes in HUD and DOT certification procedures (primarily in acquiring common reviewing criteria), for federal operating subsidies for transit and the use of highway trust fund monies for transit. Many of these goals have come into being illustrating the importance of the consensus and priority-building conference.

The general success of this conference technique led to two UMTA-sponsored seminars, one at Airlie House, Maryland in 1975 and the sec-

[i] An excellent review of planning conferences and legislation is to be found in "Evolution of Urban Transportation," a report by Edward Weiner, manager of Office of Transportation Systems Analysis at the U.S. Department of Transportation, April 1976.

ond at Hunt Valley, Maryland in 1976. Both of these conferences related to alternative choices in transit investment with the second relating specifically in developing criteria for investments. These have proven to be important mechanisms for bringing together diverse viewpoints and gradually hold promise for the gradual development of a sound, effective planning discipline.

Federal Review Processes

Federal requirements differ significantly in scope and complexity. Since 1962 the federal government through the highway acts has required a "continuous, comprehensive and cooperative" transportation planning process, often called "the 3 C's approach" and grants are predicated on the proposed project being a part of that process. The Urban Mass Transit Act of 1964 also requires a unified approach to planning. To establish eligibility for assistance, it must be demonstrated that the project is or will be part of an activity related to the long-range, areawide planning.

The Housing Development Agency (HUD), through it's so-called 701 planning grants, has encouraged and funded regional planning. HUD regulations have set certification requirements for various planning activities that must be accomplished if any area is to qualify for certain water, sewer, or transportation grants. There are currently three certifications:

First Certification

An areawide planning area and organization must be established representing all local governments units by a majority of local elected officials.

Second Certification

Status of Comprehensive Urban Planning must be advanced to include:
1. Annual work program adopted, budgeted, staffed and underway
2. Adoption of a statement of areawide goals and objectives, including socioeconomic and housing concerns
3. Adoption of an areawide land-use element consistent with goals and objectives, and designation of both locations and densities of broad-use categories for at least 20 years hence, with transportation considerations and major public facilities
4. Citizen and public official involvement and participation in the comprehensive planning process

Third Certification

1. An adopted areawide water-sewer plan element and program
2. An adopted areawide open-space plan element program

The A-95 Review Process established by executive order in an Office of Management and Budget (OMB) memorandum requires that all federally funded projects be reviewed for compliance with regional plans. As one of the most important methods of coordinating subregional planning along the lines of the regional comprehensive plan, the A-95 review process performs the following functions.

1. Reviews all applications for federal funds to determine if the proposed project is in line with comprehensive regional plan
2. Informs all other appropriate agencies and local governments of an application for federal funds submitted to it
3. Arranges necessary follow-up conferences with interested agencies and local governments
4. Informs state and local agencies authorized to develop and enforce environmental standards, invites their comments on impact, and forwards their comments to the applicant

These represent typical examples of requirements that confront all transportation planning at some time. Because transportation is so broad in encompassing most elements of daily living, transportation becomes involved in almost all functional planning requirements to some degree. For example, the Clean Air Act amendments of 1970 require states to implement plans that include land-use and transportation controls to achieve national standards. All projects are required to have environmental impact statements. Further, the federal government requires citizen participation in the planning process. These and other federal requirements all have served to shape the transportation planning process throughout the nation.

In looking at the planning process and regionalism as a whole, it is clear that extraordinary accomplishments have taken place since the early 1960s, but, at the same time, regionalism as a reality is in its infancy. Today, every urban area has a major planning agency. Many metropolitan areas have as much as 20 years experience and several have as much as 50 years experience. Yet, the creation and strengthening of interjurisdictional regional governments is a slow process at best. Of the 250 metropolitan areas of the nation, only 11 have consolidated governments in any sense, and fewer than 20 have regional transportation governments. Until regionalism grows and develops, transportation, and other disciplines as well, must make use of multijurisdictional planning arrangements involving various combinations of states and local and bistate districts to meet immediate needs.

Commentary: Regionalism

Centralization at the national level always glorifies the importance of pieces of paper. This dims the sense of reality. With preoccupation of papers comes less understanding and less perception of the matters government should be dealing with: actual people and actual things in American life: highways, buses, drought, floods, backyards, funerals, and the price of a loaf of bread. Regionalism is the business of putting the reality back into government. It is as yet imperfect and little understood but both vital and necessary.

Appendix 3A
Planning Process History

1930s   Emergency coordinator (Transportation Act of 1933)
Presidential and congressional studies ("studyitis")
    National Resources Planning Board
    Committee of Three, of Six
    Toll Board Study (Tolls cannot finance highway construction)
Highway Act of 1934 (Hayden-Cartwright Act)
    1-1/2 percent for Highway Planning and Research (HRP funds)
    Inventory and mapping of existing highways
    Traffic surveys; economic analysis

1950s   Housing Act of 1954 (HHFA)
    Section 701: Urban Planning Assistance Program
Highway Act of 1956
    Massive construction funds ($46.2 billion over 13 years)
    No planning funds (led to highway conferences)
State ad hoc agencies
    CATS/Penn Jersey

1960s   Housing Act of 1961 (HHFA)
    "Facilitate comprehensive planning for urban development"
    "Coordinated transportation systems"
Joint report on urban mass transportation (1962) and President Kennedy's message
Highway Act of 1962
    "Coordinated, comprehensive and continuous planning" (3 C's)
    Section 134: state planning agencies
Urban Mass Transportation Act (UMTA) of 1964
    Planning and establishment of urban transportation
Housing and Urban Development Act of 1965 (HUD)
    Section 701 modified but retained as comprehensive planning
Department of Transportation Act of 1966
    Joint DOT and HUD responsibility for transit
A-95 review circular (OMB)
    Coordinates planning and implementation of federal projects

1970s   Urban Mass Transportation Assistance Act of 1970
    Extended planning to include social parameters

Highway Act of 1970

Revised Section 134 agencies to increase local decision making

Highway Act of 1973

Additional 1/2 percent for urban planning (Pl funds)

Established metropolitan planning organizations (MPO)

Appendix 3B
Planning Conferences

Federal Aid Highway Program

1958   Sagamore Center, Syracuse University
      Need for urban planning
      Cost-benefit analysis
      Land-use technology

1962   Hershey, Pennsylvania
      Emphasized teamwork
      Urban design research
      Stressed urban values

1965   Williamsburg, Virginia
      Goals in urban planning
      Evaluation of plans
      "Community values"
      Consumer-evaluation criteria
      Planning concepts broadened

1971   Mt. Pocono, Pennsylvania
      Urban transportation emphasized
      Multimodal transportation planning
      "3 C" approach recommended
      (comprehensive, coordinate, continuing)

American Institute of Planners

1971   Six seminars to improve planning process called for:
      Uniform certification procedures
      Federal operating subsidies
      Use of highway trust fund

UMTA Conferences

1975   Airlie House, Virginia
      Question of alternatives
      UMTA administration policies

1976   Hunt Valley, Maryland
      Alternative investment criteria

4

The Evolution of National Transportation Policy

Advances in transportation management have resulted more from changes in national policy than any other single factor. Keeping informed on policy and legislative matters is, therefore, a matter of critical concern to the transit manager and crucial to the development of public transportation.

Unfortunately, changes in policy follow only national crisis. This is true not just for urban transit, but for all transportation policy and for all policy in general. Democracies traditionally have lacked anticipatory mechanisms for dealing with predicted problems and instead confine most activity to obvious and apparent needs. For a long time, as long as resources were plentiful and the impact of unwanted or harmful actions limited, this method of confronting only crisis issues was adequate, no matter how wasteful or inefficient.

Times are changing. Today the government is confronted with a new generation of issues that resist old patterns of solution. Urban transportation is typical of these issues, which include, and are dominated by, the energy problem, environmental concerns, the balance of payments, inflation, and unemployment. One of the most distinctive characteristics of these problems is in fact that they are all bound together. Nor is this interconnectedness their only common characteristic; they all cut across a wide variety of interest groups; they concern shrinking economic resources; they are not subject to resolution simply by additional spending along traditional lines; they cannot be settled by the orthodox method of negotiating with competing interests or of trading-off; and, further, all involve technological and highly complicated analysis where issues are often not what is obviously perceived to be but something quite different and not easily understood. It is no longer a case of being able to simplify arguments, but of being able to complexify arguments in an understandable and meaningful way that can sustain an advocacy base.

These new issues, which are sometimes referred to as being part of the new politics of resource constraints, embody many of the characteristics that have long been evident in transportation policy. It is, therefore, of special value to examine the evolution of all transportation policy, not just of urban transit policy, to understand how issues have been handled and how solutions for newer, emerging issues might be developed.

Early Beginnings

Transportation policy had an impressive beginning in the work of Albert Gallatin, Secretary of the Treasury to Thomas Jefferson, in his "Report on Public Roads and Canals" in 1808. This distinguished analysis, which included an appendix by Robert Fulton, was a systematic, comprehensive study of the nation's transportation needs and of alternative methods for meeting these needs. Specific national objectives included resource development, industrialization, and settling of the West. Regarding the importance of transportation, Gallatin said, in words as true today as they were then: "No other single operation, within the power of government, can more effectively strengthen and perpetuate the union which secures external independence, domestic peace and internal liberty."

Gallatin intended a federally supervised national transportation effort, and his plan included proposed solutions of both geographic and engineering problems in relation to the United States budget and other priorities. It proposed an annual expenditure of $2 million a year for ten years. The plan was solidly on the side of government intervention in local affairs.

The 1800s, however, saw an era of strong state supremacy with opposition to the exercise of federal tax powers necessary for a strong federal program. The expansion of the canal and rail systems were largely state promoted and governed by the states. Consequently, until the late nineteenth century, federal transportation policy was essentially one of nonintervention. Then, a series of regulatory acts were passed to control the railroads and pipelines, in addition to the Sherman Anti-Trust Act of 1890.

It began with the Act to Regulate Commerce,[a] passed in 1887. This act was largely unsuccessful, although it marked the beginning of the federal regulatory agency, the Interstate Commerce Commission (ICC). The first ICC was without the proper tools to function adequately. It could not obtain accurate rate information, lacked the power to subpoena witnesses and information and had no enforcement power. In the Revision of 1889, the ICC was made independent, given limited enforcement power and directed to report directly to Congress. This marked an important step in policy development since it recognizes (1) the need for information and performance data of all kinds and (2) that implementation activities must be combined with analysis.

The Character of Transportation Policy

With the exception of regulatory-type policy, there existed no transportation policy as such before the turn of the century. Roads had been considered a rural problem, handled by the Office of Road Inquiry in the Depart-

---

[a] A history of transportation acts is summarized in appendix 4A.

ment of Agriculture. Since railroads dominated all forms of transportation, secondary road systems declined to a level that had not existed since Revolutionary times. The rapid development of the automobile, and World War I, ultimately led to the Federal Aid Highway Act of 1916, the first of a long series of highway acts. A history of subsequent legislative policy for rail, air, sea, and surface modes is presented in appendix 4A.

In reviewing the evolution of transportation policy, three factors are at once apparent:

1. Policy changes occur primarily in times of crisis or stress.
2. An existing policy, having once set a precedent, is frequently applied to a new situation even though there is little resemblance to the past act.
3. Each mode, whether air, sea, rail, or surface, is treated independently from the others, although in practice there are strong interactions among modes.

Pressures in a democratic society arise from many sources including social upheavals, labor disputes, depressions, recessions, and military threats. Such a crisis, sensed by the entire nation, impinges on the political leaders who take action by executive order, legislative action, or administrative directive. Sometimes the action directly removes the source (A) of the crisis, such as in a military threat. Other times, the crisis may relieve itself by other means, and the resulting actions simply become precedent for entirely unrelated needs, part of the bureaucratic machine running on its own resources (B). The ideal solution (C), if such exists, would be a rational, pragmatic approach, examining alternatives and consequences, relating back to the political leadership and eventual impact on policy. (See figure 4-1.)

One of the most interesting and, unfortunate, characteristics of transportation policy is the lack of coordination between legislation of various transportation systems even though they are closely interrelated.

The Shipping Act of 1916 was carried out independently of any effect on railroad and highway goods movement. The Transportation Act of 1920, although directed toward promoting an adequate national transportation system for the country as a whole, was in a practical sense directed toward modifying some of the most punitive legislation against railroads. Yet, the following year, the Federal Highway Act of 1921 took place with virtually no regard to its effect on railroads, although this legislation was to have an enormous influence on the character of national transportation and the role of the railroads. When the Motor Carrier Act of 1935 was enacted to protect the growing trucking industry, then numbering 89,000 private carriers, no thought was directed toward the conflicting interests and diverse government involvement among water, rail, and truck modes or how these could be resolved.

Any new legislation to improve or modify previous work was always

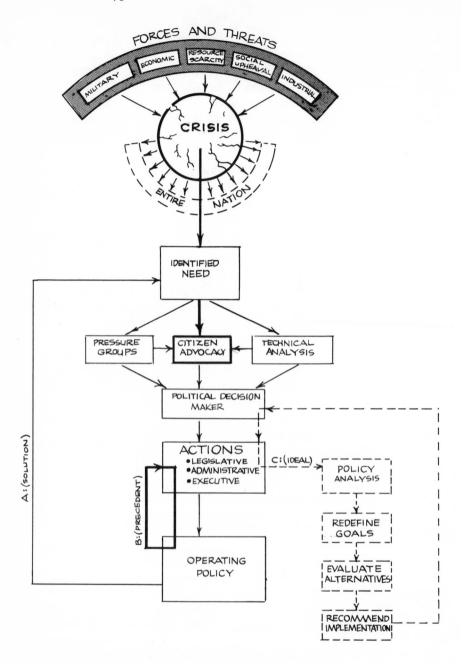

Figure 4-1. Crisis-oriented National Policy.

undertaken in terms of the specific mode.[b] It was really the first era of government intervention in the private sector. The legislation during the 1930s, in every field, not just transportation, was designed to prevent further economic catastrophe brought on by the Depression. The legislation was of a simple sort, such as Social Security and the Federal Housing Authority, to bring stability and promote economic expansion in the private sector. Although public transportation had declined drastically during the late 1920s and early 1930s, transit stabilized dramatically in 1931 and so was considered to be in sound health or at least not headed for imminent demise. It may be, in fact, that transit's apparent economic stability was one of the factors that kept transit from being included in this first wave of government intervention in transportation generally and that later posed some difficulty when it became necessary during the 1960s to bring transit into the fold of government involvement. This may account for the fact that, even today, transit is not considered as logical a choice for direct government intervention as are, say, the highways.

Highways are interesting because they span several different eras of government involvement. For example, when the first Highway Act of 1916 was passed, many states were opposed because they had already spent local funds on road-building programs and did not feel it proper that their funds, contributed to the federal government, should be dispersed to other states that had not invested in highways. Note that the act provided only for 50-50 government sharing with local funds, a concession to these other states that had been investing on their own. The concept of building an interstate highway system (Highway Act of 1921), that is, a network having special value to the central government, was in part a response to resistance to federal intervention in local affairs, and very early set the pattern that highways were not to be thought of as other federal programs, but rather as a special program that somehow circumvented traditional arguments, as a program of loftier goals and involved with national purpose in a different way than previously considered.

In 1956, under pressure from what was called [14,15] "the most unique and massive coalition of single-minded pressures ever to hit the American scene," the Federal Aid Highway Act of 1956 was passed. Under this act, 90 percent of the costs of interstate highways were covered by federal funds. These massive funds proved to be an irresistible lure for the states and served to meet many needs other than that of the transportation objective. (See figure 4-2.) The act also established the Highway Trust

[b]Other independent legislation would include the Merchant Marine Act of 1936, and all of the aviation legislation beginning with the Air Commerce Act of 1926, the Air Mail Act of 1934, and the Civil Aeronautics Acts of 1938.

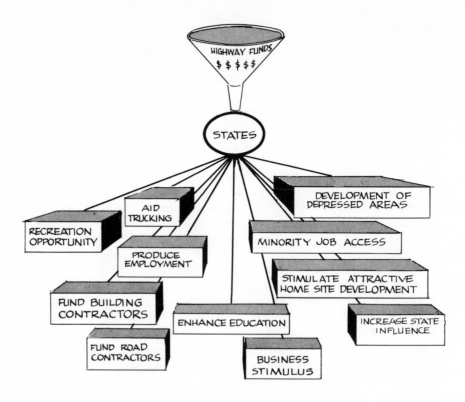

Figure 4-2. Varied Use of Highway Funds.

Fund, from which all highway expenditures were made to be made.[c] This fund identified certain taxes assessed on motor vehicles and materials to be used for highway development and for no other purpose.

So effective was this legislation in developing the highway system that other legislators saw it as a means of effecting new policy, although the Highway Acts have generally been resistant to change. For example, it was believed in 1962 that the Highway Act would serve as an excellent means of promoting nationwide comprehensive planning. Consequently, the highway legislation that year carried the provision that highway funds could only be obtained when comprehensive planning processes were carried out by the states and municipalities. The intention was to use the trust fund allocation as a lever and driving force in establishing the policy of integrated planning. It did not work quite this way, because of the basic inflexibility of the highway network already planned. Since the first task

[c] (For a detailed discussion of the trust fund, see Chapter 7, Financing and Marketing Structure.)

of comprehensive planning is to examine the earlier plans, the planning process itself was seriously compromised.

Any federal policy that funnels enormous funds into local governments will naturally be resistant to change because of the legislature pressure to fund withdrawal from affected areas. Certainly transportation development has been used to accomplish ends unrelated to surface goals. States have determined their transportation needs by a myriad of dispersed and sometimes conflicting considerations, such as the need to stabilize their regional economics through large government expenditure, to produce employment opportunities and fund building and business contractors, to aid trucking throughout the region, to accelerate redevelopment of depressed areas, to improve minority job access, and enhance educational, recreational, and attractive home-site development. When all of these factors become closely linked with, and dependent on, a strong ongoing federal funding program, a change in policy is difficult to achieve because of the vast, yet tenuous nature of the affected areas.

Many authorities have said [16] that if anyone had realized the sheer magnitude of the interests affected by our public policy of developing the road system while neglecting other transportation, that legislation never would have been adopted. It has taken learned pleas [17, 18], and the eloquent and lucid warnings of concerned organizations [19] and public officials [20, 21, 22], to bring about significant change in the Highway Act. This occurred in 1973 when trust funds for the first time were permitted to be used for public transit projects as well as highways. Although some of the most recent policy analyses [11] from within the Department of Transportation still predict a continuation of massive highway expenditures, in comparison to transit construction, there are distinct signs of change [13].

Highway legislation is especially interesting in that it reflects but remains apart from general legislative patterns evolving with changes in national character. There have been several distinct stages to this gradual evolution:

1. Prior to the 1930s, government intervention in the private sector was not embraced and welcomed. Highways proved an exception to this rule in the two decades proceeding by relating well to national goals of defense, which requires an interstate system, and locks all states together on an individual basis in developing a system needed for national survival. No other physical process has really done this.

2. During the 1930s, the federal government began intervention in the private sector, although the nature of that intervention was always under debate. All forms of transportation reflected this intervention with the exception of public transit. Somehow it seemed natural that the federal government should take a lead role in promoting air travel, in building highways, in regulating truck commerce, and become deeply involved with

the railroads, but no one suggested the needs of cities and transit be included in these deliberations and actions. This posture continued throughout World War II.

3. The 1960s opened a new era for government intervention in purely local affairs. The government began to create opportunity for those who had not had much before, and hence was involved indirectly altering the nation's social environment; the federal government also became involved directly with improving the environment and changing national behavior. Mass transit was one of these new wave goals. Unfortunately, most of these efforts did not last long and were generally underfunded; it was not so much a case of public opposition to federal involvement as it was due to an unpopular war, a shortage of money, class resentments, and the general feeling that national behavior cannot be simply redirected by federal legislation alone.

Highway legislation weathered the transition in government intervention very well. Because of the vast resources in the highway trust fund, the new highway legislation remained outside the revitalized social legislation of the sixties. Although the trend in highway guidelines and legislative directives followed the pattern of the times (that is, the work gradually included citizen participation, opposition to freeways, more land-use planning and aesthetic considerations, and finally comprehensive planning and transit), for the most part the highways remained a separate quantity, handled through traditional state offices that had existed since the middle of World War I.

In contrast, public transit was very much a part of the social legislation of the 1960s. It began with the Housing Act of 1961, which provided a limited amount of financial assistance to aid the inner city and gave some emergency relief to the section of the population that could not afford an automobile. It produced a variety of studies and pilot projects that in turn laid most of the nation's key problems, either directly or indirectly, at the doorstep of automobiles. The dangers to the nation resulting from an overwhelming reliance on the automobile and the consequent need to develop a more "balanced" national transportation system were stressed [31].

Although this action was hailed as a beginning in recognizing the federal responsibility to public transit, it had a limited view of public transit as being only for the inner city, for the poor and handicapped, and for those automobile-owning households who worked in the central business districts (CBD). Although the CBD of any metropolitan area is important in generating employment, most of those employed worked either in the suburbs or in other regions of the area, where little public transportation exists and where most households consequently have two or more cars. The significant role public transportation could play in conserving energy and providing inflationary-caused relief to families while increasing employment opportunity has, therefore, never really been examined.

President John F. Kennedy's Transportation Message [32] to Congress in 1962 identified both the need for long-range assistance and emergency aid. Several of the most important recommendations adopted required comprehensive planning in urban areas as a prerequisite for highway grants and initiation of further public transit legislation.

Unfortunately, the nation's public transit system had so disintegrated by the time the first Urban Mass Transportation Act of 1964 was passed that all that could be done was to administer transit's most apparent ills. Today, modest improvements are planned, with increased capacity in specific areas. A general stabilization of transit has prevented catastrophic collapse.

Although recent legislation has improved the public transit funding rate, some "official plans," notably those of the Federal Highway Department [11], largely follow past policies in predicting major expansions of the highway system with only modest improvement in public transit. During the next 15 years, by 1990, the plans call for:

1. $26.8 billion a year to be spent for highways
2. $3.5 billion a year to be spent for public transit
3. A 66 percent increase in vehicle miles and auto trips
4. A 1 percent increase in public transit trips in spite of an anticipated 43 percent increase in transit routes

These figures mean that by 1990 most of the existing transit fleet will be replaced by newer cars, and only about half of the existing dilapidated stations and facilities will be replaced. The continual delay in starting new systems does not auger well for transit expansion, with little change on the almost total dependence on the automobile predicted.

Such plans are in direct conflict with stated administration energy conservation goals and are out of touch with the realities of resource management. It is doubtful that such policies will continue for long. However, it is interesting to note that as the only published official plans, these remain at present obsolete, official, and under heavy scrutiny.

The Crisis Syndrome

Change in a nation's transportation policy has occurred only in time of crisis, such as war, national depression, or major recession, or in situations where a major transportation mode was in danger of collapse. Generally, this necessity of crisis to prompt change is present in all government activities.

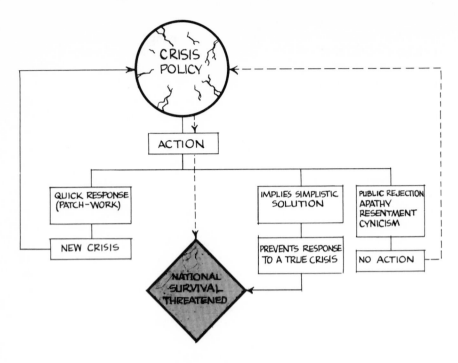

Figure 4-3. Crisis Policy Threatens National Survival.

Consequently, as one strategy to encourage change, American journalists, politicians, and special interest groups have become adept at exposing problems in debatable belief that overdramatizing issues will attract serious public attention and support for proposed solutions. Although part of this zeal reflects the growing awareness and concern of an informed public, it also reflects a superficial aspect of the national character that wants to solve problems quickly without understanding the problems in terms of their complexities.

Most of the serious problems of our time do not lend themselves to this crisis approach. Many of them, such as air pollution, congestion, and land use have solutions that require a basic change in human perceptions and attitudes, in resource allocations and perhaps in technology. Therefore, failure to recognize these factors can lead to national apathy, resentment, resistance, and cynicism, which ultimately slow progress and work to prevent any policy change.

More important, the promotion of too many crisis issues can destroy the public's ability to respond to real and present danger. There is some indication that this is happening now in conflicts between transportation and conservation policies and in the resource scarcity, inflation, and unemployment cycles. (See figure 4-3.)

One of the tests of an effective transportation network is its capability to adjust to dynamic change and crisis. The fact that this nation's transportation system has always required crisis-oriented legislation is in itself indicative of the failure of the system.

In a nation of moderate means, it is possible to correlate directly the prosperity of the people with the effectiveness of the transit policies. However, in the United States, with its vast indigenous wealth and long considered to be the world's most prosperous nation, influence of federal policy is less apparent as a tool in developing national capacity. Only when resources begin to decline noticeably, with a consequent effect on society's problems and on national prestige and power—as they are happening now—does national performance become a direct measure of the effectiveness of the federal transportation policy. The crisis is real but not apparent.

It has long been recognized, although not supported by action, that the personal automobile is not by itself suitable as a means of transport because of specific problems: the expense and wasteful use of land, roads, special servicing facilities, and both mineral and human resources the automobile demands in resolving problems of congestion, pollution, and energy consumption. Furthermore, the automobile, presently the nation's chief means of transportation, depends on uninterrupted services and supplies for performance. Any breakdown in gasoline deliveries, parts availability, or maintenance services brings chaos and disruption to national life.

The often near-total destruction of their systems through war and chaotic periods have allowed the European nations to evaluate systematically the balanced transportation needs necessary for tapping the full potential of the countries' resources, both human and material. Consequently, the strong economies and strong currencies of many European nations today are related to this purposeful coordination of transportation policies.

Many economists [29] believe that worldwide resource scarcity is the real cause for the high unemployment rate and of rampant inflation, which have so far resisted effective control. It is fair to say that until these resource problems are brought under control, the employment and productivity problems cannot be solved either. Hence, the importance of learning to deal with these pervasive problems now impinging on the nation's well-being [30]. Better policies are needed.

Efforts in Comprehensive Policy Analysis

The movement for the study and analysis to develop a comprehensive transportation policy began in the 1930s and produced several landmark works.

The federal coordinator of transportation, created under the Emergency Transportation Act of 1933, carried out some of the first comprehensive, long-range analyses designed to develop the concept of a full-fledged, unified, national transportation system. One underlying assumption was that separate, competing, private industries could be convinced to concede certain advantages for the common good. The arguments were not pursuasive and individual modes preferred retaining separate policies and separate legislative action.

Although this work produced little in the way of separate overt action, it did provide a broad perspective and information base for subsequent policy evaluations. Unfortunately, the work also presaged future difficulties in altering existing policies on the basis of intellectual judgment in the face of long tradition, well-established pressure groups, governmental bureaucracy, and all the factors that exert a tenacious influence over policy formation.

The various studies [2] of the 1930s and early 1940 awakened interest in coordinated policy and indicated an appreciation of the common problems affecting various transportation modes. Not only did these studies represent an attempt to examine the dimension of policy in greater depth than had been considered before, they also can be said to have had some effect on subsequent legislation, beginning with the Transportation Act of 1940.

Following World War II, a wide number of transportation studies were produced by a variety of groups. One of the most comprehensive evaluations was presented by the Hoover Commission [3], which not only urged the need for an integrated policy but advised centralizing institutions in a Department of Transportation.

These studies also noted the serious shortcomings in effective planning strategy and a general inability to predict, or even consider, possible consequences to certain actions. Certainly the need [23] to improve, especially in the technical aspects of planning, so that all the relevant factors in an evaluation are included, has never been satisfactorily addressed, and that remains a critical problem. Furthermore, the task of convincing the nation as a whole—especially competing agencies and organizations—to consider what the likely consequences of a given action can be, eludes us almost as much today [19, 24, 25] as it did previously.

Another key observation of the Hoover Commission found that sole reliance on the economic aspects of decision making in transportation policy could lead to national catastrophe. This point is crucial today in terms of policy implementation. Evidently unaware of this warning, for years the official policy on public transportation dictated that capital improvements would be undertaken by federal financing only with extreme caution, since it was argued that such improvements could impose serious long-term burdens on local resources unless the resulting services were guaranteed to be self-supporting.

As late as 1974, the Secretary of Transportation [26] presented to Congress his concept of transportation as being a system of individual modes, as if the main goal was to have financially successful, independent companies operating different modes of transportation [27].

Fortunately, this substantial policy error was addressed in the National Transportation Assistance Act of 1974, which for the first time authorized the use of federal funds for transit operating assistance. However, the lapse of 25 years between the commission's recommendation and the first steps of implementation has not been without cost to the nation.

It is difficult to assess the true impact and significance of transportation studies made in the past. The evidence shows an increasing capacity to support recommendations by facts, data, and by logical analyses of trends, rather than by intuitive judgment and opinion alone.

Transportation has always followed a model orientation with the rule of "separate policies for separate modes." Thus, depending on the crisis which developed, each mode—whether rail, air, water, or public transit—has been the object of separate legislation and funding. The administrative department, whether Department of Commerce or of Transportation, has limited scope in distribution of authorized funds. This leads to a serious imbalance in the transportation system as a whole, and to the inefficiency that has produced the energy crisis. (See figure 4-4.) Although the hope for a fully coordinated, comprehensive transportation policy is still some time off, there are important movements, through public pressure and technical analysis, encouraging political decision makers to create comprehensive policy models and to guide administrative agencies in an allocation of general, authorized funds to individual modal needs. (See figure 4-5.)

Although some high level studies of recent origin reveal a distressing lack of objectivity and understanding of urban transportation issues [28], on the whole most have been of reasonable caliber and responsible for providing a focus on key problem areas, developing good data bases in the process. Yet, in the overview, the long-run influence of these studies must be regarded as peripheral at best. The primary thrust of federal policy remains what it has always been, modally oriented, dominated by traditional influences and a complex maze of affected organizations. This observation suggests then that policy change cannot come through more elaborate analysis or through better-formulated papers and publications

PAST POLICY

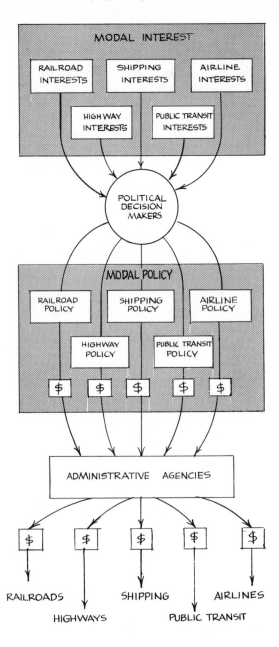

Figure 4-4. Past Policy.

EMERGING POLICY

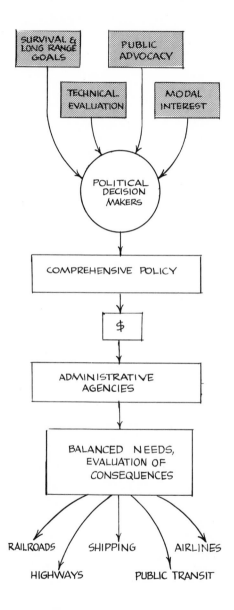

Figure 4-5. Emerging Policy.

but only through direct action—oriented toward breaking barriers and inflexible traditions. The goal is to effect change in a system designed to resist change.

Management Problems at the Federal Level

The announcement of a proposed Department of Transportation brought deep concern to the transportation industry [4]. Rumors that the new department would meddle in politics held untrue inferences that transportation policy had previously been nonpolitical [5]. Traditionally the transportation industry has always been deeply concerned over change, of course with good reason.

To allay this concern, the department was formed on a purposefully weak base as a "management shift" to maintain modal orientation with separate offices for each transportation mode, where no substantive changes were to occur in affected areas [6]. In 1968 public transit (UMTA) had 58 employees and FAA over 40,000. The respective sizes of each department are shown in figure 4-6. The highway mode has more than ten times the public transit mode indicating the disparity in balance among ground transportation modes. Although these factors were primarily a result of concerns of the railroads and shipping industries worried about regulatory policy, the impact has been profound on public transportation matters as well by essentially freezing the transportation management structure at a time when federal aid to public transit was still in its infancy.

A key factor in the congressional debate was whether DOT should have authority to make decisions on transportation investment. The chairman of the House Public Works Committee recommended [8] that DOT be limited to an advisory role to bar its disapproving highway construction under the Federal Aid Highway Act or the possibility of its shifting funds to other purposes in an action that did not foresee the energy crisis and the need for change. Each transportation interest, with its traditional, separate ties to the federal bureaucracy and Congress and its history of separate funding, backed a department organized along modal rather than functional lines [9].

In the final version of the bill creating the new department, the powers of both the department and the secretary were carefully circumscribed and limited [7]. In practice the secretary has always had more influence than planned. The large number of programs in which the department is engaged alone extends the power base [12]. The pervasive nature of transportation, interacting as it does with broad reaches of government encompassing regulatory agencies, courts, Congress, and the executive offices

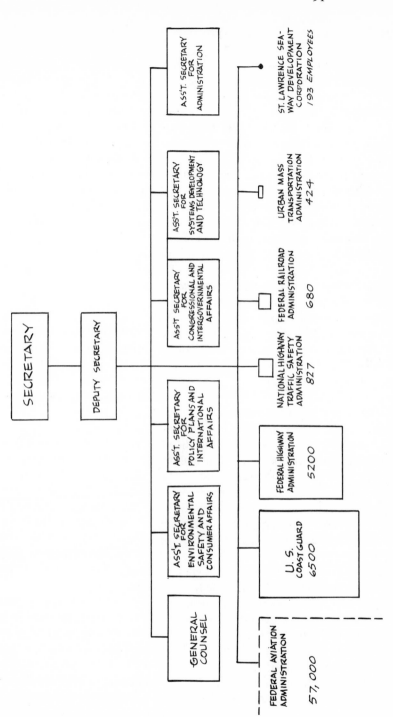

Figure 4-6. U.S. Department of Transportation Organization (1975).

of the White House including the president make it difficult, if not unfeasible, to limit department functions.

The large number of programs the department directs automatically extend the scope and influence of department activity and policy-making ability [10]. Although a past secretary has remarked that "policy tends to be confused with programs," there is another aspect to the extent that programs are often the tools that form policy, something every manager knows well. A striking example of this was revealed in a national survey [11] that provided data showing the necessity of channeling transit funds directly through cities, rather than traditionally through the state agencies as established in 1916. The report predicts this important change in policy will occur within the near future.

Another example of how learning through programs affects policy, although less direct but nevertheless as instructive, involved the legislation change in 1974 that permitted operating subsidies to be used for transit for the first time. Although previous policies had been firmly against this, experience through various programs showed that unless such changes were made, catastrophic events would occur.

One danger of any large bureaucracy is its tendency to do the convenient, even if such tasks are simply procedural and nonproductive, rather than tackling the harder problems of policy formation. This is especially true in the Department of Transportation where the formation has been based on the assumption that only management and not substantive changes would occur. In DOT the emphasis has been on managing existing policies and given administrative procedures rather than on true attempts to remedy problems.

Consequently, it is not unusual to discover that the department often becomes involved in local decision making on detailed engineering and design reviews that in no way relate to the federal responsibility of efficiently administering federal grants. Federal agencies also suggest and encourage changes in local policy that can ameliorate traffic situations or other problems. However, the existence of these problems may be directly or indirectly due to long standing federal policies and can only be remedied by changes in federal level activity. The fact that municipalities probably can make improvements to alleviate some of the detrimental results of federal decisions is not a prime federal concern. It displays a confusion at the federal level as to what is a proper activity and what is not. Such activities may well rise from the frustration that comes with an inability to act directly on policy at the federal level and to substitute activities in policy-making decision at the local level, and both are related to a lack of broad definition of national goals [1].

A different type of malfunction involves an inability to become directly concerned in transit financing decisions. While the department has examined the severe financial limitation [33, 34] and lack of alternative means of improving this situation, there is a marked tendency to substitute hoped-for panacea projects to overcome the lack of funding with technical miracles. From the early 1961 public transit study projects, there has been a tendency to concentrate on intellectually interesting studies, but ones that in total are very far removed from a plan of action and that in total fail to come to grips with the real problems of public transportation. At worst, demonstration programs have become defense supports for marginally funded, technological feasibility projects where excessive promises are made and little produced. By giving only to those who promise vast benefits, such programs discourage valid technical investigations and true technical advance.

Considerations of convenience also have been a factor in preventing the agency from entering into crucial problem areas that demand attention but where procedures and workable guidelines are not defined. For example, although it is generally recognized that existing regulatory policies are highly inflationary [35], little has been attempted in a technical way to provide data and information on how best to deal with transportation regulation. Labor relations and transit problems in general are other equally sensitive problem concerns. Most authorities agree that, however difficult, a different approach to productivity and wage increases must be implemented; the special management and personnel problems of transit operators require a more specialized approach.

The long history of the transit industry's decline and the resulting paucity of good management personnel represent a special challenge, and one in which some progress has already been made through the special academic training programs. It is an understandably difficult task for the department to undertake, since concurrent with trying to improve the most discouraging aspects of current transit management, it is continually exposed to the lack of perception and awareness that is sometimes all too evident in existing management. Within the past decade, the improvement in transportation management has been significant nationwide.

The greatest danger to progressive policy evolution lies in the tendency to confuse habits of convenience and a preference for staying within well-established procedures and guidelines when analyzing potential benefits of a new course of action.

The energy policy decisions of the past year are an unfortunate example of this tendency to make policy decisions based on convenience and tradition rather than on technical merit or need. The published policy [36] evaluating public transportation's potential contribution erroneously concluded that public transit could be of little use. This conclusion was based, first, on the assumption that any addition to existing transit would only be made equally to all areas since this was the most convenient way, rather than to selected areas that would require additional effort and analysis. Second, it was assumed that any increase in transit would have to stay within the present plan of limiting transit to a 43 percent route increase by 1990, clearly too small an increase over too long a period to permit transit to make any contribution in energy conservation.

The facts show [37] that public transit has the potential of greatly reducing fuel consumption with only relative increases in cost. Clearly the policy should be to follow the course that holds the greatest benefit rather than the one most convenient.

Significant improvement in the nation's transportation policies will require a different role for the Department of Transportation. If the department is to be expected to improve policy, especially toward developing a comprehensive policy and direct activities to correct the ills of the transportation system, the department must play the role of a full-fledged partner in this endeavor.

There can be, and probably will be, disagreement among competing interests but the dispute and resolution must be among partners. Otherwise, the full potential of the country, in terms of both human and material resources, cannot be realized.

Federal Influence on Mass Transit

The Department of Transportation, in spite of the aforementioned difficulties, serves as an important focusing mechanism for public transportation issues. It is instructive to review progress in public transit legislation both before and after DOT formation, taking into account other events and changes in public thought and advocacy position.

Early Progress

Although it is difficult to imagine now, the promotion of urbanization was once among the earliest and most important activities of the federal government. At the time of the Revolution, the nation was almost completely rural and directly supported from the soil. Only two cities had more than 25,000 inhabitants, and only 24 places had more than 2,500 people. New York, the nation's largest city, did not pass the 100,000 mark until after 1820.

The young revolutionary government was in debt and dependent on foreign nations for almost all manufactured goods. The government used incentives and strategies of various kinds of promote manufacturing and commerce, to increase exports and reduce imports, to aid invention, discovery, and industrialization. The building of large urban centers was a natural part of this process. By 1835 over 10 percent of the population was urban, the growth of industrialization was well underway, and the national debt had been extinguished. The federal government then disengaged from active urban development.

The present era of major federal concern for urban areas is usually considered to have its beginnings with the Standard City Planning Enabling Act of 1928, under then Secretary of Commerce Herbert Hoover. This act promoted long-range, comprehensive planning for the physical development of cities. Although the Great Depression interfered with these objectives, many of the concepts were later used in regional planning activities of the 1930s and in connection with the comprehensive transportation planning under the previously mentioned emergency coordinator of transportation. Although these endeavors produced results only peripheral in the overall transportation matters, these were important beginnings in changes in perception on how things ought to be and in changes in the language, which are evident in the National Transportation Act of 1940.

The matter of public transit does not appear in federal legislation until the Transportation Act of 1958 when certain changes were made in regulatory procedures to permit railroads to divest themselves of commuter service under specific conditions to help build the overall financial health of the railroads. Although not in the interests of public transit, it did serve to bring to attention transit stress.

Prior to the late 1950s, little federal activity was evident in the public transit field. The entire BART project in San Francisco, for example, from early planning to construction was done without relation to federal interests. Then, in 1957 bills began to appear. The so-called Green Bill, sponsored by Congressman William Green of Philadelphia, was introduced into the House but never reached the floor, having been buried in committee. Other efforts to interest the U.S. Department of Commerce were also unsuccessful.

However, in 1960 the Department of Commerce issued the "Federal Transportation Policy and Program" document, which mentioned the relation between federal programs and the resulting impact in terms of congestion and public transit losses. This document described the greater efficiencies of public transport and urged reexamination of the highway program with respect to urban transportation; it suggested that some highway funds might be used in better comprehensive planning. In spite of these encouraging words, the Department of Commerce and the Eisenhower administration, with the extensive commitment to build the highway system, were not receptive to suggested legislation.

The first sure movement of action came instead from another source, that of the Senate Committee on Banking and Currency, which had jurisdiction over the Housing and Home Finance Agency. A bill, the Urban Mass Transit Bill of 1960, which authorized $100 million in loans and demonstration grants to transit, was approved by committee; the Senate passed the measure but it did not get out of committee in the House.

Another, and similar bill, introduced in 1961, shortly before President Kennedy's inauguration, was found to be short of support. Consequently, the major request for $100 million in funds for low-interest loans and experimental or demonstration programs was eventually reduced to $42.5 million and included as part of the Housing Act of 1961, then under the Housing and Home Finance Agency (HHFA). It was a small start, but a start nevertheless.

The change in national position was also evident in a major administration speech, President Kennedy's Transportation Message of 1962:

To conserve and enhance values of existing urban areas is essential.... The ways that people and goods can be moved in these areas will have a major influence on their structure, on the efficiency of their economy.... Our national welfare therefore requires the provision of good urban transportation, with the properly balanced use of private vehicles and modern mass transport.

These newly developing attitudes were reflected in highway legislation to a small degree. The Highway Act of 1962 contained provisions for comprehensive planning including mass transit alternatives as a requirement for receiving federal highway funds, as already discussed in an earlier section. In spite of these announced intentions by the administration, the Urban Mass Transit Bill of 1962 did not survive the 87th Congress, although an extension to the Housing Act did succeed in passage.

Another "new" Urban Mass Transportation Bill of 1963 did pass the Senate, by a vote of 52-41, but was not expected to pass the House. After months of delay and considerable legislative effort on the part of transit interests, the House did pass the measure by a margin of 212-189 in June of 1964 producing the foundation of transit legislation: the Urban Mass Transportation Act of 1964.

In part, this act extended some of the work initiated under the Housing Act of 1961, and followed the guidelines originated in 1961 that the funding would be on a sharing basis of at most two-thirds federal to one-third local, in contrast to the highway sharing of 90 percent federal to 10 percent local. It provided $375 million for a three-year period, and gave funds for capital grants as well as for demonstration studies, and continued the low interest rate loans.

Recent Legislation

It was generally recognized that the 1964 legislation was correct in intention but grossly insufficient in funding. For a time, a variety of bills were considered to significantly increase the funding level. However, it was an age of fiscal conservatism and such amendments did not receive favorable support. In 1966 amendments permitted an additional $175 million for one year only and provided training funds for the first time. It passed with little opposition: 47-34 in the Senate and 235-127 in the House.

Another provision of the 1966 amendment was that the transit funding should fall under the newly formed Housing and Urban Development (HUD) Department. It was the first year that mass transit had funds to examine long-range projects and higher technologies. In 1967 the Urban Transportation Administration (UTA) undertook these promising studies. Shortly after DOT was formed in 1967, mass transit activities were moved to the new department under the Urban Mass Transit Administration (UMTA).

During this period, support was gaining momentum to use portions of the highway trust funds for purposes other than highway construction. In 1969 Secretary of Transportation John Volpe added support for this activity and for the formation of a general transportation trust fund.

However, in August 1969 President Nixon proposed a $10 billion program for mass transit to be extended over a 12-year period, but without trust fund monies. In 1970 the Nixon administration succeeded in getting this legislation through Congress. There was now growing support for transit. The Senate passed the legislation 83-4 and the House, 327-16.

Meanwhile, pressure continued for transit funding from the highway trust fund. In the 1970 Highway Act, some monies had been allocated for transit-related purposes. Specifically, funds were allotted to construction of exclusive bus lanes under certain conditions, special traffic control mechanisms, bus passenger loading areas, bus shelters, and certain types of parking facilities for public transit patron's use. It was also clear that when the trust fund came up for renewal in 1972, some further concessions were likely.

The issues in the trust fund debate were sufficiently volatile that a consensus could not be reached in the election year of 1972. Accord was finally reached in 1973 and under strong administration support, the trust fund was opened to mass transit usage. The House vote, for example, was 382-34, showing the growing support for transit programs. The percentages of total highway funding that could be used for mass transit were small (see appendix 4A), but the principle was established. It further increased the percentage of federal sharing to 80 percent from the previous maximum of two-thirds, and permitted 100 percent funded planning grants.

The need for operating assistance, long misunderstood and thought to be merely a way of rewarding poor management, came into prominence in 1973-74. Gradually it was realized that transit could not be supported out of the fare box. These concepts became part of the National Mass Transportation Assistance Act of 1974.

The true indication of the turning point for mass transit, however, was not in the passage of these bills alone but in the growing momentum that marked the passage. Prior to 1973, the Senate always offered a hardcore liberal vote of about 30 votes, and could be counted on to pass moderately liberal transit legislation. In House, however, there were at most 160-170 transit votes, which were of insufficient strength and would require special circumstances, such as a major crisis, to promote action.

Yet, in 1973 the so-called liberal Anderson Amendment, named for Congressman Glen Anderson of California, failed the House but only by a vote of 190-215, and this happened with six important New York votes absent. When vote counts reach close to the 200 mark, it becomes at once clear that the strength can be sufficient to pass major legislation. Members of major committees know that when this type of strength exists on the House floor, they then must mark up a bill with care, lest corrective action be taken on the House floor, embarrassing the committee chairman and members. Thus, it was clear that although the House was not quite willing to pass outright a liberal amendment, it was close and, later, much of this "Bust the Trust" Anderson Amendment was included in the passage of the final bill that was worked out in committee with the Senate. These amendment votes, even in defeat, are the key indicators rather than the final compromise version of the bill.

The shift in factions is also evident in the margins between types of funding for the same objective. For example, the compromise version of the Senate Bill S502, for opening the Highway Trust Fund to transit, passed by the narrow margin of 49-44 on March 15, 1973. But in a separate outlay, authorizing $800 million transit expenditures from general tax revenues, the Senate voted in favor, 59-36. Similarly, the original transit operating subsidy bill, S386, passed the House on October 3, 1973, by a vote of 219-195 showing further evidence of the growing strength.

In less than two decades, federal legislation has progressed from refusing loans and grants to transit and being completely committed to an unbalanced program in highways construction to funding significant, if still unbalanced, transit funds for loans and study projects (1961) to capital grants (1964), to opening of the Highway Trust Fund (1973), and to operating assistance (1974). The comprehensive policy and a general transportation trust fund are still to be realized. (See figure 4-7. Also see appendix 4A.)

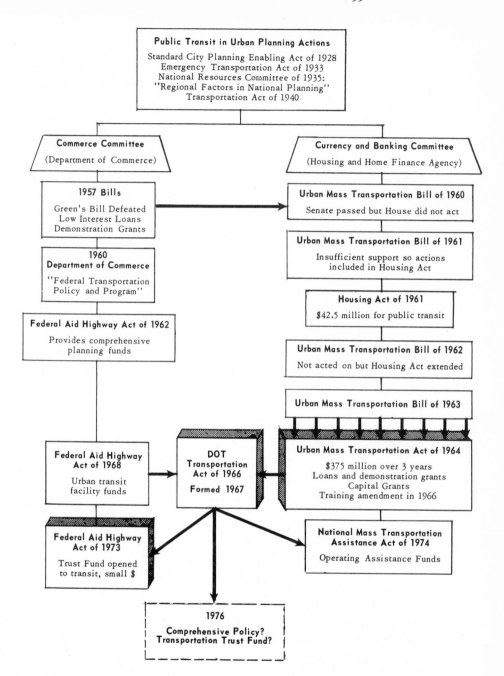

Figure 4-7. The Course of Public Transit Legislative History.

Directions in Transit Policy

In September of 1975, the Secretary of Transportation, William T. Coleman, Jr., issued a "Statement of National Transportation Policy."[d] In a foreword, he indicated that this statement was an initial attempt to set forth broad policy considerations. He invited and urged criticism and comment.

To put together such a document took courage and foresight. Changes can occur only if a first step is taken. This in itself is an accomplishment. Nevertheless, taking all such considerations into account, this policy statement must be regarded as something of a masquerade. It takes tacit positions that are known not to be the case. The statements about what goals and objectives of the various transportation modes are, and what is being done, are all true enough; yet, behind it all is a kind of obvious false mask as if to say, "what we show is not what we really believe."

Perhaps the most curious charade is the pretense that the federal government is weak and powerless in setting things right. This concept pervades the entire document. The statement contends that the federal government is inherently weak in bringing about change and in meeting national objectives; it contends that decision makers are limited by a paucity of information when in fact there is more information and data available to legislators than in any time in history. Always the statement seems to emphasize a need for a consensus, of being either ignorant or afraid of true experimentation, of wanting to hide behind generalities even when it is known that the resulting action or lack of action is contrary to national goals and needs.

Certainly the statement does address in many different ways the various key issues facing the nation, and ways in which mass transit plays a role in these issues is also clearly stated. The need for vital cities, control of air pollution, conservation of energy, mobility for all citizens, movement toward full employment, a more compatible use of land and open space, and a better quality of life and an improved relationship between man and his environment are beautifully articulated. Consequently, on page 8 of the statement, strong federal support for transit is recommended. But nowhere does the statement actually tie together, say, prospects for better land-use and transportation decision making. It becomes clear that although transit policy acknowledges land-use needs and the relationship with transportation decisions, there is no marriage of the concepts. The statement in this sense does not really bring rational land use into the policy at all but seems instead to leave it as something local-regional planning groups should address, implying a vague hope that these groups will

---

[d] A summary of pertinent portions of the policy statement that relate to urban transportation is presented in appendix A.

make something out of it. The important and necessary federal role that must be developed, the concerted efforts between transportation and federal policy as the dominant factors in land use, are simply not there.

The question of energy use is handled in precisely the same way. Energy crisis questions are addressed and the role of transportation delineated, but the question of what effective action should be taken is again brushed aside somewhat casually as something some other governmental entities should address. Worse, the statement simply reiterates the congressional policies of the past of calling for more and better super highways, resulting in even greater intensive oil use. Thus, the question of transportation dependency on oil and the rapid depletion of oil is related in the statement, but as vaguely exclusive to highway construction; instead, mention is made with regard to local officials finding better ways to discourage automobile use, in what can only be considered as rather strange and evasive for such a powerful governmental agency.

It has been said that it is easy to criticize but hard to do better. Yet, one must question if this is really any way to bring the Department of Transportation to the point of "biting the bullet". Is, in some sense, DOT addressing the wrong sets of questions and trying to define the wrong tasks to avoid the painful and disruptive?

One clue comes on page 49 of the statement, which concludes: "Policy helps direct decision making along more rational lines toward national goals and provides the reasons for proposed changes." Although this is a laudable and noncontroversial conclusion, one can only gasp in astonishment at what is missing. There is, in these words, no hint or clue as to whether there even needs to be massive change in this society, or what is wrong with what we are doing; it more resembles a massive whitewash to gloss over unsightly matters as if to wish to keep the masquerade going until after midnight, leaving on the masks.

Certainly, the way the tax system works in this nation, the federal government is the only body that can take on enormous public works' efforts; only the federal government has the tremendous power to bring about rapid change. The notion that one of the most important agencies within that government, namely DOT, can only make vague suggestions is close to preposterous and illustrates the paralysis an entrenched bureaucracy can produce.

What, then, should the policy be? Certainly, it must involve deeply, interrelated national needs with federal power and recognize the uses of that power. Effective federal transportation policy must define federal strategies and tactics for using federal assets to lead toward activities related to nation problem solution. It must be understood that the vast transportation investments made by the federal government have had more to say about land use than any other single factor. There has to be rational direction based on analysis and understanding of information and not a hackneyed retracing of worn-out policies and procedures. There has to be a genuine accounting of subsidies and a desire for consistency in allocating revenue sources and in facing up to the general revenue-raising problems. New kinds of priorities and alternatives are needed. Somehow a new leadership posture must be developed and only then will the nation arrive at a true transportation policy statement that can serve national needs.

Commentary: The Evolution of National Transportation Policy

Never a captive of logic, transportation policy continues a course of responding only to crisis and little else. This pattern of behavior has been fostered by the knowledge that the United States is the most powerful and technically advanced society in human history, powerful enough to surmount any crisis. A series of ominous events, having a somewhat intractable quality, such as the Arab oil embargo and the problems of inflation and unemployment, portend much needed changes.

Appendix 4A
Highlights of Transportation Legislation

Legislation	Content	Policy Implications
Rivers & Harbors Act of 1823	Allocated funds for projects at one-, two- and three-year intervals.	Set policy of providing federal funds for justification and planning did not arise until amendments in 1882.
The Act to Regulate Commerce of 1887	To control and restrict railroads; set up Interstate Commerce Commission (ICC); set up guidelines to require publishing of rates, prohibited pooling undue preference or prejudice against selected commodities.	The first major statement of federal transportation policy, and was conceived as a foundation for future legislation and policy formation. "Invented" the regulator agency.
Revision, 1889	Required the ICC to report directly to Congress. Attempted to give the ICC better tools to analyze rates, and obtain testimony, and limited enforcement powers.	Created the first "independent" regulatory agency. Was directed at monopoly control, as a forerunner to the Sherman Anti-Trust Act of 1890.
Hepburn Act of 1906	Placed oil pipelines under control of the ICC. From their inception in 1865, pipelines had been free of regulation.	Set a pattern of following policy used by railroads. Set policy of federal government reacting to business excesses.
Shipping Act of 1916	Created U.S. Shipping Board to protect a transportation mode in trouble, to strengthen overseas shipping, and to meet World War I needs.	Crisis-oriented legislation pattern set as policy. This crisis legislation and federal assistance made possible technological advance. Tried to both control and promote a transportation mode.
Federal Highway Act of 1916	Set present pattern of sharing road construction cost on a 50-50 basis and established state departments to manage and construct roads.	Policy established for creating large state organizations, and the subsequent array of private interests, as recipients of massive federal funding.
Transportation Act of 1920	Primarily to modify punitive legislation against railroads. Relaxed regulations against cooperation among railroads, permitted joint use of terminals, etc.	New policy set for "a fair rate of return." Also, in a minor provision for waterways, set policy of using legislation to preserve a certain mode of transportation just to keep a balance.
Highway Act of 1921	Set the basis for first interstate highway legislation and increased and strengthened federal-state flow of funds.	Set policy of enacting legislation (favoring roads) that directly undermined objective of previous 1920 legislation to strengthen railroad travel.

Legislation	Content	Policy Implications
Kelly Act of 1925	Funded private air carriers to carry the mail if they also carried passengers. Previous air mail funding had been in direct grants to the post office beginning in 1916.	Federal policy is used to promote a specific modal development.
Air Commerce Act of 1926	Federal government assumes responsibility for maintenance of civil airways, aids to navigation, and safety regulation.	Set basis for future expenditures of large magnitude based on small dimensions of the need at the time of legislation.
Emergency Transportation Act of 1933	Liberalized rail control, established Office of the Federal Coordinator of Transportation.	Crisis planning, largely unsuccessful, to extensive analysis and evaluation of federal policy.
Federal-Aid Highway Act of 1934 (Hayden-Cartwright Act)	1½ percent of funds set aside for highway planning and research (HRP). Inventory and mapping of all highways. Traffic survey, economic projections.	Identified need for planning as a valid national process. Work directed toward relieving unemployment of the Depression.
Air Mail Act of 1935	Primarily concerned with safety, as a result of tragedies with army fliers.	Another example of crisis legislation.
Holding Company Act of 1935	Required all public utilities to divest themselves of transit properties.	Unintentionally contributed to the demise of public transit.
Merchant Marine Act of 1936	Provided funding for a long-range program of ship building and promotion.	Another example of crisis legislation oriented to trade and national defense needs.
Civil Aeronautics Act of 1938	Established the Civil Aeronautics Board and began regulatory involvement. Another "grandfather" clause favor airlines in operation in 1934, having presumptive rights.	This shows how oriented the government is to individual modes, "for aviation." Note that the ICC was not considered suitable for regulation so new CAB is formed, even though legislation is similar.
Transportation Act of 1940	Brought water carriers under closer control of the ICC, with a new grandfather clause. Established a board to research transportation systems and intermodal relationships.	First declaration of a national policy for all modes and recognized need to improve policy.
Cole Act of 1941	Provided "risk" capital for the "Big Inch" pipeline from Texas to the Atlantic.	Policy used to advance technology.
Federal Highway Act of 1944	Wartime act to call attention to the need for a nationally integrated highway system.	Laid the foundation for the vast influence of federal policy on nation's roads.
Housing Act of 1954	Section 701 allocated funds for the planning assistance program.	Major stimulus for funding urban planning groups; tied transit planning to housing.

Legislation	Content	Policy Implications
The Federal Aid Highway Act of 1956	The federal share of highway costs is increased to 90 percent, authorizing $46.2 billion over a period of 13 years, for 41,000 miles of highways. No planning funds were included.	The most costly and far-reaching legislation ever enacted. In a policy departure, the Highway Trust Fund was created, which earmarked certain taxes assessed on motor vehicles and accessories for highway development only. Speeds postwar decentralization of population and industry.
The Transportation Act of 1958	Concerned primarily with ICC authority and gave the ICC right to guarantee loans to railroads.	Another example of crisis legislation taken with a view toward examining railroads alone.
The Seaway Act, 1959	Created the St. Lawrence Seaway Development Corporation within the Commerce Department and provided about $140 million for the joint seaway development with Canada.	A significant deviation from standard federal practices.
Housing Act of 1961	Was instrumental in providing initial federal funding to public mainly with a view of providing for central-city needs, and for the poor and handicapped.	First encouragement for mass transit, but viewing public transit only from the central urban city needs.
Federal Aid Highway Act of 1962	Called for coordinated, comprehensive, and continuing transportation planning at a regional level.	Policy used to force integrated planning, through Section 134 state organizations.
Urban Mass Transportation Act of 1964	Authorized a $375 million grant program over a three-year period where grants could only be applied to capital costs with two-thirds matching from federal sources.	Crisis legislation to keep the remaining public transit systems operating. Did not address problem of unbalanced system created by massive highway commitments.
Housing & Urban Development (HUD) Act of 1965	Comprehensive planning; modified "701" funding.	Crisis legislation for cities including transit needs.
High Speed Ground Transportation Act of 1965, Amended 1972	Authorized research, development, and demonstration of new public transportation systems.	Indicative of growing awareness of long-term consequences of growing urban transit needs.
Department of Transportation Act of 1966	Organized the Department of Transportation as a cabinet-level department consolidating 30 different functions and 7 major agencies. DOT is restricted from policy formation and Congress retains power to allocate funds to separate modes.	An example of how legislative compromise and special interests can be used to weaken the intent of the legislation. DOT purposefully formed on weak and modal lines rather than on functional lines.

Legislation	Content	Policy Implications
Federal-Aid Highway Act of 1968	Extended interstate program two years until 1974 and authorized an additional 1,500 miles of highway above the 41,000 already covered. Funds also included for parking facilities in urban areas.	Supported by DOT, this extended act more than doubled the original estimate, making it the most expensive system in the world.
Airport & Airway Development Act of 1970	Funds to improve and modernize airports. Creating the Airway and Airport Trust Fund modeled on the Highway Trust Fund.	Extended concept of user charges to finance federal expenditures.
Railway Passenger Service Act of 1970, Amended 1973	Created a national railroad passenger system (AMTRAK) and provided funds for modernizing and operating rail service.	A further example of crisis legislation designed to prevent collapse of rail service.
Emergency Rail Services Act of 1970	Authorized financial assistance to railroads undergoing reorganization under Section 77 of the Bankruptcy Act.	Piecemeal, crisis-oriented policy.
Federal Aid Highway Act of 1970	Created the Urban System that includes highways other than extensions of intercity roads.	Emphasis is shifted to road service for the urban area.
Urban Mass Transportation Act of 1970	Authorized $10 billion over a 12-year period for public transit; authorized research, development, and demonstration program as adjunct of planning.	A substantial increase of previous $100 million per year funding but did not recognize crucial operating needs such as fare subsidies.
National Environmental Policy Act, 1970	Required an environmental impact statement (report) to be prepared for all federally funded projects.	Set a policy of requiring a study of alternative before approving federal transportation funds.
Clean Air Act Amendments, 1970	Established automobile emission standards. Financial assistance provided to state and local governments to develop air pollution and control programs.	First environmental constraints against the automobile. Only other legislation of this type was the Traffic and Motor Vehicle Act of 1966 regarding safety factors.
Noise Control Act, 1972	To establish federal noise emission standards.	Viewed as antirailroad legislation but may force better use of fuels, eliminating engine idle.
Regional Rail Reorganization Act, 1973	Created a process by which rail networks could be restructured, and authorized funding for modernizing rail facilities.	Together with 1970 legislation, provided important funds on an emergency basis to keep commuter rails operating.
Federal-Aid Highway Act of 1973	Authorized shifting of funds from planned interstate routes to transit projects, thus allowing trust funds for either highways or transit. Raised federal share of matching grants for transit from 66-2/3 percent to 80 percent. $1 billion a year for public transit.	The first comprehensive urban legislation in the spirit of the 1940 act. Funds are still highly restrictive for public transit, but do give some flexibility for local governments. The 55 mile per hour speed limit on highways was first official reaction to energy crisis.

Legislation	Content	Policy Implications
National Mass Transportation Assistance Act of 1974	Authorized federal funds to be used for operating assistance for first time, on a 50 percent local matching basis. Provides $11.8 billion in funding over next six years. Funds can be used either for operating assistance or capital investment.	With this act, legislative tools are now in place in terms of both policy and financing to provide a true, comprehensive approach to urban transportation.
Deepwater Port Act of 1974	Provides for the licensing of offshore bulk handling facilities for handling oil.	Federal involvement supportive of the automobile needs.

5 The Capital Grant Program

Any comprehensive study of urban transportation will cover the need for and the evolution of an organization, or authority, to regulate as well as to remedy the ills of the nation's transit systems. But when the point is reached where one has the knowledge of what must be done, when one has the authority to take action, one then must have the financing to carry out policy and plans.

Without assistance from Washington there would be very little in the way of mass transportation facilities in the average-size American community. This is especially true since the states individually have been increasingly moving into financial and power vacuums in the area of local transportation.

It has been in a relatively short time that the transit industry has progressed in proving its need for federal assistance. Washington finally recognized this need when in 1964 Congress passed the Urban Mass Transit Assistance Act. With that milestone in transportation legislation, the federal government declared it to be a public policy to support mass transportation financially.

This public policy was reaffirmed in subsequent legislation [1], resulting in the adoption of a program in 1970 to provide $3.1 billion in a five-year period for improving and expanding mass transportation systems, with federal grants representing two-thirds of the costs.

As a result of this federal action, a significant number of states, cities, and other local governments also joined in the movement of coming to the aid of public transportation systems. In substance, this has been an ideal development. As a public obligation, financial aid to mass transportation should be a triparte undertaking, with the federal, state, and local governments making their respective contributions in accordance with their capabilities [2].

Although one can present a case against federal subsidies to local mass transit systems—and we will examine the dangers in the approach to a local problem through the administration and viewpoint of a huge bureaucracy—these problems are minute compared to the problems that would confront the American city left without any form of mass transportation facilities at all.

So, the question is not whether the federal government belongs in the area of local transportation, but rather to what extent and to what degree it should be a partner.

But before examining the impact of the federal government on local transportation policy and planning, it is necessary first to cover, in detail, the entire capital grant program of the funding agency with which we are concerned, the Urban Mass Transportation Administration of the Department of Transportation (UMTA). This will include the basic eligibility factors and application procedures, the additional statutory requirements, and the guidelines for project selection and grant level.

Applying for a Capital Grant [3]

Although only public agencies are eligible as applicants for grants, private transportation companies may participate in assisted projects through contractual arrangements with a public agency. (Public bodies include states; municipalities and other political subdivisions of states; public agencies and instrumentalities of one or more states, or of one or more municipalities or other political subdivisions of states; and public corporations, boards, and commissions established under state law.)

Eligible projects include the acquisition, construction, reconstruction, or improvements of facilities and equipment for use in mass transportation service in urban areas. At present, repairs, maintenance, and other operating costs are not eligible as part of project costs.

The term facilities and equipment includes land (but not public highways), buses and other rolling stock, and other real or personal property needed for an efficient and coordinated mass transportation system.

The term *mass transportation* includes bus or rail or other conveyance, either publicly owned, serving the general public (but not including school buses or charter or sightseeing service), and moving over prescribed routes.

Application for a grant is prepared and submitted in two stages: a preliminary application, for the purpose of ascertaining the probable eligibility of the applicant and the project and the availability of funds; and a final application, in which the project is fully detailed, including all available engineering, planning, financial, and legal data. (See appendix 5A.)

The purpose of the two-stage application is two-fold: It avoids the costs of preparing and processing a full application in cases where it can be readily determined that the applicant or project is ineligible or that funds are not available; and it allows for a period of discussion and negotiation between the applicant and UMTA to facilitate preparation of an acceptable final application.

The preliminary application consists of a letter (original and five copies) addressed to the Urban Mass Transportation Administration, Department of Transportation, in Washington, and signed by an authorized representative of the public agency. As prescribed in UMTA's "Capital Grants for Urban Mass Transportation, Information for Applicants," the application should:

1. Describe in detail the capital facilities or equipment for which the grant is desired.
2. Describe the transportation system in which the facilities or equipment will be used.
3. Describe the benefits to be derived from the facilities or equipment and relate these benefits to the transportation program for the urban area.
4. Estimate the total cost of the project.
5. Estimate what portion of the total cost of the project can be financed from revenue, identify the source of the revenues, and indicate how much financing will be arranged.
6. Estimate what portion of the total cost of the project cannot be reasonably financed from revenues and indicate how the local share of this amount (at least one-third or one-half) will be secured.
7. Indicate how local share of funding will be secured (20% for capital projects and 50% for operating deficit subsidy).
8. Describe the status of transportation planning for the area and comprehensive planning for the development of the larger urban area.
9. Describe the program that exists or is being developed for a unified or officially coordinated public transportation system in such an area.
10. Describe the arrangements to ensure satisfactory continuing public control of the facilities or equipment, whether publicly or privately operated.
11. Indicate whether the project will adversely affect employees of the existing transportation system or result in the relocation of families or businesses, in compliance with Section 13c of the labor-protection agreement and Department of Labor regulations.

This preliminary application should be supported by any engineering, planning, or financial reports that have been prepared and are pertinent to the project. It should also be supported by an opinion of counsel clearly showing that the applicant is a public body authorized by law to carry out the described project in the manner contemplated. As part of the project budget, the applicant must provide a table that shows the actual disbursement of federal funds required, by year, to complete the project using the federal fiscal year of project approval as the base year.

Following a review of the preliminary application, the Department of Transportation will advise the applicant concerning the eligibility and the availability of funds and the procedure to be followed in preparing a full application. In most cases, a conference with the applicant will be requested before preparation of the final application is begun. Full engineering, planning, financial, and legal data will be required for the final application.

According to UMTA, in the evaluation of capital grant applications, priority is given to projects where the demonstrated community need is most urgent and where state and local governments have made substantial efforts to preserve or improve public transportation service in the urban area involved. (This is a significant point, discussed later.)

Statutory Requirements and Planning

Additional statutory requirements made by UMTA include:

1. *Areawide Planning*: Affected general-purpose governments and areawide comprehensive planning agencies must have an opportunity to review projects, and applications must include their comments.

2. *Protection of Private Transportation Companies*: Projects must be essential to a unified or officially coordinated urban public transportation system. Private mass transportation companies affected should participate in all stages of development. Where acquisition of the franchise or property of such a company is involved, "just and adequate compensation must be paid." When a private bus firm is acquired by a public agency, the charter bus service cannot be retained, although the employees, who often are paid premium charter wages, must be retained. (Retaining charter service, especially school bus service, but a public agency is considered unfair competition to private carriers.)

3. *Land Acquisition*: In the acquisition of real estate by eminent domain, the applicant must make every reasonable effort to acquire each property by negotiated purchase before instituting eminent domain proceedings against the property.

4. *Relocation*: The applicant must submit acceptable assurance that an adequate relocation program will be established for families displaced by the project. It is important to note that the UMTA Act has authorized 100 percent federally supported grants for the relocation of families, individuals, business concerns, and non-profit organizations.

Maximum grant is 80 percent of net project cost (that part that cannot be financed from system revenues) if the community has a completed mass transportation plan and program as part of a comprehensive community plan. If planning is not yet completed, a community may qualify under the emergency program for a 50 percent grant; the balance will be reserved for payment if the community meets the full planning requirement within three years. The local contribution may include direct contribution to the project of labor, materials, land, or other property of ascertainable value.

If financing cannot be obtained otherwise at reasonable terms, loans are also available. Loan applicants must also meet the planning requirements. The aggregate amount of grants for projects in any one state cannot exceed 12.5 percent of the funds authorized.

Categories, Priorities, and Guidelines

A review of these application procedures and statutory requirements reveals some of the potential influence that UMTA has on local agency policy and planning, but it is in the following guidelines for capital grant project selection that present the greatest impact. Later, the proposed changes in these guidelines are discussed, but for the present, the concern is with what is presently recommended and required by UMTA.

This study is important, because, according to UMTA: "...a project selection system based on explicit purposes and objectives should ultimately assist the attainment of those purposes and lay the groundwork for meaningful reporting on the progress and value of the program."

UMTA sees its capital grant program as having three objectives, although, according to that agency, the priority among the following three may vary in differing circumstances:

1. To provide mobility to those segments of the urban population that may not command the direct use of motor vehicles, specifically, the young, aged, poor, handicapped, unemployed, and "secondary workers."

2. To improve mobility by improvement in overall traffic flow and specifically, in reduction of travel time in peak hours.

3. Achievement of land-use patterns and/or environment conditions that effectively contribute to the physical, economic, and social well-being of communities. Specifically, this is interpreted to mean "the ultimate attempt is to reduce or minimize the need for transportation facilities and the urban space demands made by them." Alternatively stated, this objective committed the program to attempting to produce concentrated urban patterns of the New York-San Francisco sort, rather than diffused patterns of the Los-Angeles-Houston type [4].

In pursuit of these objectives, UMTA states three priorities:

1. Preservation of existing transit services that otherwise would be abandoned.

2. Provision of new transit services for persons who otherwise would not

have reasonable access to employment and other social and economic opportunities.

3. Improvement of existing transit services within the priorities established by the transit development program for the locality.

Clearly then, the stated objectives of the program show that preservation of existing systems has higher priority than investment in new systems. The program was drafted to provide only for capital grants, precluding operating subsidies; preservation could be accomplished only by grants assisting public bodies to assume transit ownership or grants to public bodies for reequipping transit enterprises. Providing federal funds for an assumption of public ownership was "stabilization" in UMTA technology, and provision of federal funds for reequipment was "preservation."

The capital grant application caseload [5] is managed by separating it into three size categories: under 250,000 population, 250,000 up to 1,000,000, and 1,000,000 or over. According to UMTA, "this is a meaningful classification, because in planning and financing capabilities, public transportation needs and transportation problems differ by size of the urban area." It does recognize, however, that in some cases, projects involving the smaller components of large metropolitan areas are not of regional significance and can be treated more flexibly than grants such as those for metropolitan systems.

In the small areas, congestion is not thought to be a major problem, owing to the general absence of high concentrations of traffic-generating activity. In these areas, UMTA believes, the principal criteria for grants is provision of mobility to disadvantaged groups, typically to be achieved through bare survival of the city transit system. Priority is to be given to projects to ensure survival of systems and to projects tied with the model cities program.

In some areas over 250,000 and especially 1,000,000, public transportation is viewed as a comprehensive force for enhancing the quality of urban life in contributing to all three of the goals of the capital grant program: relief of congestion, mobility for nondrivers, and improvement in land-use patterns.

Specifically, applicants from smaller systems are directed to identify current geographic areas of service, composition of ridership, trip purposes, origins and destinations of passengers, and related matters. Applications are to identify the project's immediate and longer term (two to four years) impact on ridership, and to specify the means proposed for maintaining and increasing use of the system. The applicant is required to present a five-year financial statement, projecting revenues and costs of the project, and if a deficit is projected, the source of funds for continued operation. The guidelines specifically do not require break-even operation, but they note that an identification of the break-even level of fares and services would be useful for evaluation of the prospects of the system.

Applicants are also required to demonstrate coordination with other transit operators in their areas to document the need for replacement vehicles. To the extent that UMTA's research, development, and demonstration programs produce appropriate vehicles, technology, and methodology, applicants are "expected to take notice and to make appropriate choices."

Applicants are expected to adhere to methods of specifications clearly understood to be prevailing industry standards, and also are required to adopt devices for noise and emission control. Financial support by local governments in the past, as evidenced by "fiscal effort relative to fiscal capacity," is also a criterion for evaluation. Applicants are expected to take corrective measures if the systems are demonstrably inferior to industry standards in average cost per vehicle-mile, vehicle-hour, passenger-mile, or passenger, or in average vehicle-miles per man-year.

For a medium-size system, usually of under 500 buses in metropolitan areas of 250,000 to 1,000,000, the first priorities are to keep the system running and provide service to riders at or below the poverty level. Secondarily, priority is to be given projects that promise to reduce traffic congestion through tie-in with Federal Highway Administration projects. These include such devices as exclusive or preferential streets and bus lanes or expressway ramps, bus priority at traffic lights, fringe parking lots, and grade-separated pedestrian walkways. Third, priority is to be given projects integrated with noncapital-intensive techniques for reduction of traffic congestions. These include staggering of working hours, encouragement of car pooling, pricing adjustments on bridges and tunnels, and similar activities to regulate automobile use and encourage transit ridership regulation of the supply of off-street parking, increased parking charges in central areas on work days, banning automobiles from central business districts on workdays, and liberalization in licensing taxicabs.

The general criteria for small bus systems are also applied to bus projects of medium-size systems. In addition, applications for grants for medium systems must be related to metropolitan transportation plans.

The larger system category encompasses metropolitan areas of 1,000,000 or more, with bus fleets generally over 500. Applications for rail systems are expected to be entirely from these areas; in fact, all applications for funds for rail systems are subject to the criteria for this category. In general, the criteria for small metropolitan areas are also applied here. In addition, for rapid transit, suburban rail, or grade-separated bus systems, the applicant is required to submit evidence of an evaluation of the alternatives considered, including use of existing investment, the state-of-the-art technology available, the adaptability of the method adopted to future technological advance, relative costs over two five-year periods, and net effect on riders in door-to-door travel time, waiting periods, comfort and convenience, protection from weather, and facility for the aged and handicapped.

For projects over $10 million, UMTA reserves the right to require before-and-after analysis of impact. Applications for investment in buses in large cities are required to be accompanied by plans for integration of bus service with rail or grade-separated bus service, either currently operating or projected within the next five years.

For rail or other grade-separated transit, UMTA states that: "These systems are primarily applicable to the more intensively developed metropolitan areas, with populations exceeding or forecast to exceed 1,000,000, and which already have grade-separated systems or which will have one or more corridors with traffic volumes requiring such capacity within 10 years. Differentially increasing the use of transit and improving the quality of urban development are the basic objectives for these systems."

For these systems, UMTA requires a comprehensive urban plan, considering geography, population, alternative transportation modes, and land-use pattern, with a workable timetable for completion. Financing must be given in periods of one to three years, three to five years, and five to ten years. Environmental impact, changes in zoning, provision for displaced families, integration with conventional transit, and prospective effect on congestion must all be spelled out. Data must be provided on anticipated daily passengers boarded and daily passenger-miles produced, cost, and prospective increase in passenger miles per day and per man-years.

When projects cannot be evaluated by these criteria, UMTA then ranks them in descending order or priority on the basis of probable effect on ridership and return investment:

1. Additions to existing car fleet on lines already in operation
2. Extension of existing lines or addition to their capacity
3. Construction of new lines and provision of rolling stock for such lines
4. Replacement of existing cars
5. Improvements to existing stations
6. Other construction or improvement of facilities

In addition, operating data are required in order to establish system efficiency on the basis of average cost per car-mile, per car-hour, per passenger, and per passenger-mile, along with average car-miles per man-year. For suburban railroad commuter service, the same criteria are imposed as for rapid transit, but a separation of costs and benefits from the freight operations on the railroad is required.

After reviewing the lengthy and much detailed list of federal guide-

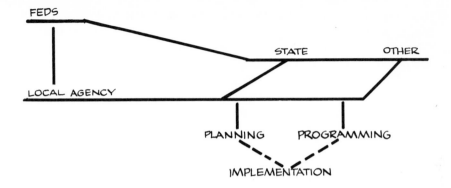

Figure 5-1. From Guidelines to Regulations.

lines, or criteria, one can clearly see there is little in the area of transportation that has not been covered. Unfortunately, these guidelines are not always based on the best information, and often they are limiting, for they attempt to tell the various local transit agencies what cannot be done.

The guidelines, in general, are too sweeping and do not take in certain regional or local considerations. Each area has its particular problems and needs, and UMTA does not always know, or is not aware of, the particular regions's needs or circumstances.

The major problem with these guidelines is that too often they turn into regulations. When UMTA tells a local transit agency how to design equipment, the guidelines become specifications, and the federal government is actually directing the specifications of a local mass transit system.

So far, the transit industry has not been well-organized enough to eliminate harmful guidelines. A concerted effort on the part of the various mass transit organizations throughout the nation would have some effect on Washington, but at present, each area falls into line and lets UMTA's guidelines become its criteria for policy and planning, often, at the expense of the agency's local needs.

When a local agency tailors its policies and planning to the federal criteria, one of the dangers is the possibility of its going overboard in capital expenditures. Because the federal agency will fund certain capital equipment, the local transit agency will invest in it, not so much out of necessity but because the government will fund it.

Another problem stemming from the guidelines is that of identifying funds; the funding rules are not clearly defined. At present, each department tends to get into the other's way. Each has its special field of involvement, from planning to programming. This, as well as interagency rivalry, influence, and overlapping of interests, are not in the best interests of local transportation. (See figure 5-1.)

Proposed Changes in UMTA: A Brighter Picture for Local Transportation?

The outlook for the transportation industry is much brighter now with the changes in the UMTA grant program accomplished through enactment of the Public Transportation Assistance Act of 1974, particularly in that Section 5 creates a new program that includes funding of operating costs as well as for capital assistance. An aggregate amount of $3.975 billion is authorized for this program for fiscal years 1975 through 1980 [6].

This major change is of great significance for the future of mass transportation. For the first time, federal funds will be available to assist localities in meeting the operating as well as the capital costs of maintaining and improving their mass transportation services. For the first time, the transportation industry will be able to look at the total picture, equipment versus operating expenses.

Until now, any changes that should have been made in the area of operations were made in capital expenditures. For example, although an inefficiency in a local agency's staff may have been recognized, rather than correct this inefficiency in personnel, because of funding limitation, money would have gone into equipment to discover where the inefficiency was. But with the proposed changes in the grant program, the transportation industry may be able to remedy this and many other operational problems.

Section 5 of the UMTA Act of 1964, as amended, provides a six-year mass transportation program for urbanized areas apportioned on the basis of a statutory formula. Urbanized areas, according to UMTA, may use Section 5 funds by developing specific capital-assistance projects under the statutory requirements as described in the guidelines.

Apportioned funds will be made available subject to required UMTA approvals, and cash disbursements will be consistent with current UMTA practices. Funds apportioned each year in each year of the program are available for project approval through the end of the second fiscal year following the fiscal year in which they are apportioned. UMTA makes an annual determination that its planning requirements, previously discussed, are met prior to making Section 5 approvals.

The basic elements of the proposed program include the following: The governor, responsible local officials, and publicly owned operators of mass transportation services, with the concurrence of the UMTA administrator, shall jointly designate the recipient or recipients for Section 5 funds in urbanized areas of 200,000 or more population. In any case in which a statewide or regional agency or instrumentality is responsible under state laws for the financing, construction, and operation, directly, they must include such agency as a designated recipient. For areas under 200,000, the governor is the recipient or he may designate a recipient.

A single annual program of projects for each urbanized area shall be submitted for UMTA approval by the recipient or recipients through the Metropolitan Planning Organization (MPO). This program must be consistent with the comprehensive urban transportation planning procedures required by the federal statutes governing the Federal Highway and Urban Mass Transportation administrations.

For each Section 5 project included in the approved program of projects, the recipient must submit an application for UMTA approval.

An agreement for undertaking each Section 5 project shall be executed between UMTA and the recipient. Cash disbursement will be by UMTA in accordance with performance under the terms of the project agreement.

The new regulations require the submission of a program of projects to UMTA for use of Section 5 funds. The annual program of Section 5 projects must be consistent with the current approved Transit Development Program and the comprehensive planning process.

The amount of federal assistance requested under Section 5 cannot exceed the apportioned funds available to the area. Section 5 requires that the program of projects results from the planning process undertaken cooperatively by the state, responsible local officials, and local transit operators. The submission of the program of projects by Section 5 recipients must be submitted through the Metropolitan Planning Organization, which must endorse the program.

According to UMTA, "It invites the inclusion of projects in the annual program which are designed to supplement regular route service such as neighborhood and community level transit service. Such projects may include demand-responsive transportation, jitneys and special services for the elderly, handicapped, and transit disadvantaged."

The capital-assistance project application will follow the existing format for projects funded under Section 3 of the UMTA Act, with the additions required by Section 5. The federal share will be up to 80 percent for capital-assistance projects.

According to UMTA, an operating-assistance project must address the statutory requirements as described in the guidelines. The federal share for an operating-assistance project may be up to 50 percent of the project cost, subject to the availability of Section 5 funds and local matching share.

In accordance with the FHWA and UMTA intent to combine procedures for urban transportation planning, a proposed regulation has recently been issued that will merge the administration of the respective statutory planning requirements in urbanized areas.

The most recent guideline changes proposed by UMTA [7] have been the subject of much controversy and criticism. Under the new guidelines, metropolitan areas would be required to build mass transit projects one step at a time, rather than as a single, massive project.

To qualify for financing under these new guidelines, urban areas would be required to make an intensive analysis of various alternatives to major transit projects in order to determine the most cost-effective way of meeting local needs.

For example, if a city wished to build a subway, which would be very costly, and the required analysis showed that a reserved busway could do an effective job much more cheaply, then UMTA would grant only enough federal funds to finance 80 percent of the busway. Therefore, if the city still wanted a subway, it would have to raise the additional financing locally.

According to UMTA [8], this policy would encourage communities to blend various forms of transit—"light rail" trolleys as well as "heavy rail" subways, for example—into a single system, serving varying needs in different parts of the community.

Also, under the proposed step-by-step approach to construction, a city would be required to identify, plan, and build one usable segment of a system before it proceeds with extensions. This particular criteria may subsequently prove to be detrimental to a number of cities' transportation plans.

Programming: Its Role in the Capital Grant Process [9]

To attain success in any capital grant program requires a number of essential factors, but certainly a paramount one is that of communications. This involves communications not only among levels of government but among the various interest groups as well. It is in the interpretation of these planning guidelines, that the role of communications becomes so vital.

Because of the increasing variety and complexity of local transit programs, it has become increasingly more difficult for a federal agency to maintain an equitable and rational process for reviewing the results of the planning process and making fund decisions. This problem has also arisen at the local level. Urban areas have developed public transit components of regional transportation plans that meet local and regional goals, but these components are often beyond available local and federal funding capacities.

A crucial step in the capital grant application process is having the programming procedures of the local agency reviewed and approved by the funding agency. For, as important as the planning process is, there remains the practical need of making the most of the available funds. It is this major function of programming to decide what programs are eligible for funding—to decide into what projects the funds will be directed.

Consequently, the role of the local agency, such as the CTA or RTA, in programming cannot be underestimated, for it is the local agency that best understands the local environment in which the end results of the granting agency must be accomplished. If programs fail because proper procedures are not followed, it will be the local agency that is embarrassed; for the public and its representatives are most likely to blame it for failure.

The higher level granting agency is seeking an end product—a result, something that is close to uniform throughout the country or state. Therefore, the programming must really be done where these dollars are converted to this objective.

One must stress adherence to the fundamental federal and state performance objectives, provided that flexibility as to how that objective is obtained, in each local instance, is given equal recognition.

As an example, the goal of a guideline may be ready access to public transportation on the part of the handicapped passenger. Every responsible local service accepts that premise and everyone wishes to provide it.

Local programmers and engineers are best equipped, however, to determine the most efficient and safe method of attaining the objective on their own system. The operating modifications and construction specifications to do this may well vary in each area, but to pinpoint these specifications in the guidelines may often prolong completion time and foster economic waste. As stated previously, the local agency should avoid the tendency to be so eager for a particular type of funding that it allows itself to get boxed into unrealistic and unworkable guidelines at the local level.

It is the local programmers who have the responsibility to conduct continuing analysis of how their programming is working out in implementation—in other words, how well it is doing in meeting the end result objectives of the grant.

The overall goal of the funding agency should be to increase the level of analysis being carried out by the local agency, the consistency of feedback as the programming proceeds. Concerning the responsibilities of the local agency in the performance of its role: it must provide a soundly analyzed program, one in which all possible alternatives—not just one major formula—should have been considered. The advocate of each alternative should have had an opportunity to make his arguments.

Programming acts as a checkpoint on planning because it applies resources to plans that have been made in an unconstrained framework.

Therefore, the programmer should carry no personal or implied responsibility to the planner to prove his work. For this reason, it is best to make planning and programming separate departmental functions, as is the case at the CTA and the Chicago Department of Public Works.

The local agency also bears the responsibility to be actively involved in the formulation of the national and state guidelines. Any oversights in

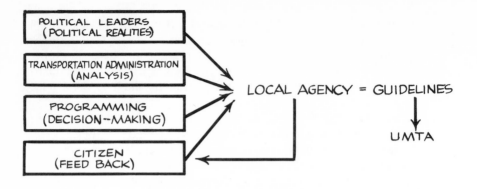

Figure 5-2. Programming Input.

policies promulgated by funding agencies cannot be recognized until they are pointed out.

The particular knowledge and case experiences of the local agency provide the only way the federal or state agency has of recognizing the variations that must be accommodated. The local agency is the proper focal point for the decision making on the nature and time phasing of the program in that area.

The local agency also is where the inputs of four major audiences can be most readily collected and analyzed. (See figure 5-2.)

First, there are the political leaders. Not only are these individuals acutely sensitive to the needs and desires of their constituents, but they are aware of political realities, of what projects can and cannot be accomplished within the local climate.

Second, there is the transportation administrator. This office has the resources to analyze the changing needs of users of the service, because, in essence, that is the total business of the office. It is the transportation administrator who ensures objectivity in the evaluation of effect on the rider, potential rider, and never-ride-at-all.

But it is he programmer who must have the most professional attitude of all these four. He must look thoroughly at the various alternatives without being a prejudged advocate of any one. He must remain cool under political pressure; however, he must also respect political input as an essential part of citizen involvement—and not allow himself to regard it as political interference.

Finally, there is the citizen. If a faulty program is being implemented, the citizen is the last link in the chain. It is the responsibility of the local agency to keep the citizen informed in order that he can express himself, should he so desire, and as early as possible.

This is one of the reasons why the local agency needs an information function, familiar with meeting the needs of the community media. Consequently, then, it is the local agency that is most responsible for whether the program is workable, efficient, and effective in the attainment of the funding agency's overall goals.

In summary, one should state that the real danger of the capital grant program would be for local transit agencies to rely almost entirely on the federal government and cease to function independently of thought and action. Excessive reliance on Washington would be a grave mistake and might well in the long run negate any good to be accomplished through the infusion of federal money into local transit problems.

It cannot be overstressed that local officials and local transportation agencies must stand on their own two feet, and long-range planning and operation must be handled purely from a local standpoint. If a vacuum is created, it could easily become an ugly sore in the community, eventually leaving transit operations in a more serious state than ever. Therefore, this is the real danger, and the problem that must be squarely faced. The local community must maintain control of action and planning and the federal government should only be relied upon for general assistance and advice in addition to financial help.

Political factors should play their proper role in any decision regarding mass transportation. One thing is certain, and that is that slide rules and charts cannot relate transportation to the economic, social, and cultural facilities of the area. This is especially true if the concept of an area's problem is taken "through the view from Washington outside looking in, rather than from the inside of a community looking out" [10].

The Capital Grant Program Commentary:

Appendix 5A illustrates a mass transportation grant process [11] from its initial request through both state and federal approvals. It also describes purchase and payment procedures. In addition, the exhibit portrays UMTA procedures for preliminary and final application submittals. (For details, see the section on "Applying for a Capital Grant" in this chapter.)

Important activities and interrelationships illustrated in appendix 5A include how:

1. Private transit companies or local agencies initiate a grant request
2. Local regional planning agencies provide comments and review the application early in the process
3. The Illinois DOT Regional Office (Local Transportation Services) provides the initial contact and assistance for preparing mass transportation grants

4. The Illinois secretary of transportation and UMTA representatives review and approve preliminary applications early in the process
5. Environment and safety reviews are conducted by both Illinois DOT and other agencies
6. Illinois DOT Planning, Programming, and Environmental Review recommends priorities for state mass transportation grant applications

**Appendix 5A
The Capital Grant
Application Process**

Grant Application Process: Part I

Example: Local box company requests capital grant assistance to purchase operating equipment

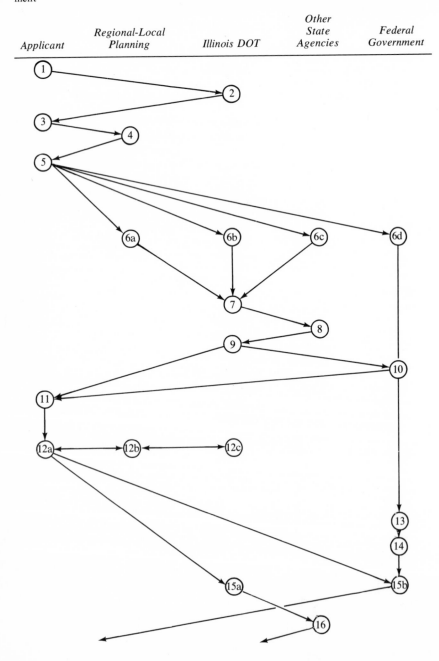

Description of Activity

1. Applicant contacts region or central office of Illinois DOT Local Transportation Services for initial conference.

2. Local Transportation Services counsels on eligibility and recommends how to proceed.

3. Applicant contacts regional planning staff before preparing a clearinghouse request.

4. Regional planning staff advises applicant whether proposed equipment is consistent with the regional plan.

5. Applicant prepares and files preliminary application with regional clearinghouse (e.g., NIPC), Illinois DOT, State Clearinghouse (Office of Planning and Analysis, or OPA), and Urban Mass Transit Authority (UMTA).

6. a. Regional Policy Board requests staff position before acting on request. Staff provides position. Policy board acts on request. Local A-95 letter indicating board action sent to applicant. Copy sent to Illinois DOT.

6. b. Illinois DOT reviews and evaluates application and forwards to other state agencies.

6. c. State A-95 Clearinghouse (OPA) reviews for consistency with statewide plan. Requests planning position from Illinois DOT Planning, Programming, and Environmental Review, and from other agencies.

6. d. UMTA reviews and evaluates application and forwards to other federal agencies.

7. Planning, Programming, and Environmental Review coordinates with Local Transportation Affairs and sends planning position to OPA.

8. OPA sends State A-95 letter to applicant with copy to Illinois DOT.

9. Illinois DOT coordinates comments, reviews priorities, and informs applicant and UMTA of preliminary state approval.

10. UMTA informs applicant on whether project meets legal requirements and if funds are available.

11. Applicant holds public hearings to meet federal requirements and publishes public notice to meet state requirements.

12. a. Local bus company with assistance of local or regional planning agency and the
    b. Illinois DOT Local Transportation Services prepares the final grant application,
    c. which contains 15 essential elements involving such items as civil rights provisions, labor exhibits under Section 13C of 1964 UMTA Act, areawide transit planning requirements, financial capabilities of local bus company, results of public hearing, and copy of public notice. Final grant application is submitted by applicant to Illinois DOT and UMTA.

13. Department of Labor reviews project and determines effect on labor after review of exhibit prepared in compliance with Section 13C of 1964 UMTA Act.

14. HUD determines if region meets the areawide planning requirements. (Note: This step may take place before or during the application process).

15. a. Illinois DOT coordinates with UMTA, conducts final state review, and recommends approval to the governor.

15. b. UMTA coordinates with Illinois DOT, conducts final federal review, approves, and notifies applicant and Illinois DOT.

16. Governor approves and notifies Illinois DOT and applicant.

Grant Application Process: Part II

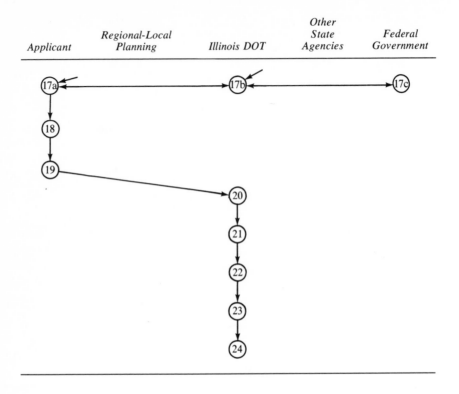

Description of Activity

17. a. Applicant, Illinois DOT, and UMTA enter into contract agreement.
    b. —
    c. —
18. Applicant advertises and competitive bids are received. Contract is awarded with concurrence of Illinois DOT and UMTA.

19. Applicant accepts periodic delivery of equipment and requests Illinois DOT to make progress payments in accordance with the terms of the related contract.
20. Local Transportation Services authorizes fiscal management to make progress payments in accordance with the terms of its contract.

21. Fiscal management issues progress payments upon receipt of authorization from Local Transportation Services.

22. Local Transportation Services, upon delivery of all equipment and completion of proper inspection activity, authorizes final payment and completes closeout of project files.
23. Fiscal management completes final payment as prescribed by terms of the contract.

24. Fiscal management postaudits completed project files to determine compliance with contract terms as originally prescribed by Illinois DOT.

130

Sample Documents

STATE OF ILLINOIS

OFFICE OF MASS TRANSPORTATION

APPLICATION FOR CAPITAL GRANT

APPLICANT _____

FOR OFFICE USE ONLY

GRANT APPLICATION NUMBER

DATE RECEIVED

The Applicant hereby applies to the State of Illinois through the Office of Mass Transportation for a Capital Improvement Grant, under the Transportation Bond Act. Required resolutions, documents, schedules, and exhibits in support of this grant request are attached. The attachments are to be considered a part of this application.

Project Description (briefly describe the nature of the proposed project).

Grant Request	Amount	Percent
Federal Grant Requested	$ _____	_____%
State Grant Requested	$ _____	_____%
Local Matching Share	$ _____	_____%
Total Project Cost	$ _____	___100___%

Application is made for:

$_____ under the 2/9 State funding, 2/3 Federal funding provision [sec. 49.19(6)]

$_____ under the 5/6 State funding, Federal eligibility provision [sec. 49.19(7)]

$_____ under the 2/3 State funding—no Federal funds provision, [sec. 49.19(8)]

$_____ under the Emergency funding provision [sec. 49.19(9)]

$_____ under the Soft Match funding provision [sec. 49.19(10)]

$_____ under the "No Match" Capital Grant provision [sec. 49.19(11)]

I certify that the statements and the supporting documents contained herein are correct and complete.

By: _____   Date: _____
    (signature)

Name (typed): _____   Phone: _____
Title:

Sample Documents

STATE OF ILLINOIS
OFFICE OF MASS TRANSPORTATION   APPLICANT _____

GRANT APPLICATION—EXHIBIT 4.7

INCOME USED FOR OPERATING OR DEBT SERVICE EXPENSES FROM SUBSIDIES
AND TAXES SINCE JANUARY 1, 1968

DESCRIPTION AND SOURCE[1]	PERIOD APPLICABLE (GIVE DATES)	SUBSIDIZER[2]	AMOUNT[3]
	TOTAL	$	

[1] Specify the source of funds, e.g., property taxes, motor fuel taxes, etc.
[2] Name the agency or government unit which provided the subsidy.
[3] Funds used for capital purposes should not be included.

Prepared by: _____ Date: _____
Certified by: _____
Title: _____ OMT-cap-04
November 1, 1972

6

The Cities and UMTA

The most distinguishing feature of American cities is that no two are alike, especially in ways that matter to a transportation planner. Consequently, progress is slow in developing uniform criteria for evaluating competing proposals for scarce federal funds. The problems of a single federal agency attempting to administer to the needs of such dissimilar entities has produced an interesting and checkered history.

Although the nation's cities are admittedly unalike, the decline of public transit in each is distressingly similar. The flight to the suburbs has resulted in decline in every city with the possible exceptions of Washington D.C. and San Francisco, and most central business districts (CBDs) have similarly deteriorated with perhaps only those of Chicago and Atlanta surviving the holocaust intact.

As a result of the coming of the automobile age, only ten cities in the nation have commuter rail service (New York, Baltimore, Boston, Pittsburgh, Philadelphia, Chicago, Detroit, Washington, D.C., Cleveland, and San Francisco). Only seven have rapid transit service (New York, Boston, Chicago, Philadelphia, Cleveland, San Francisco, and Washington, D.C.). Of the 948 transit companies listed by the American Public Transit Association, most (928) are bus companies, and many very small bus companies.[a]

Only cities having rapid transit have high percentage of trips in the journey to work. Many cities have comparatively high percentage of households without cars as do rapid transit cities but fewer use public transit in the journey to work. Transit availability is a factor in reduced automobile purchases. (See figures 6-1 and 6-2.)

Yet, for all the lack of commonality among cities, their experiences with UMTA have been remarkably similar. Large or small, experienced with transit or not, all find themselves victims of an agonizing slowness in federal bureaucratic processing, confronted with incompatatibility of federal and local approaches and always the spectre of rising costs.

It is of special interest to trace these elements of national transit life through the experience of a cross-section of the nation's cities:

1. A city in the Southeast, having low density but where geographic constraints produce a potential for rapid transit (Atlanta)

---

[a] 333 companies (35 percent) are now publically owned, due mainly to UMTA grants, and carry 90 percent of all passengers over 86 percent of the miles. By contrast, New Jersey has, for example, 165 private bus companies each having one bus.

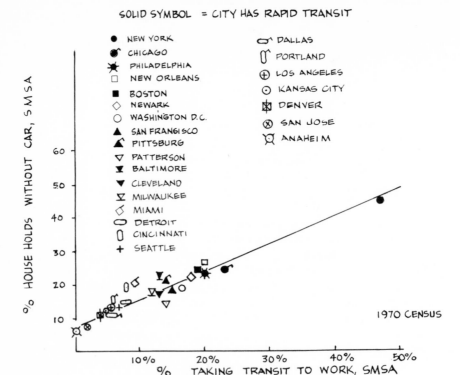

SOLID SYMBOL = CITY HAS RAPID TRANSIT

Figure 6-1. City Households without Cars as a Function of Persons Taking Transit.

2. A major eastern industrial center, traditionally committed to rail service, dependent on annual state grants (Baltimore)

3. A historic New England city with large and complete transit services but aging (Boston)

4. A midwestern, industrial complex with excellent transit but in need of refurbishment and new addition (Chicago)

5. A moderate-size industrial city of high density (Cleveland)

6. A Rocky Mountain urban center of moderate size and low density suffering from air pollution from automobile emission, requiring a new type of low-density rail service (Denver)

7. A West Coast city, and world's largest in land area, wishing to break the complete dependence on the automobile (Los Angeles)

8. The largest city by population, and the most dense, having the largest subway system in the world but beset by deep financial problems (New York)

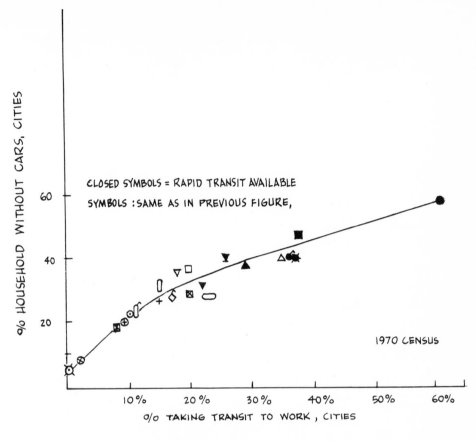

Figure 6-2. SMSA Households without Cars as a Function of Persons Taking Transit to Work.

9. A West Coast urban center, with a high percentage of transit riders, that built and took the financial responsibility for a new, innovative rapid transit system (San Francisco)

10. The Northwest's largest city, a relatively new city with a high quality of life and only the beginnings of a comprehensive transit system (Seattle)

11. The only capital of a major industrial power that has not had an operational subway and comprehensive transit system (Washington D.C.)

Each of these cities has experienced some failure, protracted delays, pressed for new alternatives when old courses proved unrewarding, and known some success. What has worked for one city has sometimes worked for another, sometimes not. Each city has had to solve the prob-

Table 6-1
Capital Grant UMTA Funding, 1964 - January 1, 1976 (in millions of dollars)

New York - New Jersey	$1,129
San Francisco - Oakland	492
Atlanta	473
Chicago	468
Boston	350
Philadelphia	233
Baltimore	184
Pittsburg	102
Washington, D.C.	88[a]
Los Angeles - Long Beach	79
Seattle	57
Minneapolis - St. Paul	52
Detroit	41
Cleveland	31
San Juan, Puerto Rico	29
Dallas	26
Denver	25
Honolulu	22
Kansas City	22
Portland, Oregon	22
Miami	21
Cincinnati	21
Rochester	20
Salt Lake City	18
San Diego	17
New Orleans	16
Buffalo	15
St. Louis	14
Orange County, California	13
Syracuse	12
Norfolk	11
Houston	11
Dayton	10
Omaha	10

[a]Does not include Metro funds, which are directed from Congress.

Note: Total funding to all cities = $4.66 billion. Capital grant UMTA funding does not include transfer from operating assistance ("Section 5") funds or from highway funds. Number shown does not include local share, which was 33-1/3 percent before 1973 and 20 percent thereafter.

lems with which it was confronted according to differing state laws; some could win with a bare majority, others lost with a greater percentage of the votes, when special laws required minimum percentages for bonding powers. Some cities managed to obtain a firm source of funding to be used for deficits and matching funds; others must still rely on annual appeals with the legislators. Thus, the story of each city is different, yet has common elements with others. The general pattern is one of persistence with limited but continuing successes. (See tables 6-1, 6-2, 6-3, and 6-4.)

Table 6-2
Urban Transit Capital Grants from Transferred Sources, Year Ending July 1975

1. Transferred from Section 5 operating assistance funds

Dallas	$1 million
Denver	2 "
Houston	9 "

2. Transferred Interstate Highway Funds

Washington, D.C.	$286 million
Boston	66 "
Philadelphia	51 "

3. Transferred from FHWA Urban Systems Funds

New York	$43 million
San Francisco	2 "
Portland	2 "
Chicago	2 "
Cincinnati	1 "

Note: UMTA encourages transfers from Section 5 (operating assistance) in the belief that such transfers indicate good management, although this may actually not be the case. If funds are used for highways, the federal matching ratio is 90 percent; if for urban transit, the ratio was raised in 1973 from 66-2/3 percent to 80 percent, except for urban system transfer, which is 70 percent.

Table 6-3
Land Area of Major Cities, 1970 Census

City	Area
Los Angeles	512 sq. mi.
Houston	397 "
Indianapolis	351 "
New York	300 "
Dallas	265 "
Kansas City	239 "
Chicago	222 "
San Diego	213 "
Detroit	138 "
Atlanta	132 "
Philadelphia	129 "
Seattle	112 "
San Francisco	99 "
Denver	95 "
Baltimore	78 "
Cleveland	75 "
Washington, D.C.	61 "
Pittsburg	55 "
Boston	46 "

Table 6-4
Population Density, 1970 Census

Rank	City	Density/Sq.Mi.	Planned/Existing Mass Transit
1	New York	24,400	X
2	Philadelphia	15,200	X
3	Boston	13,900	X
4	Chicago	12,300	X
5	Washington, D.C.	12,300	X
6	Baltimore	11,600	X
7	Buffalo	11,200	
8	St. Louis	10,200	
9	San Francisco	10,000	X
10	Cleveland	9,900	X
11	Miami	9,800	X
12	Pittsburg	9,400	X
13	Milwaukee	7,500	
14	Twin Cities	7,000	
15	New Orleans	6,900	
16	Los Angeles	6,100	X
17	Cincinnati	5,800	
18	Denver	5,400	X
19	Seattle	5,200	
20	Atlanta	3,800	X

Atlanta, Georgia

Atlanta is the largest city between Washington D.C. and New Orleans and is the financial and commercial capital of the southeast. Atlanta owes its existence to railroads, which began in 1836. Although originally incorporated as a circle with a radius of 1-3/4 miles (which had its center at the old Union railroad station), the city is the only metropolitan area in the nation that has developed along a single, strong, linear spine, designated as Peachtree Street.

It is primarily this geographic concentration of business that gave impetus to the present-day rapid transit development. Another factor has been the development of the city to neighboring, rolling hills along radial streets, with no circumferential streets. This circumstance results in long, winding bus routes with little opportunity to transfer to other routes as can be done in cities laid out along grid works. These factors act to produce strong traffic corridors and make Atlanta a suitable site for urban transit, even though the density of the city is comparatively low compared with other communities in the nation.

The entire SMSA of Atlanta has 1,728 square miles with an urbanized area about 435 square miles and the city of Atlanta proper of 131.5 square

Table 6-5
Population of Atlanta as a Percentage of SMSA Population

Year	Population, City of Atlanta	Percentage of SMSA Population
1950	331,000	46%
1960	487,000	48%
1970	496,000	36%

Table 6-6
Percentage of Population in Atlanta Using Public Transit and Private Transportation to Work

Year	Percentage Using Transit to Work		Percentage Using Auto to Work	
	Atlanta	Entire SMSA	Atlanta	Entire SMSA
1960	30%	18%	60%	73%
1970	21%	9%	71%	85%

miles. The city ranks 21st in the nation according to population but 13th in density. The population density is about 3,775 per square mile, less than normally required for rapid transit, but is actually several times this along rapid transit corridors. In general the city has not suffered the devastation of the move to the suburbs that other cities have endured during the post-World War II period. Although the growth of the suburban areas has been more rapid than for the city, the city itself has maintained a strong position (see table 6-5).

The shift in population distribution to the suburbs is reflected in the decline in public transportation usage. (See table 6-6.) Atlanta traditionally has had good public transportation. Until 1963 the city had both trolleys and buses and since that time has been served only by a bus operation, the Atlanta Transit System (ATS), which by public votes in 1971 was purchased by the Metropolitan Atlanta Rapid Transit Authority (MARTA).

As early as 1950, the Atlanta region Metropolitan Planning Council (AMRPC) began publishing reports for the electorate on the need for extensive transit, especially rapid transit. Called "Up Ahead," "Now for Tomorrow," "Rapid Atlanta," and "Atlanta Region Comprehensive Plan-Rapid Transit," the system eventually called for by the planning commission was 60 miles, 32 stations. The first stage of this system, for an initial 13.7 million miles of rapid transit, was placed under construction in February 1975 under $800 million in UMTA grants.

The history of rapid transit development in Atlanta is one similar to other cities: long delays, opposition, failures followed by moderate successes, and uncertainty in federal intentions, all accompanied by seemingly endless studies.

Realizing that the UMTA bill would soon be passed in the early 1960 period, transit advocates in the Atlanta five-county region placed a proposition on the 1964 ballots leading to the creation of the regional authority, MARTA. The proposition passed all five counties of the SMSA, but just barely.

In successive years, a number of detailed transit plans were studied by such firms as Parsons, Brinkerhoff, Quade, and Douglas (PBQD), Stanford Research Institute, Parsons-Brinkerhoff, Tudor and Bechtel, and Alan M. Voorhees & Associates which were involved in BART planning. For a time, controversy erupted over the possible use of exclusive, express busways. Later a study showed that the relative costs of the exclusive busway system and the rapid system were not very different, and voter preference surveys showed a strong preference for rail service.

The first public vote for a rapid system in 1968 met with defeat. The plan was based on support through increased property taxes and found strong opposition among suburban property owners. Suburban voters also rejected the plan partly on the basis that the city of Atlanta, being the key beneficiary, was another indication of the strong polarization of city and suburban interests that occurs nationwide. The referendum defeat also in part reflected the poor treatment MARTA received in General Assembly debates and the veto given a MARTA bill by Governor Lestor Maddox.

By 1971 the local political situation had improved considerably in transit's interest. Further, the new referendum was greatly enhanced by additional terms sensitive to local concerns. The bus fare was to be reduced from 40¢ to 15¢. A 1¢ sales tax rather than the unpopular property tax was to be instituted, which was pledged to be reduced to 1/2¢ in 1981. The plan included both dual-lane busways and rapid rail and a short automatic guideway system. The referendum passed, although by a balance of strong city votes against the more rural counties of the SMSA, namely, Gwinette and Clayton counties, a trend found in other sections of the nation. Opposition to highway construction was considered an important factor in the favorable electorate response.

Although the amount of federal contribution to capital grants has risen from 66-2/3 percent in 1971 to 80 percent today, the majority of federal money available cannot logically be directed toward one small city, albeit a promising and important community, having less than a million people.

Atlanta has received some $200 million for planning and initial construction and in May 1975 received a promise for an additional $600 million to be allocated over a six-year period to develop the core system. An additional request by MARTA for another $200 million in 1976 is still pending.

Although the cost of the system has increased from $1.3 billion to $2 billion, an indication of a need for increased federal assistance, it must be remembered that the amount of UMTA funding already represents 10 percent of the entire UMTA capital-assistance funds available for the entire nation. To expect much more is unrealistic. However, there is evidence of overreaction on the part of Atlanta transit supporters who feel they have been let down by insufficient federal assistance as originally promised. Yet, the history of all transit development is one of incremental, piecemeal progress requiring patience and persistence.

Baltimore, Maryland

One of the oldest cities in the nation, Baltimore, was established primarily as a tobacco port in the early seventeenth century and remained strong in mercantile trade until a gradual change to large-scale industry occurred at the end of the last century. The combination of rail facilities and port operations transportation have been key in the city's development, as has the close proximity to Washington D.C.

Traditionally, Baltimore has always been committed to rail. At present, only two commuter lines remain active, a branch of the Penn Central, now Conrail, and the Baltimore and Ohio (B&O). The high city population density of about 12,000 per square mile accounts for part of this rail orientation, and the large and growing resident population of over 2 million in the SMSA encourage this trend.

In addition to a strong city bus system of about 1,022 buses, the first phase of a new rapid transit system is under construction. When completed, the first phase will have 28 miles of subway in metropolitan Baltimore with 20 downtown stations, at a cost of more than $1 billion. Construction began in 1974 with UMTA grants of nearly $60 million, of which $50 million was for the first 2.6 miles of subway, the remaining portions of the grant for 155 new buses. UMTA officials have continually announced support for the project and the intention to continue through annual incremental funding.

Baltimore faces however, a unique situation in their local funding share appropriation by virtue of the fact that each year the local share must be voted by the General Assembly, and funding allotments handled through the state Department of Transportation offices. In this arrangement, all funds collected from road taxes, airport fees, waterway tolls,

Table 6-7
Percentage of Population in Baltimore Using Public Transit to Work

Year	Percentage of Population in Baltimore	Percentage Using Public Transit to Work
1950	65%	—
1960	53%	30%
1970	44%	26%

and the like are placed in a unified fund and then dispersed to individual modes as needs arise. As in most metropolitan areas, the distant suburbs within the local SMSA generally favor highway construction and oppose more funds for transit. This means, in Baltimore, the officials must each year request and argue in behalf of continuing transit construction. Such citizens are highly sensitive to announcements of UMTA officials as to the likelihood of funding being cut because of excessive or rising costs.

The polarization between city and suburban areas is reflected in the suburban trends typical of other cities. The city has lost population and the suburbs have gained. This is reflected in the use of transit for the journey to work (see table 6-7).

In maintaining a strong journey-to-work ridership, Baltimore has not reduced fares. The Mass Transit Administration (MTA) has maintained a constant fare of 30¢ and retained high level service since 1969, with special fares for the elderly, handicapped, and students. The MTA deficit is about $18 million for 1976 and expected to be over $23 million in 1977. The MTA at present is considering a peak/off-peak fare structure and increase of the fare to 40¢ at rush hour as well as 10¢ zoning charge. Baltimore currently charges one of the lowest fares in the country and is one of the few operators to have maintained a constant fare since 1969. Analysts note that if the consumer price fare had kept pace with the consumer price index, the fare would have risen from 30¢ to 46¢ over the period from 1960 to 1975.

As of 1976, UMTA has offered to commit $500 million for the completion of the first segment of the new subway system and had previously given a total of $73 million toward the subway. This will place 10-3/4 miles of rapid transit in service by 1982 if delays are not encountered, taking about six years to complete. The additional states share over the six-year period will be about $148 million ($25 million per year). Maryland is perhaps the only state where the federal share of mass transit is more assured on a continuing basis than the local funding.

Table 6-8
Percentage of Population in Boston and in SMSA Using Public Transit to Work

Year	Percentage Using Transit to Work in Boston	Percentage Using Transit to Work in SMSA
1960	43%	25%
1970	38%	19%

Boston, Massachusetts

Historic Boston is the nation's eighth largest city, the third most densely populated, but the smallest in land area of the nation's 20 largest cities. The decline through decentralization began early in Boston: between 1940 and 1950, Boston increased only 2.6 percent in population while the surrounding areas increased over 8 percent. Many small cities are clustered together around Boston forming a metropolitan district that controls water supply and the park system and more recently, transit.

Traditionally, Boston has been known for many small factories and great diversification and since World War II has become prominent in electronics and research, in addition to the older, established industries, and strong in many service and financial areas. In this respect, Boston differs from cities such as Atlanta in that it is surrounded by many smaller cities having various kinds of small industry and older rail facilities rather than rural, underpopulated regions. Boston has over 15,000 people per square mile and even the surrounding areas have at least 3,000 per square mile, which is nearly an order of magnitude greater than the few hundred per square mile found in the rural regions of many SMSAs.

Boston traditionally has had excellent public transit. The first subway in the nation was built in Boston in 1897 (and is still in use); commuter rails have a long history as well. Although the number using transit in the journey to work has dropped, it is still large compared to other cities, second only to New York City, and is significant also in the outlying regions of the SMSA (see table 6-8).

The Massachusetts Bay Transportation Authority (MBTA) operates 37 miles of rapid transit, 43 miles of street cars (now called light rail), 3,538 miles of bus service, and 480 in miles of commuter rail, in addition to a small 8-mile route of trackless trolley or electric bus. The rapid transit, made up of four main lines call the Red, Orange, Blue, and Green, makes use of a variety of cars and operational systems; much of the system is in need of extensive repair and improvement on a major scale. The operating deficits are larger per passenger served than for any system outside of New York City and in part are due to an unusually high wage scale with a minimum wage for any transit employee of $14,000 a year.

During the 1960s, Boston began evaluating their entire ground transportation system in part as a reaction to opposition formed in neighborhoods about to be displaced by new and extensive highway construction. Deficits mounted on the transit operating expense and the aging system continued to deteriorate. In 1970 a moratorium was placed on further highway construction, and a project, referred to in transit circles as the "Boston Restudy," began under the Boston Transportation Planning Review (BTPR).

Prior to the restudy, Boston had not received much encouragement from UMTA on transit projects. The MBTA established by the legislators in 1964, eventually joining 79 different communities in a regional relationship, had worked with other planning groups in identifying and analyzing transit needs and objectives; these groups included the Metropolitan Area Planning Council (MAPC). The Joint Regional Transportation Committee (JRTC), the Central Planning Transportation Staff (CTPS), and the Executive Office of Transportation and Construction (EOTO). They developed a sound program of projects and priorities to extend and improve transit service. In anticipation of such projects with anticipated UMTA assistance, the state authorized bonds of $124 million for transit projects. Yet, such encouragement from UMTA was not forthcoming.

Against this background the restudy continued, eventually taking 18 months, concluding that transit needs should take priority and highway construction should be deleted from several approved projects within the Boston area. Presumably, because of stipulation of the 1973 Highway Act, which allows authorized transfer of certain interstate funds to be redirected toward transit projects, it might be thought that the needed funding would be forthcoming immediately. Such was not the case.

First, working out the details of the interstate transfer was time consuming in part since known criteria and authorized procedures did not exist before. The delays involved have caused many to wonder about the feasibility of trying to exchange highway funds into transit funds, even though the law states such can be done. The flexibility promised by the Highway Act of 1973 is undermined by cumbersome and inflexible administrative procedures. Clearly a state wishing to transfer funds from highway to transit may simply end up with no funds whatever.

Another problem is within UMTA itself. The UMTA staff refused to accept Boston's reports and analysis. Months were wasted on revised environmental impact statements, when in fact such statements had already been accepted for highway development; it might be considered reasonable that if an area could withstand the environmental damage produced by any highway, a transit system would always be an improvement. These circuitous involvements allowed a direct comparison to be made between UMTA staff and the highway staffs in analyzing and processing grants for a given situation; it became increasingly clear to any state organization watching the proceedings that the reason the nation has billions of miles of highways and few operational transit systems does not result from funding limitations alone. Here was a distinct case where the funds were available and the breakdown was due in large part to an unresponsive bureaucracy.

The $600 million Boston is receiving from the interstate highway transfer overwhelms anything than could ever be realized under present funding arrangements from UMTA sources. The outlook for a greatly improved transit within Boston is, therefore, very encouraging.

Chicago, Illinois[b]

Chicago's public transit history covers a rich blend of innovative transit vehicles beginning with the horse drawn omnibus in 1850, to horse drawn rail cars, to cable, steam, and electric rail systems. At present, the Chicago Transit Authority (CTA), the principle carrier in the city, formed in 1954 from a consortium of independent surface carriers, operates 135 bus routes over 2,000 miles with about 3,000 buses, and 6 rapid transit routes covering approximately 110 miles of subway, and surface and elevated track, with over 1,000 cars. (The city's 8 major commuter railroads are operated through agreement with the Regional Transit Authority[b]). The three subway systems were built in 1943, 1951, and 1971. Three of the major expressways (Dan Ryan, Kennedy, and Eisenhower) have rapid transit in the median strip and intermodal passenger transfer stations built over the rights-of-way.

The Chicago SMSA has a higher percentage of residents using public transit to work than any other outside of New York. The dramatic reduction in ridership the system suffered in recent years was primarily due to off-peak usage; the journey to work trips even in 1970 were 70 percent of what they had been in 1956, and on the rapid transit system, the percentage is higher, approximately 80 percent.

Chicago's ability to maintain this ridership, now about 650 million per year, is due in part to the $200 million bond issue passed in 1971 by the state legislature for mass transit, and to UMTA for $350 million for a variety of projects and refurbishing. The Chicago system remains in need of extensive repair and improvement.

---

[b] The Regional Transit Authority of Northeastern Illinois is covered in chapter 3.

Chicago is generally regarded as the nation's transportation center: Illinois has more miles of rail than any other state, O'Hare International Airport is the world's largest and busiest, and more trucking firms are located in Chicago than any other city.

Most transportation statistics show a similar conclusion as might be expected for so large a city located centrally in the nation. Consequently transportation planning was always a necessity and began in the last century. The well known Burnham plan was one of the first formal and complete plans of its type, dating from the 1890s; this plan emphasized total city planning incorporating transportation planning.

Today Chicago works with a multi-layered set of planning organizations. For long range, comprehensive planning, the predominant agencies are the Northeastern Illinois Planning Commission (NIPC) formed in 1957 which is also the A-95 review agency, the Northwest Indiana Regional Plans Commission (NIRPC), and the Department of Development and Planning (DDP), a municipal organization in City Hall.

Technical transportation planning is carried out by the Chicago Area Transportation Study (CATS), dating from 1955, the Indiana State Highway Commission (ISHC) and the Department of Public Works (DPW) in City Hall.

Coordinating agencies include the Regional Transportation Planning Board (RTPD) created in 1971, and the Bi-State Commission (Bi-State) with both NIPC and CATS historically also involved in coordination.

The chief operating organizations are the Chicago Transit Authority (CTA) and the Transit Carriers Coordinating Committee (TCCC) which includes the suburban railroads and suburban bus companies.

Most of the aforementioned organizations share several common directors and by means of ad hoc task forces and other institutional arrangements have developed effective coordination producing some of the most innovative and successful transit development in the nation. With the formation of the Northeastern Illinois Regional Transportation Authority (RTA, see chapter 3), many of the individual responsibilities of the above organizations have changed with the RTA having an umbrella responsibility in planning generally and gradually developing specific planning responsibilities for the six-county Chicago area.

Two major projects are pending UMTA approval. The first, the Chicago Urban Transit District (CUTD) project is made up of two new subways: one, a shallow subway called the Distributor that will coordinate with a new deep subway to increase the viability of the entire central Chicago area, removing the Loop elevated system and bringing the commuter railroads within easy reach of the downtown areas, the new North Michigan Avenue John Hancock Center and the Standard Oil and Sears Tower areas, and the University of Illinois. This project to cost over $1 billion, will bring to Chicago a coordination of transportation modes unique in the nation. The second major project pending at UMTA is the extension of the Kennedy rapid transit service to O'Hare. A third major project, the southwest corridor study, is examining the feasibility of rapid transit service to the underserved southwest side of Chicago.

Chicago's experience in improving urban transit is related directly to lack of major funding. Although certain controversy over choice of sites and routes are bound to occur in any major project development, the task of knowing what to do is reasonably obvious. The recent history has been one of trying to hold an old and aging system together, to maintain the viability of transit usage generally while keeping preliminary design work current until construction funds become available.

Cleveland, Ohio

Cleveland, the 7th largest city in 1950, suffered a 10 percent decline during the last census decade and dropped to 12th in population among the nation's cities by 1970. This was the lowest population for Cleveland since 1910. However, the city still maintains a population density of about 10,000 per square mile, an important factor in urban transit design. Cleveland, one of the nation's oldest and important industrial centers, founded in 1836, has long had good public transportation with one of the few rapid transit systems built since World War II. About 1912, Cleveland's several transit systems were mergered into two interests called "Little Consolidated" and "Big Consolidated" operators; these two later merged in the Taylor franchise. Later the Van Swerington family, real estate promoters, acquired much of the transit operations. One parcel of land, purchased from a religious sect known as the "Shakers" gave the name to Cleveland's first rapid transit line.

Thus, Cleveland's first rapid transit system was constructed by a private developer as a selling point for a home-development project called Shaker Heights in 1928. The Shaker Heights light-rail system covers 13 miles using about 57 cars. Today it is integrated with the main rapid system, which covers 19 miles and uses 116 cars, most of them the 80 passenger Pullman Standard cars with a few older St. Louis cars. The city is served by 835 buses.

Before the Cleveland Transit System (CTS) was absorbed into the newer Regional Transportation Authority in 1975, the CTS was responsible for Cleveland's development. This included building the original rapid transit system in 1955, extensions in 1958 and the airport line in 1968. They have an impressive record in refurbishing their bus system and lead the nation in construction of bus shelters. Twelve million dollars of the $18 million rapid transit extension to the airport was funded through UMTA, as was 50 percent of ten new transit cars costing $2.5 million and several small grants for new buses and other capital equipment.

In July 1975, the CTS was struck by transit employees for 17 days. The effect was devastating and many believe that the system has not yet recovered. Almost 30 percent of the rapid transit ridership was lost. In an effort to bring back riders, the system reduced fares, from 50¢ to 25¢ with free transfers. Senior citizens ride free in nonrush hours (7:00-9:00 A.M. and 4:00-6:00 P.M.). Ridership is said to have increased by 26 percent. Total ridership for the RTA, including the six suburban bus companies is over 100 million annually.

Cleveland is served by a single commuter rail line, a three-car train of the Erie Lackwanna operating one trip a day from Youngstown, Ohio. It is planned to remove this line from service in the near future, replacing it with an express bus, if regulatory bodies consent.

Taking a broad view, Cleveland has done as well as could be expected under the limited UMTA funding. Considering the size of the city, however, and the density, their transit system is far from adequate. Comparing respective areas, each mile of Cleveland's rapid transit must serve twice the area of Chicago's system. Although the RTA is presenting a five-year plan to UMTA for new project development, part of the agreement for the 1 percent tax sales tax transit received was that the systems could not expand for 5 years. This move was requested by the city to prevent possible use of city funds for development of suburban transit systems. The 1 percent sales tax provides about $3 million a month to use for federal matching funds and cover operation deficit.

These factors combine to give a somewhat slower possible development for Cleveland transit than might be considered desirable. However, with the financial base now stable, prospects are greatly improved for revitalized transit service.

Denver, Colorado

Traditionally, Denver has not been a transit-oriented city. More households own cars (89%) than in any other city of comparable size except Dallas, and fewer people travel to work by transit (4%) than in any other city larger than Denver. There are no geographical barriers that produce density corridors so the Denver area, with its low population density of 5,400 per square mile, is considered ideal for the private passenger car.

Unfortunately, the automobile has produced air pollution so severe that Denver is ranked as one of the worst in air quality nationwide. Consequently, in 1971 Denver began examining the possibilities for a rapid transit system capable of serving a low-density population.

Transit planning has been carried out principally by three bodies: the Joint Regional Planning Program (JRPP), which represents the Regional Transportation District (RTD); the Colorado Division of Highways (CHD); and the Denver Regional Council of Governments (DRCOG). The various planning groups and consultants have generally agreed that some type of advanced technology system such as a Personal Rapid Transit (PRT) or Automated Rapid Transit System (ART) is most attractive for the region. Originally, newly designed vehicles using advanced technologies were considered although at present more conventional, mass-produced vehicles have gained favor. Although UMTA did not reject the PRT concept, there was a continuing delay owing to frustrations and failures experienced in Morgantown, Virginia. Consequently, the ART system seemed suitable with less risk.

Almost all designs considered call for a rapid transit system of about 80 miles in length. Considering that the 1/2¢ sales tax and a 2-1/2 mil property can be used to back bond sales to $425 million, which in turn act as a local share (20%), the maximum amount of project cost is limited to about $2 billion, assuming the federal government will provide the maximum share. Analysts feel such a system can be constructed if design is limited to either at-grade or elevated structures without subway. To date, Denver has received $20.7 million for capital equipment mainly buses, and an additional $2 million for technical studies. Denver is one of the few cities to request a shift in Section 5 operating funds to capital equipment.

Los Angeles, California

Los Angeles is a much misunderstood city in terms of transit. Although it is true that the city relies to an excessive degree on the automobile, as evidenced by severe smog problems, over 6 percent of the population goes to work on public transit. This compares reasonably well with 7 percent in Seattle and 9 percent in Atlanta, considered reasonable by present, deteriorated standards.

Most transit analysts have agreed, since the early 1960s, that Los Angeles needed some type of rapid transit development, although no one knew how to pay for it. It must be remembered that Los Angeles is one of the largest cities in the world with over 500 square miles of area; this is 50 percent larger, for example, than New York City, so, consequently, the cost of any transit system will be enormous simply because of the massive area to be covered. Although the average density is low (owing to a mountain range that consumes 24% of the area within the city), there are large traffic corridors having population densities of about 14,000 per square mile, which is well above that needed to support rapid transit. The question is how to cover the tremendous distances with a suitable system with costs than can be managed.

In the city's early beginning, one of the most complete interurban electric railways had been constructed and eventually merged into a single company called the Pacific Electric with over 1,100 miles of track. As freeways were built, buses were substituted for railcars and in 1961 the last electric car was withdrawn from service.

When bus service began running large deficits during the 1950s, the state legislature authorized the former Los Angeles Metropolitan Transit Authority (MTA) to buy and operate the existing bus service lines. Later, the MTA was replaced by the Southern California Rapid Transit District (SCRTD) with the explicit mandate of designing and implementing rapid transit service in addition to maintaining bus operations.

In 1968 the first of the rapid transit plans was submitted to the voters and defeated. It called for an 89-mile, $2.5 billion rail system to be financed by a general sales tax. In 1971, in conjunction with the Southern California Association of Governments (SCAG), and the Orange County Transit District (OCTD), a new plan was devised that called for $3.3 billion for a 116-mile rail system and 24 miles of exclusive bus lanes. Later, consultants working primarily for SCRTD recommended a 145-mile transit system. This plan was defeated in the election of November 1974.

In analyzing the defeat it was clear that the solid opposition was, as in other cities throughout the nation, from the most distant suburban areas. The plan did receive broad support from across economic stratas of society including the Los Angeles lower income groups (56%) to upper middle of Santa Monica (61%) and the prosperous Beverly Hills area (54%). Many began to wonder if there was a single plan that could succeed in overcoming this distant suburban block. The total vote was only 46.4 percent "Yes" from Los Angeles County.

Although the vote for large composite systems was not favorable, other events occurred to encourage transit development. In 1971 the state legislature had voted passage of Senate Bill 235, a sales tax on gasoline to be used for public transit; in 1972, the first year of its effect, Los Angeles received approximately $55 million, called "SB 325 funds." Later, Proposition 5, approved by the voters in June 1974, diverted state gas tax money to rail transit (called "Proposition 5 funds"). These funds can provide a local matching share for federal grants for good "starter" lines even if the funds are insufficient for the massive systems invisioned by the planners.

Consequently, a new plan was drawn and approved by both the city of Los Angeles and SCRTD for construction of a rapid rail system stretching from the San Fernando Valley through the Los Angeles CBD down to Long Beach and San Pedro. If the federal government will agree to share in the costs, this system can be financed without additional funds and without requiring voter approval.

At present, Los Angeles continues to be completely dependent on a bus company of moderate size. Although some observers like to point out the use of exclusive bus lanes on the expressways is increasing, and the number of buses has increased (primarily through $120 million from UMTA) from 1,771 to 2,111 between 1974 and 1975, the bus system is still only about two-thirds the size of Chicago's bus system, which serves an area just half the size of Los Angeles. More years and additional struggle may one day be bring an adequate transit system to Los Angeles.

New York City, New York

New York City has the largest transit system in the world and, as such, must necessarily be included in any discussion of urban transit. Yet, New York is unlike any other city. At any moment, for example, 10 percent of the New York traffic is made up of circulating, empty, taxicabs. New York probably has more taxis, for example, than Ames, Iowa has people. In fact, New York has more people on welfare than any other American city has people. The first question then is how to put the city in context with other urban transit arguments. (See tables 6-9, 6-10, and 6-11.)

Legal New York City is made up of five boroughs and has not grown in size since 1898 and is not growing in population either; the population is just under 8 million within city confines, barely 1 percent more than in 1960.

The New York metropolitan area is another matter; it is constantly growing in size and in numbers. The newspapers, for circulation purposes, define New York as including 1 county in Connecticut, 14 in New Jersey, and 6 in New York state, in addition to the 5 counties that define legal New York City. Usually called "The Big Apple," it defines a region where 18 million people work, live, and move about without regard to geographical limits.

Whether they realize it or not, these 18 million people, as well as millions more throughout the nation, derive a major portion of their economic well being mainly from the New York confined within the boundaries of the previous century, and in particular to the unique "centre ville," as the French call it, the lower one-third of Manhattan, said by many to be the world's leading center of finance, commerce, trade, entertainment, and culture. A dominating 65 percent of the people arrive by public transportation. Without public transit, the city, and much of the nation's economic well-being, could not exist.

Table 6-9
SMSAs and Cities Ranked by Population, 1970 Census

Rank	SMSA	Population (Millions)	Central City (% SMSA)	City Rank
1	New York	11.58	68%	1
2	Los Angeles	7.04	45	3
3	Chicago	6.99	48	2
4	Philadelphia	4.82	40	4
5	Detroit	4.20	36	5
6	San Francisco	3.11	35	6
7	Washington, D.C.	2.86	37	7
8	Boston	2.75	23	8
9	Pittsburg	2.40	22	18
10	St. Louis	2.36	26	16
11	Baltimore	2.07	44	10
12	Cleveland	2.06	36	12
13	Houston	1.99	62	9
14	Newark	1.86	21	25
15	Twin Cities	1.81	41	13
16	Dallas	1.56	54	11
17	Seattle	1.42	41	17
18	Anaheim	1.42	31	24
19	Milwaukee	1.40	51	14
20	Atlanta	1.39	36	21
21	Cincinnati	1.39	33	23
22	Patterson, N.J.	1.36	21	27
23	San Diego	1.36	51	15
24	Buffalo	1.35	34	22
25	Miami	1.27	26	26
26	Kansas City	1.26	40	20
27	Denver	1.23	42	19

In view of this profligate crossing of geographic boundaries, how should operating subsidy needs be handled? Indeed, how can decisions be made on transference of, say, "interstate" highway funds, which with respect to the New York area has an entirely different connotation than elsewhere. The New York area alone has ten federal aid "urbanized areas" covering three different states, giving rise to special multijurisdictional problems in transfer of highway funds to transit.

It is probably fair to say that the massive New York system could have prudently used the entire UMTA capital grant funding of over $20 billion in the period between 1964 to 1976; yet, New York received only slightly over $1 billion from UMTA. In 1975, Section 5 operating deficit share for New York City was placed at $42.7 million, about 10 percent of the actual value and very far from the 50 percent share contemplated for most regions. It is clear that even if all UMTA funds were directed toward New

Table 6-10

Passenger, Revenues, and Operating Subsidies on Public Transit in the New York Region in 1973-74

	Passengers (Millions	Revenues (Million $)	Subsidy (Million $)	Subsidy as a Percent of Total Operating Expense
New York City	1,929.8	701.5	456.9	39.4%
MTA rapid transit (NYCTA & SIRTOA)	1,099.9	392.6	392.0[a]	49.9
MTA bus (NYCTA & MABSTOA)	720.3	260.7	52.9	16.9
Private bus	89.9	47.2	—	—
Ferry	19.7	1.0	12.0	92.4
Suburban NY State	127.7	162.9	91.0	35.8
MTA commuter rail (PC & LIRR)	85.7	143.7	87.0	37.7
MTA bus (MSBA)	17.7	9.0	2.7	23.1
Other bus	24.3	10.2	1.3	11.0
Suburban New Jersey	268.2	164.5	70.9	30.1
Commuter rail (PC, EL, CNJ)	34.5	33.9	22.7	40.1
Rapid transit (PATH, TNJ)	40.2	13.1	32.3[b]	71.2[b]
Private bus	193.5	117.5	15.9	11.9
Suburban Connecticut	20.7	20.3	6.7	24.7
Commuter rail	8.2	14.5	4.3	22.9
Bus	12.5	5.9	2.4	28.8
Region Total (23 counties)	2,346.4 S	1,049.4	625.2	37.3
			Total operating expense	$1,674.6

[a]Includes $167.5 million transit debt service paid by New York City; excludes transit police costs of $89.5 million.

[b]Amount overstated compared to the others; includes debt service on World Trade Center terminal of PATH and a share of the Port Authority's general overhead.

Sources: Tri-State Regional Planning Commission Technical Manual 1017-3305, and NYCTA Transit Record.

York, it would scarcely be sufficient and such a policy would leave the entire nation outside of New York barren of any transit. It is an unresolved conflict for transit.

For years, New York transit was directed by four regional groups and a fifth major bistate agency:

1. The Metropolitan Commuter Transportation Authority (MCTA)

2. The New York City Transit Authority (NYCTA)

Table 6-11

Section 5 Federal Transit Assistance Funds Allocations per Transit Rider in Selected Urbanized Areas (*1974 Riderships; 1975 Federal Fiscal Year Dollar Allocations*)

	Available for Operating Subsidy, Cents per ride
New York portion of the N.Y. - N.E.N.J. urbanized area	2.07¢
Pittsburgh	3.86
Baltimore	3.95
New Jersey portion of the N.Y. - N.E.N.J. urbanized area	3.98
New Orleans	4.12
Atlanta	4.13
Boston	4.35
Philadelphia	4.64
Chicago	5.01
Denver	11.71
Houston	13.75
Los Angeles	14.20
Louisville	15.47
Albuquerque	17.34
Tulsa	18.29
Dayton	18.90
Fort Worth	26.71
Tampa	28.07
Wichita	31.62
Akron	35.25
Grand Rapids	35.25
National Average: 5.09¢	5.09

Sources: *Federal Register*, January 13, 1975 "Capital and Operating Assistance Formula Grants; Interim Guidelines and Procedures"; American Public Transit Association, *Monthly Transit Traffic*, January 30, 1975.

3. The Manhattan and Bronx Surface Transit Operation Authority (MABSTOA)

4. The Triborough Bridge and Tunnel Authority

5. Port Authority of New York and New Jersey (PATH)

Then, in an effort to unify transportation policy and practice under a single board, the MCTA board was expanded in 1968 to include the NYCTA, MABSTOA, and the Triborough, and the Metropolitan Transportation Authority (NTA) was created. If the MTA were a comprehensive regional authority, it would be, of course, the nation's largest, larger than Chicago's RTA. However, the MTA has been likened more to a public holding company, in providing unified direction to the related transit operation.

The same 1967 state legislation that authorized the MTA also provided $1 billion for mass transit facilities and for use as matching funds for federal grants. This legislation was prior to the financial problems of New York that have affected transit budget in addition to all others. In an effort to maintain service under mounting fiscal pressure, the basic New York fare of 35¢ was raised to 50¢. The New York transit system is closely tied to a series of financial and management crises the city still faces. The solution to these problems involves complex questions of jurisdiction, obsolete geographical boundaries, political and legislative limitations, and a need for structural in government change that is inevitable, but slow in coming.

San Francisco, California

San Francisco, one of the true metropolitan cities of the world is tightly constrained by geographical elements, namely, the Pacific Ocean on the west and San Francisco Bay on the east. Occupying only a narrow land strip of less than a hundred square miles, San Francisco could not physically accommodate even a single expressway and still remain intact. As a direct consequence, San Francisco citizens staged an early revolt against the fast expanding federal highway system, stopping construction in San Francisco.

Having agreed to lose the billions in federal highway funds destined for the area, the San Francisco region then indebted themselves, with no thought of state or federal assistance, to the largest bond issue ever undertaken by a local area ($792 million). The Bay Area Rapid Transit (BART) project was strongly opposed by state highway agencies and officers.

A major resource of business and financial centers such as San Francisco, New York, and Chicago is the concentration of highly skilled business and management leaders who, when working together with political leaders, can shape a powerful force in bringing about change. Such a coalition was a key factor in San Francisco. It provided not only a local source of technical direction for the challenging engineering problems of building BART, but provided as well the strength and know-how to bring about important legislative changes.

Under California law, local bond issues had to be approved by 66-2/3 percent of the electorate and each county had to be considered as a basic political unit. Unfortunately, many of the bedroom communities of San Francisco that provide the daily commuters, such as those located in the big counties of Alameda and Contra Costa across the bay to the east, have large rural regions. Although the economies of these counties benefit significantly from their proximity to San Francisco, this benefit is usually viewed by the more rural voters as a one-way obligation of the city toward the county, and support for reciprocal responsibility is not large, nor well understood. Consequently, one of the first tasks was to have the voting percentage dropped to a more reasonable level and have the entire region vote as block and not according to individual county. Achievement of such compromise measures was complicated by the fact that many of the legislators, especially the chairman of the Senate Transportation Committee and others in the legislature who had been influential in building California's massive highway plan, strongly opposed urban transit. Eventually, through skilled political maneuvering and persuasion, special legislation was passed lowering the required voting percentage to 60 percent and permitting the total vote of participating counties to be shared so that lower voting percentage of the more rural counties could be balanced by the anticipated higher central city vote. A further stipulation was that each county's Board of Supervisors could determine whether the county should enter the BART project.

Support for the BART referendum, as might be expected, soared in the city proper to 67 percent. Alameda and Contra Costa counties, the home of San Francisco professionals, voted approval by 60 percent and 55 percent, respectively. San Mateo County, directly adjacent to San Francisco on the southern portion of the peninsula, withdrew, partly owing to the projected high transit tax burden of $112 per person considered high for the area, and also because of the Southern Pacific commuter rail line that already provided service. Marin County to the north, connected to San Francisco only by the Golden Gate Bridge, withdrew for reasons of accessibility, as did the other counties of the SMSA.

Design of the 75-mile rapid transit line also required extensive coordination with other services in the area. Most prominent was the Municipal Railway (Muni) system and streetcars and the famous cable cars. The Alameda-Contra Costa Transit District (AC Transit) is another large bus operation about half the size of Muni. AC also operates the bus system resulting from the old Key Service, the last interurban electric rail across the Bay bridge withdrawn from service in 1958 when, incredibly, the rail decks were removed and replaced with paved lanes for cars and buses. BART's ridership falls third, about as projected, behind these other two services.

During construction BART ran into financial trouble owing primarily to inflation effects. By mid-July 1966, a $200 million shortfall was predicted. Then federal funds entered the project for the first time. A $13 million grant in August 1966 was the first of a series of UMTA grants that eventually reached $304 million, about 20 percent of the project cost.

The design concept for the BART system involved use of single automated cars, much wider and more comfortable than traditional rail cars.

Unfortunately, this new design ran into serious safety problems with failures in the automatic equipment, and generally poor mechanical reliability. Rising costs and deficits also troubled the system. With special sales taxes revenue from the state legislature and a variety of other taxes levied for capital development, the system is soundly financed.

A number of organizations assist in the planning and direction of various aspects of BART activities. The oldest of these, Muni, was formed in 1900; the Bay Area Rapid Transit District (BARTD) was formed by the legislature in 1967. The regional planning agency for the nine-county area is the Association of Bay Area Governments (ABAG); the regional transportation planning agency (which includes airports and waterways as well) is the Metropolitan Transportation Commission (MTC), which is also the designated A-95 review agency and the designated Metropolitan Planning Organization (MPO). Extensive technology assessment and analysis programs are currently in progress emphasizing environmental impact.

Although San Francisco began work in earnest on a comprehensive urban system before federal funds were available and at a time when only highway development was encouraged, the experience of the city in many ways reflects the more recent efforts of others. It began primarily as a revolt against highway elements, factors that had a role in both Atlanta and Washington, D.C. It was one of the first conscious uses of transit to produce a given urban form, namely, the San Francisco image: high-intensity banking, shipping and investment interests in a city of sophisticated and high-quality life-style.

Seattle, Washington

Seattle, built on mountain tops rising from nearby lakes and bays, is frequently listed first among the most desirable cities in which to live. Almost completely surrounded by water, with Puget Sound and Lake Washington the largest bodies of water, and many smaller lakes and ponds, the dense trees and greenery testify to a moderate if wet climate; the city offers good air quality and a high quality of life generally.

Although Seattle is the largest city in the northwest, the work force has traditionally been dependent on the aerospace industry that is in turn dependent on often capricious defense spending.

The severe problems the aerospace industry encountered in 1970 account in part for the downturn in Seattle population (see table 6-12). The loss in transit ridership in the journey to work is less than might be expected considering the 1970 unemployment (see table 6-13).

Seattle traditionally has had good bus and trolley bus service. Efforts

Table 6-12
Decline in Seattle Population as a Percentage of SMSA Population

Year	Seattle Population	Percentage of SMSA Population
1950	468,000	55%
1960	557,000	50%
1970	531,000	37%

Table 6-13
Percentage of Population in Seattle and in SMSA Using Public Transit to Work

	Percentage Using Transit to Work	
Year	Seattle	SMSA
1960	19%	12%
1970	15%	7%

to introduce rail service have not been met favorably. During the early 1950s, when the major freeways were being constructed, efforts were made by certain planning groups to have rapid transit placed in the median strip as in the Chicago design. This approach to expressway design was debated several times and each time the decision was to eliminate rail transit.

In the first of the major transit systems to be put before the voters, the so-called Forward Thrust plan included both extensive express busing and 48 miles of rapid rail; the plan won a bare majority of 51 percent of the vote, which was insufficient by Washington law to pass since bonding required a 60 percent majority. In another state, the system might have passed.

The transit plan was revised and presented to the voters again in 1970. However, it failed once more, this time receiving only 46 percent of the vote, believed due to the poor economic conditions, which in turn resulted from the huge layoffs at Boeing.

Although expensive transit plans were not being well-received, economical bus systems were. A study by the Northwestern University Transportation Center showed clearly that express busing, which saved considerable time, was being used by an increasing number of former automobile drivers, to a much greater degree than for the standard bus system. A new plan was developed based on a 650-mile bus system serving four major city centers. In 1972 the voters approved a 0.3 percent sales tax to finance the bus plans. Then Metro, the umbrella authority throughout the Seattle region, took over operation of the bus company, operated under the Seattle Transit System, and several suburban bus systems. Additional funds were also made available from state legislation on motor vehicle excise tax revenues. The resulting bus program together with the matching funds made possible one of the largest UMTA grants in history for an all-bus program; when completed, federal funding will reach about $80 million.

Plans are still going ahead for alternative rail systems. Changes have come to the city that alter conditions and interests. A domed stadium, completed in 1976, acts as a major centralized attraction giving rise to the need for better transit. The World's Fair of 1962 left a cultural and entertainment center, served by a mile-long monorail linking the site to the CBD. Most important, decisions must be made on highway funds of about $500 million planned for the interstate system (I-90), which is giving rise to new total ground transportation design. It seems likely that a portion of these extensive funds will be available for rapid transit.

The future concerns of the area are largely in the hands of several co-ordinated groups: the city of Seattle, the municipality of Metropolitan Seattle (Metro), and the Puget Sound Council of Governments (PSCOG), which had previously been called the Puget Sound Governmental Conference (PSCG). With the city's economy stabilized, and the good reception to transit ridership in general, the newly available highway funds may find their way into a vastly improved ground transportation system.

Washington, D.C.

The United States was the first nation in the world to plan a capitol exclusively for the seat of government. Once the site was selected, the plan was designed primarily on positioning the capital on the west end of a region called Jenkin's Heights, "which stand as a pedestal waiting for a monument" according to the designer L'Enfant, and in direct line with the executive mansion. The irregular blocks that formed the grille of the basic plan were cut by superimposed diagonal avenues, devised to converge at the capitol and executive mansion and to form scores of squares, triangles, and traffic circles for small parks and monuments. As the city grew, the basic grid work and diagonal streets were extended into the hilly surrounding regions regardless of contours. The result was a maze of traffic complexity challenging to the transportation engineer.

To complicate matters, more people in Washington, D.C. drive cars to work (84%) than in any of the major cities in the nation. Although Chicago and Philadelphia have greater percentages of the work force employed in the CBD area, these cities have far fewer people (37% and 44%, respectively) taking cars to work. New York, which has a smaller percentage employed in the CBD, still has only 31 percent driving to work. Thus, Washington, D.C., which a high percentage employed in the central city, and with an overwhelming percentage driving to work, has, as might be anticipated, severe traffic problems.

In spite of this intense congestion, public opposition has stymied not only freeway construction, but improvement of existing arterials as well. In part, this arises from a desire to protect historic monuments and buildings and to preserve the small parks and squares that give Washington a distinctive atmosphere. With so much space given to government buildings and historic sites, housing has always been difficult in Washington and additional highways and parking areas for automobiles were thought to be unconscionable.

In 1960 Congress created a federal agency, called the National Capital Transportation Agency (NCTA), to devise a transit plan. The NCTA, together with the National Capital Regional Planning Council (NCRPC), worked to prepare a comprehensive plan for the region. A seven-line system, 83 miles long, called the "Wedge and Corridors" plan, estimated to cost $796 million, was given careful technical design, perhaps with inadequate effort on ancillary items, only to be rejected by Congress. There was no organized support for it; the president's assassination in 1962 had shifted the focus of business elsewhere. This plan was criticized specifically for lacking certain necessary components such as labor-protection agreements and protection for private enterprise.

In a new plan presented in 1965, the various objections and omissions from the first plan were corrected; in addition the plan called for a slightly larger system at a cost of $431 million. This plan received congressional approval.

In late 1966, Congress passed legislation creating, together with Maryland and Virginia agreements, the Washington Metropolitan Area Transit Authority (WMATA), replacing the NCTA. Activities began to design the regional system.

In voting for bond approval for construction in 1968, five different jurisdictions were involved in the Washington area; all five voted overwhelmingly for the construction bonds with an average 71 percent of the vote, with the understanding that the federal government would pay two-thirds of the cost and would further guarantee the bonds. Construction began in 1969 on the 98-mile system, estimated to cost $2.5 billion.

By the time Metro opened the first segment in 1976, five presidents had been involved. President Eisenhower signed the law creating the transit agency that began planning the subway. President Kennedy sent to Congress legislation providing for the original 83-mile system, which President Johnson later signed into law in 1966. President Nixon obtained the initial $1.1 billion authorization from Congress that made possible the start of construction in December of 1969, and later obtained a crucial federal guarantee making possible sale of the $1.2 billion in Metro bonds for continued construction. President Ford, when funds were running out, together with Secretary William T. Coleman, recommended completion of the entire system with unused interstate highway funds.

Rising costs plagued construction from the start and finding funds has been a continual problem. By the end of the first year, costs had increased by almost 30 percent; by 1974 the increase amounted to an incredible 80 percent overrun. A number of crisis conferences and piecemeal decisions has kept construction going.

At one point in 1966, UMTA officials considered applying their new articulated policy of encouraging metropolitan areas to build rail systems in incremental stages as the demand for transit grows. This procedure slows down construction, reorders construction priorities, and increases overall costs; it is a way of keeping programs ongoing in the face of inadequate funds. WMATA officials argued that such an approach would delay completion of the system by five years and increase costs by at least $500 million. In the face of these strong objections, UMTA then stated within a week of the first announcement, that highway funding had been underestimated making the incremental policy approach unnecessary. Many other cities no doubt wish such reverses in unwanted policies could happen as easily to them, and as quickly.

Construction continues in spite of delays and uncertainties. The first 4-1/2 mile segment "going nowhere to nowhere" according to some critics, opened in March 1976. Two other major segments will be ready for opening in 1977; the first, connecting the Mall to the Pentagon and the National Airport should be ready by spring 1977 and the second, an eastward extension to the Stadium, by fall of 1977.

On opening day of the first segment, Washingtonians by the thousands lined up for free rides. The unexpected throng overloaded the new system causing delays and crowding beyond what might be anticipated for the peak of the rush hour. On some trains there was spontaneous applause for the rapid but quiet movement, in contrast to the overhead traffic. This short segment, which takes 28 minutes in rush hour traffic, takes about 7 minutes by Metro car. Metro's car, like BART's, is wider than conventional design and fully carpeted with picture windows; they are 75 feet long, and hold 81 seated and 94 standing passengers. Unlike BART, however, the Washington system uses primarily conventional equipment and is therefore not anticipated to have the equipment failure problems that have troubled BART. Eventually, the Metro is expected to make use of automatic equipment, with a major portion of the operation could be run by computers rather than human motorman, in keeping with the BART concept.

Another feature of the Metro system is the spacious, vaulted-arch underground stations (designed by Harry Weese & Associates of Chicago). BART, too, had planned such stations to deter crime by removing all posts. Eventually, in a cost-savings move, BART redesigned their stations and used the less expensive post construction. Washington's system however has retained all of the crime deterent measures originally designed, such as the unobstructed vaulting[c] to discourage lurkers, and an elaborate system of closed-circuit television monitors.

The unresolved question of finances brings many to wonder whether the system will be finished, or cut short only half completed. Considering that the continual approach of federal government is through management by crisis, problems of any kind, financial or otherwise, are usually not seriously addressed until chaos threatens. In the case of the METRO, the omnipresent highway funds may rescue construction efforts. If not, crisis management will respond again in the traditional fashion.

Commentary: The Cities and UMTA

Cities need transit systems. Indeed, 43 cities throughout the world have subways or rapid rail of some type. Only 7 of these cities are in the United States. Yet, major urban centers of countries with no more and usually less resources have already built viable transit systems: countries such as Argentina, Belgium, Brazil, Britain, Canada, China, Czechoslovakia, France, Greece, Italy, Japan, Mexico, the Netherlands, Portugal, Rumania, Spain, the Soviet Union, Sweden, and West Germany have had subways for years. The United States is unique among modern countries in failing to build these public systems on a large scale. Whatever the cause, viable public transit seems at least to becoming part of the American landscape.

---

[c] Chicago's *Sun Times* journalist, William Hines, described the surprise on entering a subway station at least the equivalent of "what came upon Alice when she fell down the rabbit hole. There is a cathedral-like quiet splendor to the 600-foot long, vaulted-arch stations. . . ."

7

Financing and Marketing Structure

The economic rationale for public transportion, which clearly is being closely examined by many cities, is complicated by a growing inability to determine the real cost of any product or service. The concept of economic efficiency, for example, deals primarily with the cost per-unit item, whether the item is a unit of service or a unit of goods. The lowest cost is considered the most efficient. This, in turn, produces two major problems:

1. The market structure of this nation is so complex—especially considering the nature of government intervention (both hidden and visible)—as to prevent a complete cost to be assigned to any given item.
2. Cost in the long run may not be the most important factor; not only does the least expensive process often have hidden costs that later require expensive correction measures, but there are some important elements of the human condition that cannot be measured by cost alone. Value judgments are difficult to accommodate in pure cost analysis.

In transportation matters, it may seem to some [1] that the least expensive mode in terms of direct cost, and, therefore, the most economic, efficient method of arriving at a destination is through use of a private automobile. Such computations, however, usually fail to include the true cost of gasoline, for example, which has been unrealistically low through imprudent energy policy and neglect of a variety of pervasive, tax-supported, auto-related costs. These include road and parking costs, street lights, traffic control personnel, pollution control expense, the costs of death and dismemberment, dispersion through poor land use, and a wide variety of potentially detrimental effects of which we are only gradually becoming aware—all of which will no doubt be expensive to correct.

Conversely, public transit costs may seem too high as an out-of-pocket expense. Considering that the transit patron also has to shoulder the high cost of the automobile, this may be true. Transit costs are immediate and visible. A rapid transit system must pay for track maintenance and repair and for control and direction of transit traffic; electric lights must be purchased, installed, and maintained, and the electric bill paid as separate and easily identified costs. Until recently, these costs had to be paid directly from fare, by patrons who were at the same time helping through taxation to finance the real costs of the automobile.

The whole question of how to "manage the automobile" in terms of identifying real costs and getting the automobile to shoulder some of these costs is currently the subject of numerous high-level government studies [2]. It is a difficult question to address because a large portion of the employed populace is dependent on the automobile, and it would be unrealistic to impose strong economic deterrents, if no transportation alternative is available.

Given the complexity of the economic rationale, it is apparent that viable public transportation systems are needed. The question is: how can such a network be financed?

Revenue Mechanisms for Financing Public Transit

The needs and financing of urban transportation [3,4] have been the subject of numerous studies. The general conclusion from these efforts is that the needs are so great that very substantial changes will be needed in the financial mechanism to accommodate what must be done, and that no one source, such as a gasoline tax, will be sufficient.

Because of the way our tax structure works, only the federal government has the funds necessary for major public works projects. Local support is also required both for use as matching funds against the federal contribution and for other costs not appropriate for the federal level. It should be recognized, for example, that federal allocations must be consistent with the federal role, which is to distribute tax funds equitably among the states in programs that allow all states to participate. However, it must distribute funds according to predetermined criteria, directed toward achieving a set goal and not one that simply redistributes funds to those who contributed. For example, the highway program arrived at a 90 percent federal share so that even very poor states, especially those located geographically in strategic areas, could participate in the interstate highway system. Other states, such as those located at the peripheral regions of the nation, have become "donor" states, contributing more to the fund than received back, because presumably the benefits are not in dollar share of road building funds but in the economic and defense advantages enjoyed by all states throughout the interstate system.

Public transit is very similar. Admittedly, large cities are more concerned with this element of transportation than are rural areas. The advantage of a rural area in contributing to a metropolitan transit system should be evident in the total economics: public transit in Los Angeles would save gasoline and road investment funds that could be used by rural Kansas. The economic health of the nation as whole and matters of national security, associated with the oil import problem, affect everyone.

Since both public transit and highway construction are part of the nation's ground transportation system, it is natural that similarities should exist. It follows that the successful mechanism which has been, as some claim, too successful in the highway construction program will also be useful in building the needed public transit network.

Concerned transit officials [5] have expressed the opinion that the most sensible course of action for achieving a viable public transit network is through the development of a transportation trust fund. This fund would allocate funding to be spent directly on these programs, thus freeing this work from annual congressional political maneuvering. Transit systems, like road systems, take years to complete—often nearly a decade—and the trust fund is an excellent mechanism for maintaining the continuing of such projects [6,7].

High visibility is one of the key elements of the existing trust fund. It is a way of imparting specific responsibility, of providing a yardstick against which performance can be measured. It acts as a focusing mechanism on which to build public advocacy. It carries with it something of a long-term influence that is extremely important in building the long-term, advocacy-type support needed in all of our most pressing national problems. Most of these problems, such as public transit, do not have easy, quick solutions; instead, the solutions depend on developing new public attitudes, a new sense of awareness and insight, technology that requires a long time between initial stimulus and completion, and better ways of getting things done.

Another thing a trust fund does is allow Congress to group responsibility under one umbrella. Today, the humanitarian areas concerning the elevation of the lot of the poor and handicapped to become producing citizens is universally recognized as an area closely tied to public transportation. Many of the problems the country has faced in solving these welfare matters can be laid at the doorstep of the automobile. Perhaps a major part of the responsibility for the solution should be placed on the same transportation doorstep. The trust fund concept gives that opportunity, if there is the courage to take it.

Most important, a transportation trust fund is a viable way of "getting things done." It must be recognized that it is getting more difficult all the time to accomplish real progress in any field. Although any mechanism that provides a tool for getting things moving is probably also open to abuse, the critical economic consequences to this nation as a result of changing events, such as the energy crisis, require courageous action. It is doubtlessly true that the highway program and the trust fund have contributed to the present dilemma in oil scarcity—and if economists are to be believed, worldwide resource scarcity is behind the inflation and unemployment problems as well.

These problems can, therefore, be equated in a very real sense with what happened to the Highway Trust Fund, which heretofore has been too resistant to change. But the fear of what has happened should not undermine efforts to remedy the problems. Serious problems require strong remedies and it is likely that the most severe problems, such as those of energy, inflation, and unemployment, will require just as powerful tools to solve them as the tools that created them.

Some critics argue that, just because taxes are collected on automobile-associated purchases (see table 7-1), there is no reason why these taxes should be expended solely on behalf of the automobile any more than cigaret taxes are spent for cancer research or that alcoholic beverage taxes are spent for solving the alcohol problem. The fact that this trust fund has effectively financed the largest public works project in the history of man demands careful attention.

The best course of action lies someplace in between those who would abolish the trust fund and those who would continue it only for highway use. In an emotionally charged situation, common sense is frequently difficult to achieve. Clearly, the nation needs good highways, and it is not sensible to cut off the completion of the interstate system at any arbitrary point. Similarly, it is not sensible to continue building highways at an ever accelerating rate while neglecting other transportation systems.

The trust fund is simply a tool, to be used to advantage in situations where other funding mechanisms are less effective. It is only a tool and not a policy. The policy in turn, depends on how the tool is used. At present, the trust fund appears to be the only financing mechanism suitable for the needs of public transportation but courage is required to develop its potential.

Regulation in Public Transportation

Although many commuter rail lines fall under the federal regulations, typical city bus systems and subways operations do not. Therefore, combining of rail and city transit systems raises questions again about federal regulatory policy—and especially its effect on efficiency and cost.

At least two types of government regulation are clearly distinguishable. The first is that pioneered and practiced by the ICC in its regulation of the railroad industry. It represents an extensive sharing of managerial responsibilities and is called "joint public-private management." Although such an arrangement may have been initiated with an intent of protecting the public interest, it has come in practice to be concerned with "promotion" of an industry, by suppression of competition if necessary. This type of regulation emphasizes cross-subsidies in which a railroad, for

Table 7-1
Tax Sources for Highway Trust Fund

User Taxes	Rate	Net Yield Fiscal Year 1974	Percent of Total
Gasoline[a]	4 cents per gallon	$3,906,614	62.4
Diesel fuel[a]	4 cents per gallon	394,681	6.3
New trucks, buses and trailers	10 per cent of manufacturer's wholesale price. Vehicles of 10,000 pounds or less gross weight, school and transit buses are exempt	614,132	9.8
Tires	10 cents per pound for highway type, 5 cents per pound for others	837,717	13.4
Tubes	10 cents per pound	33,382	0.5
Tread rubber	5 cents per pound if for highway type tires only	24,131	0.4
Heavy vehicle use	$3 per 1,000 pounds annually on total gross weight of vehicles rated at more than 26,000 pounds gross weight	225,193	3.6
Parts and accessories	8 percent of manufacturer's wholesale price of truck and bus parts and accessories	130,455	2.1
Lubricating oil	6 cents per gallon in highway use. All non-highway use refundable	94,005	1.5
Total		$6,260,310	100.0

[a]Highway use only

Source: Highway Users Federation.

example, takes profits from a freight line and transfers them to a losing commuter line.

A second type of regulation is that found in the practices of the Civil Aeronautics Board and in some urban transit regulation. The approach here is to create, through appropriate franchising, limited but workable competition. In aviation this practice has been used to subsidize and promote unprofitable but socially desirable services.

The entire regulatory policy presently is undergoing careful study, and it is likely that within the near future the first steps will be taken to deregulate many phases of transit. Most of the original purposes to be served by regulatory agreements have passed from the scene. For example, it can be said that the railroad discriminating rate structure facilitated the economic

integration of the continental United States. It fostered regional special-
ization, afforded wide markets for products, and stimulated large-scale industrial production creating the industrial colossus that exists today [8,9].
Regulation served its purposes well.

Today, much regulatory policy is simply too expensive and it has resulted in wasteful practices the economy can no longer afford [10]. In
times of rapid change, it prevents commuter railroads from incorporating
needed changes as fast as required, and often shackles these organizations with outmoded practices and increased costs, and deters technological advance.

One of the major problems in adjusting present regulations is the extreme difficulty in analyzing benefits. Not only is the transportation system interaction so complex as to make the clear delineation of trade-off
factors difficult, but new factors are emerging, such as the need for energy
conservation, which make regulation more difficult in terms of ultimate
benefits and goals. An optimized energy policy, for example, which
would favor water transportation, is in direct conflict with other regulatory policies.

The aims and goals of regulation are often laudable although their
practical implementation is less clear. Many excellent papers and reports
have studied these problems; one suggestion has been that all transport
programs be subjected to a more rigorous economic analysis [10] than has
taken place heretofore. There have been brave attempts at the uniform
application of economic investment criteria to all modes in which public
investments occur and to draw up priority lists to differentiate those projects that will produce the largest real net benefits and make the best use of
the most scarce resources. In even a static society, it would be a nearly
impossible task. In a fast-changing society the regulatory structure itself
may be outmoded, indicating a need for new management approaches on
the part of government.

Pricing

The concept of what price can be charged for a given transportation service is closely related to urban travel demand analysis and forecasting
[11,12]. Although nearly a billion dollars has been spent on these endeavors, the field is still far from being able to produce accurate and detailed
estimates of demand functions, including all the relevant price and income
elasticities and cross-elasticities of the various transport modes. A scarcity of data and lack of control in pricing experiments have severely ham-
pered most direct attempts to obtain the needed empirical parameters.

It was not very long ago that the relationship between fare increase or
decrease and ridership was thought to be a reasonably simple function

and that "standards" could be set [13]. It is now known that what happens is a function of many parameters such as the length of the ride, type of individual traveling, whether the trip must be made as in the journey to work, types of service available, and other considerations. Consequently, there is a wide variety in reported experiences.

There are a number of ways to price transit service. In a very large city, such as London, zoning is almost mandatory but in a smaller geographic area such as Paris, New York, or Chicago, the costs of zoning have offset the advantages in the past, and, therefore, graduated fares according to zone have generally not been used. Several different kinds of fare structure are employed nationwide:

Flat Fare. Represents an average charge for an average cost of service approach. It is the basic fare structure used in Chicago. A flat rate is paid for one direction of travel no matter how long or short the trip. It has the advantage of being easy to collect, and by reducing collection time decreases transportation time and transit costs. However, it tends to be discriminatory to short discretionary midday trips, multipurpose trips, and to "transit captives" who must make all trips by public transport and must "pay" for every stop.

Reduced Midday Fares. Using the same approach on value-of-service, it has been argued that rush-hour service is more valuable and thus should be priced higher than midday fares. This generally means reduction of midday fares.

Special Fares. These are based on pricing according to ability to pay. Over 50 cities have reduced rates for senior citizens, including Chicago. Other typical reduced rates are availalable to students and the handicapped. The new 1975 UMTA guidelines require midday fare reductions for senior citizens and the handicapped in order to qualify for UMTA grants.

Transfer Charge. Most cities charge for a change in vehicles. There is an inherent problem in this approach in that the transferee pays twice and endures inconvenience as well.

Fare Collection Methods

Exact Fare. Adopted by many cities in the late sixties as a method to reduce crime, this system requires the passenger to have the exact fare in hand. The system reduces time spent in collection but is a deterent to impulse trips.

Ticket Books. Sold in advance and usually at a discount, each ticket is equivalent to the exact fare. This practice is convenient for collection—both for customer and operator. However, inflation has made even discounts such as this uneconomical in many cities.

Graduated Fare—Zone System. Uses the cost of service approach to pricing. Under this arrangement the city is divided into several zones. The commuter pays a base fare plus an increment for each zone crossed. In some cities this fare is simply additive for every zone crossed; others have a complex system for reducing the increment in that it approaches "equal fare for equal service." However, there are significant hidden costs in collection hardware, labor, and time spent in travel; further, the demarcation of zones is often controversial in that one shopping area is inevitably "discriminated" over another.

Mileage Fare. Much like taxi service, this fare is again based on cost of service. This is only feasible in a small operation.

Premium Fares. These are based more on the value of the service to the commuter. For example, many cities charge an additional increment for express (freeway service) reasoning that the in-vehicle time saved is more valuable than the additional cost.

Monthly Passes. Monthly passes are sold in advance for a flat rate. These passes then allow unlimited access to the system. One attractive modification is to require payment of a token fare (e.g., a dime) with the pass for each use. This system is especially beneficial to the transit captive who must use public transportation not only for journey to work but also for all shopping and entertainment trips as well.

Special Passes (Such as the Super Transfers). These special fares are generally aimed at the most sensitive market—as in any any discretionary midday or weekend trips. Spain is the only nation that so enjoys such high ridership on weekends as to charge higher fares on holidays and weekends.

Historically, over the years, there has been a decrease in transit ridership and an increase in fares in an attempt to make up for losses in income. For a long time, the general rule of thumb used was that for every 10 percent increase in fare, a corresponding decrease of 3 percent in ridership resulted, and thus a net gain in revenue—up to a point. Logic would indicate that fares could be raised so high as to be prohibitively expensive. In 1968 James Scheiner computed the point of diminishing returns for data in Pennsylvania [14]. He found that increases beyond 80¢ result

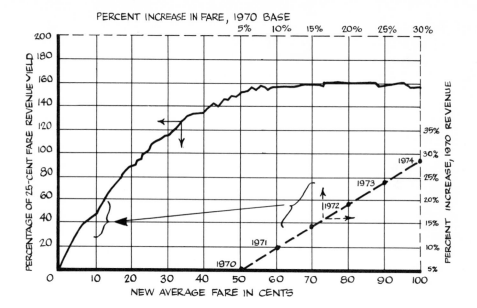

Figure 7-1. The Point of Diminishing Returns in Fare Increase. Commuter rail figures, (Chicago) shown at right, sometimes resemble the initial rise of the fare curve showing increased revenue with increased fare.

in a net decrease in revenue. Further, there are diminishing returns in revenue for fare increases beyond 30¢. (see figure 7-1.)

Obviously, this break-even point not only differs from city to city, but from area to area within the city. Short-haul trips are more affected by fare increases than long-haul trips. Research indicates [15] that long-haul rail commuters are more willing to accept substantial increases in fare without appreciable dropoffs in ridership under some circumstances.

The Chicago railroads are an interesting case in point. In 1956 the Chicago and Northwestern (C&NW), experiencing serious losses in commuter service, borrowed $50 million to purchase new bilevel cars, finance new stations, and inaugurate a monthly ticket and numerous service amenities. It put on an intensive public relations campaign—being the only railroad in the nation at that time to advertise commuter service—investing about $300,000 a year in advertising, which included radio and print advertisements, direct mail, welcome wagons, and contacts with large realtors (note that in the U.S., 25% of households move each year). In spite of almost annual increases in fares, the ridership held steady and the operation was run at a profit. Note, also, that the fare increases were small and always just enough to cover increasing costs. Only recently has the line lost money on the commuter service.

The story behind other railroad fare increases in Chicago and elsewhere has been less fortunate, partly for geographic reasons and changes in demand, and partly because these organizations were prevented during certain periods from raising fares, owing to equipment and financial assistance agreements with the federal and state governments that usually prohibit fare increases one year after emergency funding. The result is that when fare increases came, they were larger than the systematic, incremental increases asked by the C&NW, and detrimental to ridership with an obvious impact not experienced by C&NW.

Experiences with fare reductions as a means of increasing ridership have also been highly dependent on external factors, different for bus service than for rapid transit: Bus ridership is more sensitive to fare increases than is rapid transit. A study of New York patronage showed that subway patronage dropped 10-20 percent for every 100 percent increase in fare, and bus patronage decreased 15-20 percent.

Atlanta reduced fares from 45¢ to 15¢—a 66 percent reduction—and increased its ridership only 28 percent [16]. Analysis of a fare reduction in Toronto showed that a decrease in fares of 1 percent will increase patronage by 1/3 of 1 percent. A Boston study indicated that a 1 percent fare reduction brought only 1/6 of 1 percent increase in passengers. These disappointing results are more or less typical nationwide [17].

Chicago has been found to be sensitive to fare decreases to a greater extent than to those services mentioned previously. Some Chicago experiments include the following:

1. Reducing the fare from 45¢ to 25¢ on Sunday has resulted in a sustained 100 percent increase in ridership.
2. Free bus service between the Evanston elevated stations and neighboring areas resulted in over a 1,400 percent increase, from 150 per weekday to 3,665 per weekday.
3. Reduction of fare from 45¢ to 10¢ between adjacent stations on two different elevated lines increased ridership by an order of magnitude, from approximately 300-400 per day to 3,000 to 4,000.

One key problem is estimating ridership increase when transfers are involved. In Chicago, the Super Transfer, a 70¢ transfer, good for unlimited rides during a weekend period, complicates analysis of the special 25¢ Sunday fare. There is at present no practical way of counting transit riders—only of counting total revenue.

The special relationships that hold for fare increases also hold, in general, for fare decreases. That is, short-haul trips and discretionary trips, such as shopping, seem to be more responsive to decreases in fare. In At-

Table 7-2
Federal Funds Allocation among Ten Cities, July 1975-76

City	Section 5 Allocation (Million $)
New York	$42.7
Los Angeles	24.0
Chicago	18.1
San Francisco	10.1
Washington, D.C.	6.9
Boston	6.5
Twin Cities	3.3
Seattle	2.7
Denver	2.4
Atlanta	2.4
Total	$119.10

lanta, for example, an across-the-board decrease produced a 37 percent midday increase in ridership compared with a 19 percent rush-hour increase. This also may be a function of the amount of less-crowded conditions, off-peak hours versus rush hours. In many systems, such as Chicago's, there simply is no additional capacity available in rush periods.

Federal Fare Assistance

A striking reversal in federal funding posture occurred in 1974 when a new section, Section 5, was added to the UMTA act. This section for the first time provided funds for transit operating deficit, thus recognizing that transit companies cannot be expected to operate from fare box revenues alone.

Section 5 provided a block grant of $3.975 billion to cities. The proportion allowed each city is computed by a formula that takes into account population and population density of each city. The money can be used for either operating costs or for capital equipment.

The maximum allowable federal assistance for operating expense is 50 percent of the operating deficit; capital grants require only 20 percent local matching share. This action was taken in the belief that efficiency would be encouraged.

Operating deficits nationwide are of course growing, since fares have been stabilized and costs rise rapidly with increasing inflation and labor rates. The total deficit in 1975 approached a half billion dollars and is rising. Consequently, virtually all transit operators plan on using their maximum subsidy for operating assistance. The July 1975-July 1976 allocations for major cities is presented in table 7-2.

Curiously, no allowance is made for the differences in fare structure. Thus, federal funds are used to preserve a very low fare, such as the 15¢ bus fare in Denver, but a 25¢ fare in Chicago and 50¢ fare in New York City. In a sense, Chicago and New York riders are paying a portion of the Atlanta rider's cost. This type of inequity illustrates the complexities involved in federal assistance and portends future adjustments in fare structure.

Socioeconomic Questions

Another important feature of fare structure variation is socioeconomic and deals with the question of who is served by public transit. At present, 45 percent of the Chicago riders are called "captives"—they have no other form of transportation. The rest are transit independents—in other words, they have chosen public transportation over the use of a private automobile. Reversing this, 63 percent of "no-car" commuters take public transportation compared with 20 percent of persons owning one car and 5 percent owning two cars.

There are significant differences in these user groups. First, the transit captive tends to live in the city, with nearly half living in large apartment buildings; over half have incomes less than $6,000, and tend to come from single-person households (45%). The transit independent, on the other hand, has a much higher income, tends to live in detached housing (low density) and comes from larger households. Within these two groups, each making up about 50 percent of the ridership, lie important demographic differences as well.

Higher income commuters going to the Loop, Chicago's central business district, will pay for the speed and convenience of a commuter train, that is, personally absorb the costs. The transit captive has no choice until a threshold is reached where he will bear the expense of a second-hand car. The lower income blue-collar worker, whose destinations are shorter distances and are generally served by bus, often has a car and will not absorb increased fares—and thus is very sensitive to fare increases.

An interesting anomaly exists among lower income bus riders. Those having a car are sensitive to fare increases, as previously stated, so that automobile ownership becomes an important variable in the analysis. Yet, transit captives, who have no other form of transportation, are insensitive to fare increases because they have no alternative [19]. One study [18] at Northwestern University showed a fare elasticity of -0.96 (one of the highest in literature) *if* transit captives were not considered. If they were, the elasticity "dropped" to -0.08.

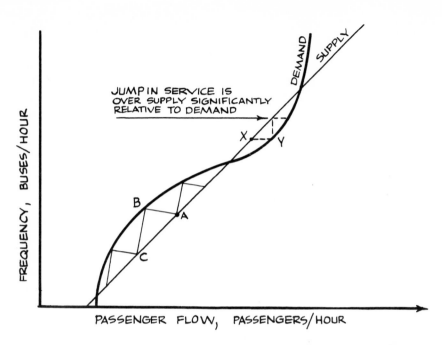

Figure 7-2. Passenger Demand Supply.

Scheduling

All of these considerations are based on an analysis of "what happened" when the fare was either increased or decreased and little is said about the kind of service that was offered simultaneously. When Los Angeles offered a Sunday fare of 10¢ for any distance within the 500 square mile area—and in a region not known for ready acceptance of public transportation—the bus system could not handle the patronage. If ridership is going to increase, the operator must be able to anticipate and serve the number of additional service required.

Therefore, the problem is shown in the shape of the demand curve, and what variables the curve depends on, are generally not known. (See figure 7-2.) There is a purposeful intent, to conserve costs, to stay somewhat below this curve at rush hours (shown by Point A), which unfortunately has the natural tendency to force a downward trend (to Points B and C). Most transit operators undersupply at rush hour in this fashion. In regions where it is hoped to encourage ridership, an oversupply might be financed as indicated by Point X building toward Y and Z. This is the situ-

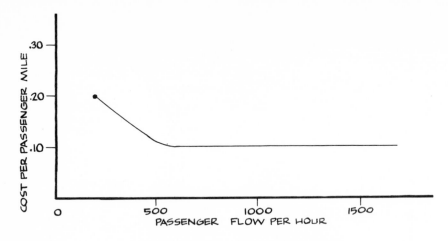

Figure 7-3. Costs per Passenger Mile.

ation on some new bus services now being introduced in Chicago suburban areas.

E.K. Morlock has shown [20] that the cost of providing transportation services follows a curve indicating that costs of operation sharply decrease and level off as the number of passengers (density) increases (see figure 7-3).

In March 1974 the fare in Chicago was reduced on Sunday from the standard 45¢ to 25¢. The ridership increased but not enough to offset a loss in total revenue. Although the number of originating riders increased dramatically on some bus lines, being as much three or four times the previous average value during the previous year, the total average ridership including transfers increased an average of only 25 percent. Later, the supertransfer, a 70¢ transfer that permits unlimited rides over the Sunday period, showed a steady increase in sales. Because 67 percent of Chicago riders normally transfer, and no charge was made in the normal 10¢ transfer (good for one hour), it is not surprising that the major ridership increase was experienced in the originating riders, up an average of 100 percent during some periods, rather than in total ridership, which includes transfers. Another point of interest was that increased ridership has been primarily noted on the bus service and not on the rapid transit. The reason for this is believed related to the fact that the rapid transit serves primarily employment areas, usually not open on Sunday, while the bus service includes more recreational and culture centers of interest to Sunday patrons. (See figure 7-4.)

These pricing concepts mentioned above primarily reflect the theoretical aspects of the problem. In practice, price is apt to depend as much on

177

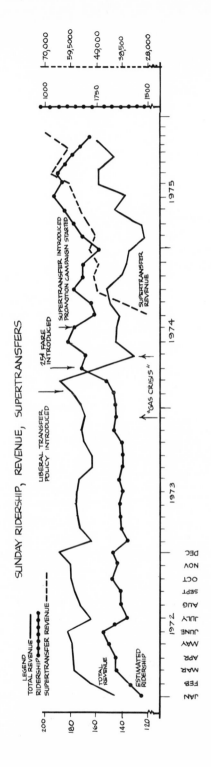

Figure 7-4. Chicago Transit Authority Sunday Fare Reduction Program.

historical background than any other factor, and the costs incurred may mainly reflect the type of union agreement the agency has, relative to meeting the demand. Scheduling, especially concerns of premium time, are often based on union commitments more than any other factor.

These subject analyses regarding demand and pricing do offer valuable insight into what is happening and in future times may provide useful guides to more efficient operation. Much of the present endeavor, especially some of the newer analyses, will be increasingly useful in marketing programs.

Scheduling by Run Cutting

In practice, scheduling for a large transit system is dominated by the union work rules. The complication in work scheduling arises from the fact that most transit runs do not correspond to a normal work day. A round trip on a bus route, for example, may take nine hours, not eight, or it may be seven hours with the driver guaranteed a full day's pay. Further, routes must be organized to provide for maximum service in the morning and evening rush hours. Most unions do not permit part-time work, they limit the amount of overtime, and they charge premium time for split shifts.

Consequently, the scheduler has to break the routes into a number of possible and logical segments, and try to fit the segments together in the most economical way. This process is called "run cutting."

In general, there are two types of run-cutting methods: (1) that of "chopping" each vehicle route into various pieces of work and then trying to match these pieces into workable shifts for the operators with appropriate meal breaks, and (2) the process of "dovetailing" where a piece of a run, cut from one vehicle, is carefully matched to another piece. The dovetailing method is used by the Chicago Transit Authority [21] and most large systems.

The process begins with a prepared service plan made by the organization's operational planning group. This plan prescribes the need for vehicles throughout the system at primarily rush hour and roughly the time of service between vehicles. The scheduling group then begins work with a listing of vehicles and departure times from a specific garage, which is somewhat flexible, to conform in a general way to the planning requirement. This set of runs is placed on "spread sheet" showing length of run, overtime committment, and so on. The complexity of the process is described in the following quotation from a paper presented by N.W.

Worcester, director of scheduling, Chicago Transit Authority, at a 1975 workshop on automated techniques for scheduling:

The first move will be to cut the owl runs, which have already been coupled with lunch fall-backs. We will then cut the latest finishing evening train back within the spread, if possible, and find a piece of work that will fit ahead of this piece to make a reasonable sized run. If the vehicles will not cut back into the spread, there is probably no need of making these portions of work too long, keeping in mind that if we cannot get a piece of work into the spread, the piece might as well be a couple of hours as a couple of minutes out of spread. Doing this will reduce the number of undesirable runs that work only a short piece of work, have a meal relief and then work a long piece of work. Keeping in mind using up the AM rushes of work, we construct runs until we have no piece of work left with a finishing time outside of spread. We match the latest morning rush pull-out time with the latest finishing work time for each evening rush piece. If this does not produce any "overspread condition", we say "we are in spread."
If we find we are not able to match up the morning starting and afternoon finishing times with the spread limitation, we then build more evening straight runs with the latest finishing PM rush pieces until we are in spread. We then proceed to build the straight day runs. . . . No one will ever make a run cut without a great amount of trying, changing, shifting and correcting.

This procedure is designed to furnish maximum evening rush hours service and if slips must occur in the system, they are automatically moved back into the little-used owl service periods, that is, midnight until 6:00 A.M. Obviously shifting routes or adding new service creates many problems for the jigsaw puzzle of matching reasonable service with reasonable pieces of operator run time. Although computerized scheduling techniques have been devised, such as the RUCAS system by Mitre Corporation, these are just being tried by smaller organizations, and must be considered as embryonic in nature. This serves to illustrate the significant gap between theoretical research work in demand analysis and methods of common practice.

The Importance of Marketing

In order to encourage transit operators to make use of marketing techniques, UMTA recently issued a new requirement that all transit operators expecting to receive federal grants must have a marketing program and an in-house marketing manager.

Essentially, there are two objectives in present-day transit marketing:

1. To improve the general climate and acceptance of public transportation, so as to build nationwide advocacy to both support transit legislation and transit expenditures

2. To increase ridership on existing services

Because the nation has only 40,000 buses and less than 10,000 rapid transit cars, a significant impact on the nation's auto using public will require an expansion of the system. The major expansions required can only take place if the public supports these extensive programs, which in turn require that the public be informed as to the nature of, and the extent of, the need for such systems.

To some extent, the building of ridership is also dependent on increased services. Many communities simply do not have service available that is in any sense convenient or reliable. Others, such as Chicago, are already used to capacity at rush hour. Ridership increase, therefore, becomes a matter of increasing off-peak service usage, and of judiciously placing new equipment. Professional level papers [21] are appearing on the use of marketing analysis in attracting riders and understanding market behavior.

Certainly, one of the major problems facing the transit industry and government is determining the potential market for public transport services and then persuading travelers to use that service. Essentially marketing is the combination of these two elements. Without an understanding of the bases upon which travelers choose a mode of transport, there is no way to know what the content of advertising, communication, or persuasion should be. Conversely, if knowledge of traveler decision making is known and no means of communication are developed, little change in transit use will occur—certainly not rapidly. Hence, the object of any marketing research program is to develop the basis for the application of persuasion techniques that will produce the maximum shift in travel modes in the shortest time at the least cost.

However, there is another element in the marketing process that is essential. This is the characteristic of the transit service itself. Basically, transit provides a series of transport services within a set of operating constraints. Certain of these properties can be modified, for example, routing, scheduling, fare, transfer, etc. Others cannot be easily modified, for example, accessibility, total travel time, minimum waiting time, vehicle comfort factors, etc. Given a basis for traveler decision making, transit can, up to a point, change its operating regimens more nearly to match travel priorities. Depending on the nature and limitations of the service, transit can adapt to traveler requirements. Therefore, an overall marketing approach is concerned not simply with persuasion, but also with the adaptation of transit service to the same set of basic needs. In sum, a complete marketing program involves the integration of service characteristics and communication methods to match the basic priority concerns of potential users.

Clearly, the foundation of any marketing effort is an understanding of requirements of travelers. The question is: what are the attributes of transport that determine what modes will be chosen? There are three factors that determine the decision to use a particular mode: One is the objective properties of the mode relative to the traveler's trip goal. Another is the subjective perception of the alternative modes, and a third is knowledge of the properties of the alternative modes.

The first factor determines the ultimate size of the market for transit. Given optimum routing of transit, there will be a certain proportion of the travel market that will still be unable to use it. Either it does not service the traveler's origin or destination, the time required to make the journey is excessive, or the amount of transferring required is too complex for people to manage or comprehend.

The second factor involves the personal, social, and functional determinants of transit use. If, for example, the traveler perceives transit as a low status means of travel, an insecure one, or an uncomfortable one, he will avoid its use. These subjective and often nonrational factors are fundamental and often irreducible biases in mode choice. Given an alternative to transit, people will choose it in preference. The question is: how large a fraction of potential transit users are using other modes because of these subjective perceptions? Since they are difficult to modify by normal persuasion techniques, they represent a hard core of nonusers whose numbers must be subtracted from the total potential market.

The third factor concerns the knowledge potential users have about the operating properties of the system. It should be recognized that in the larger urban areas, transit is a complex system. Few travelers understand the area's route structure to use it very extensively and have limited knowledge of transit's structure and operating characteristics. Clearly, if more reliable and fail-safe routing information were available, a major barrier to expanded use of the system could be eliminated. One of the primary problems in current transit information systems is that they are not human engineered, that is, adapted to the processes by which people locate themselves in time and space. If such subsystems can be designed and developed, it should at least increase the perceived utility of the system.

Beyond the within-system information, there is the general problem of mass communication. This is the advertising or mass-media information processing and presentation. The issue is less one of presentation than of rules for content. Principles of media presentation are well-developed but to what elements they should be applied and to what characteristics of transit service would people be sensitive are not well-known. Clearly, it is these issues that are fundamental to any mass communication effort and must be founded on an understanding of traveler requirements.

Consequently, it is obvious that marketing transit service involves three major activities:
1. User perception of transit
2. Transit service parameters
3. Communications of transit services

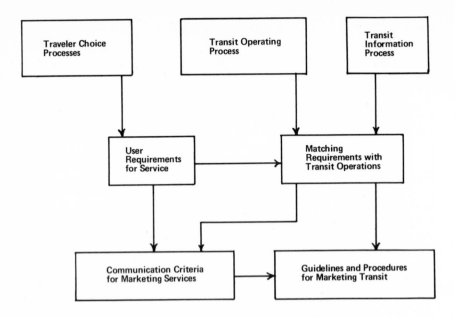

Figure 7-5. Transit Marketing Research Program.

User perception of transit service is the foundation of any marketing effort. It represents the primary area for research effort. The second area is the identification and establishment of criteria for transit level of service needed to most efficiently match traveler requirements. Third is the information content requirements needed to relate transit services to user requirements. Each of these areas represents the major elements of any proposed transit marketing research program, and each of these is described in detail. (See figure 7-5.)

The final goal of an overall marketing research effort is two-fold: to define the basic criteria for maximizing the attractiveness of public transport to potential users, and to provide a set of procedures that can be used by any transit agency in developing a cost-effective marketing program. The research effort is designed to answer the following questions for any target region:

1. What are the attributes of transit that are most attractive to potential users?
2. What are the attributes of transit that are least attractive to potential users?
3. What level of service parameters that can be modified would increase transit attractiveness the most?

4. Given objective and subjective criteria of attractiveness, what is the potential market of public transit in any region?

5. What information do travelers need to have about transit in order to maximize the likelihood of their using the service?

To achieve these goals, a coherent and integrated research program is essential. This would involve four specific tasks. As may be seen, there are three independent but related areas for research that combine to produce the operational and communication criteria for transit marketing. Given these criteria, the final phase is a marketing procedure that will be geared to general application. Within the context of this proposal, such a procedure would be directed specifically to any city with viable transit for test and evaluation.

The following describes each of these tasks.

Perceptions of Transit Acceptability

As has been previously discussed, the willingness to use public transportation and, hence, its marketability depends upon the perception of that service by potential users. Acceptability appears to depend upon three factors:

1. Perceived operational performance of transit
2. Perceived quality of transit service
3. Knowledge of system, all relative to alternative modes

In essence, the probability of a potential user taking transit relative to another mode is some weighted product of the first two factors, that, is, on a relative basis:

$$P_{tc} = \Pi(K_a\, p_a)(K_b\, p_b) \tag{7-1}$$

Knowledge of the system, that is, the degree to which the traveler's perceptions of the system are consistent with its operational properties, is one major determinant of the modifiability of his behavior. For example, if he perceived transit as not connecting his residence with his work place, the likelihood of his trying it is negligible. However, if transit does, objectively, provide the connectivity, then appropriate information can modify behavior. Thus, knowledge of system performance also determines probability of use and equation 7-1 may be rewritten:

$$P_{tc} = \Pi(K_a\, P_a)(K_b\, P_b)(1 - T) \tag{7-2}$$

where $(1 - T)$ is some relative measure of the correspondence between perceived and actual system performance.

Basically, the technical problem in the development of predictive equations is determination of the weighting functions. Work done over the past decade on mode choice and attributes of transport are sufficiently clear for us to know the priority attributes. Work done by a variety of researchers clearly identify the highest priority attributes. What is not known is how travelers evaluate public transit on these attributes.

The objective of this phase of research would be to define how travelers combine the attributes in arriving at a global assessment of public transport. Psychometric methods, both unidimensional and multidimensional, would determine the weighting functions. It should be borne in mind that this phase would encompass both qualitative dimensions and performance dimensions—both related to actual performance of public transport using a specific transit authority as the test bed.

With this analysis, related to specific transit routing and operations in a given city, it should be possible to estimate how closely potential user perceptions match the actual performance of the system. For example, if estimated transit travel times for trips from a given set of origins to a given destination are obtained from nonusers of transit, these can be directly compared with actual travel times. If the estimates were found to be significantly greater than actual, people's perception of transit travel time is negatively biased (and this can be compensated through media communication). By comparing the actual performance relative to perceived performance of public transport across the set of priority attributes, it will be possible to provide a profile along key dimensions of any disparity between the objective and subjective. From a theoretical standpoint, this will provide a basis for an estimate of the disparity function defined in equation 7-2.

In sum, the first phase of this effort is aimed at providing a means of defining the priority attributes forming the basis for traveler's evaluation and use of public transport. These would be defined in terms of variables within the system that are modifiable and those that are nonmodifiable. Therefore, these would provide a means of estimating the size of the potential market for transit service.

Matching Transit Service for Traveler Requirements

From the previous work, three basic pieces of information are provided.

1. What properties of public transport service are most crucial to potential users?
2. What properties are within the power of the system to be changed to conform to user needs?
3. What knowledge do potential users need about the system?

It is reasonable to hypothesize that there are some things transit can do about how it provides its services, for example, seating, environmental control, privacy. If travelers' dominant concerns are for the latter, then the likelihood of major increases in use is low.

Given the expectation of a mix of these two variables, those that are within the capacity of transit modifications will be evaluated. A research task could be devoted to determining what changes in level of service can be provided, the costs to provide these changes and a prediction of the increase in market that might be obtained by the changes.

If public transport is to meet user requirements, it is essential that potential users know or are able to learn how the systems can be so used. This basically involves two different dimensions. One involves information concerning what can be done using the system. The other involves information on how to use the system. In a recent study the issue of not knowing how to get around on the system was categorized as one of the six most important barriers to use of transit by nonusers. Basically, the problem for travelers is one of knowing how to get from where they are to where they want to go, in a system that is structured not around origin and destinations, but around routes. For single link trips, it is a matter of when to access and exit. For multiple link trips, it adds the problem of transfer points.

The link, transfer-node problem for travelers, in the context of a geographic location of destinations, quickly becomes unmanageable from a human information processing standpoint. Consequently, either the risk of becoming lost or the need for regular feedback that is only indirectly available limits use of the system. The first question then becomes: What are the human factor requirements for a transit information system that will provide people secure means of routing themselves from origin to destination? A second question emerges from this: What are the alternative technological systems that can meet these requirements in a cost-effective manner? Therefore, the study should be concerned with both of these questions.

In parallel with these human factors studies, analysis and design studies would evaluate the technological alternatives possible for providing essential information. The objectives of this analysis would be to define the most cost-effective means of providing information. It is reasonable to examine at least the following classes of information systems:

1. Graphic displays, active and passive
2. Voice communications with or without aiding
3. Trip-specific printed routing obtained off the system
4. Active, on-board routing systems

The first two types of systems are within the state of the art in one form or the other, for example, electronic route finders, map displays, transit information switchboard, plus computer display for routing operations. The last two have not been explored for transit, but represent approaches that can provide significant increments in user routing efficiency and security in routing.

Marketing Criteria

Research done in the previous three areas would define the basic dimensions underlying consumer behavior. This would result in a set of principles for actually marketing transit services. This will be accomplished at two levels. One is mass communication and the other is system operations.

In relation to the first, this task is to evaluate the transport attributes of priority importance to travelers. Of this group, which are perceived as being inadequate when objectively they are adequate? These provide a basic reeducation of the potential user. Similarly, what attributes of transit service are most salient to the potential user? These represent characteristics that when used in mass communication will reinforce and strengthen positive attitudes toward transit. In essence, this task should be aimed at defining the mass communication content that will be most salient to potential users and most likely to maximize the appeal of transit for them.

At the second level, the task is to define the feasible change in transit operations that will most meet the needs of potential users. In essence, by looking at potential user perceived requirements, it should be possible, first, to evaluate the correspondence between actual transit performance and traveler requirements. It should, second, be possible to identify changes in transit performance that would make its level of service more nearly correspond with those requirements.

Consequently, these two efforts converge in a sales, promotion, marketing program. That is, the output of this kind of task would be a set of procedures for developing the most cost-effective marketing effort. Hence, the output of this task, synthesizing the research done in the program, would be a manual containing both the methods that transit agencies might use to determine the basis of their marketing efforts. It would generalize the results in any area to provide a general set of guidelines for transit marketing anywhere in the country.

Commentary: Financing and Marketing Structure

"As a cousin of mine once said about money, money is always there but the pockets change; it is not in the same pockets after a change, and that is all there is to say about money." These words of Gertrude Stein have a particular meaning in the case of public transit.

8

Problems in a Manager's Planning Handbook

The advent of transportation planning brought with it a staggering array of data and of information. Many of these complex data sets are admittedly lacking in quality. Often, information is not available as to when given data apply and when not. In many fields of government investment, total benefits are difficult to quantify in any event so that professionals working in the field must take what there is and use it to the extent possible. Some analysis and projections turn out very well, such as the original BART projections of ridership, and increased business and employment that were predicted years in advance of the project; others are less satisfactory.

Public transportation is a particular kind of challenge. Each region differs from every other in important ways, so what might be determined as an important base file of information useful in decision making in one area is not at all essential in another. Even lacking the commonality among regions, the complex interaction of competing forces within a given area makes it difficult to sort out what is happening and why. Any experiment is automatically subject to so many uncontrolled variables that interpretation of results is always a key difficulty. As knowledge of field grows, this situation will no doubt improve to the point where decisions can be made on a more factual basis with trade-offs that are both understandable and believable to all concerned.

The concept of a manager's planning handbook, so desirable and necessary in most management situations, is, therefore, not yet a realistic possibility in public transportation. Instead, transportation is in an interim phase of development, having some data and information that could qualify for such a planning handbook, with other sections not developed. These small bits and pieces of information can nevertheless be important guides in decisions, especially those concerned with the selection and evaluation of transit systems. It is instructive to consider what some of these existing bits of knowledge and information are.

Sources of Information

During the past decade, the transit industry, with assistance from associated industries, has moved steadily forward in developing improved information sources [2, 8]. Some key sources are annual compilations of var-

187

ious types of statistical information; others are one-time collections of the costs of construction or operation; still others relate primarily to geographic or census data. It is helpful to have a basic reference list of where to go for this information.

The Bureau of the Census is the source of a major portion of referenced data. The very large 1,200-page "Journey to Work" report summarizes, first, for all SMSA regions, the number of trips made by automobile as compared to all trips, and, second, furnishes details of the labor forces as to race, sex, age, earnings, location of residence, location of employment, type of employment or occupation, years of schooling, and means of transportation to work. These data are most helpful in determining commuter patterns and much of this information has been written into computer programs with automatic plotters providing geocoding maps. The potential for this information is only now beginning to be realized.

A number of reports have emanated from the census data. The Federal Highway Administration, for example, has sponsored a series of 11 reports [7] studying in detail the driving habits of the nation. This includes not only the journey-to-work statistics, but in addition the shopping, recreation, family business, and civic and religious trips. These studies examine car ownership, as to whether new or used, multiple-car households, number of trips taken, the mileage associated with each, and a variety of other behavior indexes.

Most regions have also produced reports of local interest. The state of Illinois, for example [8], in a small report called "Where Workers Work," examines the census data primarily from the aspect of employment as to the distribution within the six-county northeastern Illinois region, including resulting trends and comparisons of various regions.

The annual *Fact Book* prepared by The Transportation Association of America is a comprehensive summary of both domestic and overseas statistics for all types of transport including freight, private and public transit, and regulatory information covering airline, shipping, and ground transportation.

The annual *Fact Book* [6] by the American Public Transit Association (APTA) is concerned only with public transit organizations giving trends in ridership revenue, number of cars and buses by operator, and other operator-based information such as taxes paid, average fares, seating capacity, miles traveled, and energy consumed.

The Urban Transportation *Fact Book*, a large, two-volume set published by the American Institute of Planners (AIP), is a comprehensive work describing land use and geographic information of the major areas of the nation in more detail than found elsewhere. It is especially useful in making regional comparisons and contains a wide variety of population and transportation information.

Some major works have been produced that remain useful even though portions of the information have become obsolete owing to inflation and changing times. "The Economic Characteristics of the Urban Public Transportation Industry" is one such example [5] . This major work is primarily an economic study and examines operating characteristics, revenue versus costs, and other economic variables relative to bus, rail, and taxicab operation.

A similar work [2] in the construction field is "Characteristics of Urban Transportation Systems: A Handbook for Transportation Planners," a report by DeLeuw Cather and Company. This work examines trends in construction over recent years as well as variations in construction cost owing to site selection and other construction variables both for grade and grade separated systems, and for subways and ventilated underground busways.

Planning agencies throughout the nation produce a variety of work relative to the interests of their respective regions. All regions are required to produce plans in order to qualify for federal grants. One of the major planning documents of each area is the "Unified Regional Planning Process" (URPP) required by the federal government. Each year the URPP document must specify the long, intermediate, and short-range planning goals of the region. It includes a description of each planning agency, the respective budgets, the individual goals and accomplishments expected of each agency, and a plan as to how each individual planning product is to be integrated into the total process. Aside from the professional value of the document in terms of the planning process coordination, the document is valuable in acquainting newcomers to the field with a multitude of practical information on the workings and interactions of the various planning agencies as well as some of the basic characteristics and features of the respective regions.

For many interests, the material provided in the various planning documents of any region will be too detailed. Many academic institutions provide useful reports that give comprehensive information in sufficient detail for many purposes but without the extensive and voluminous detail that most planning documents must contain.

In terms of practical documents, the phone book of the U.S. Department of Transportation can be one of the most important assets of a transportation analyst since much of the critical information needed at any given time is not found in handbooks but in special reports and papers— many sponsored by DOT, others by local transit organizations. The phone books are issued four times a year—an indication of the nature of change within government—and are sold by the U.S. Government Printing Office for $12.50 per year. For most professionals in the transit field, it is a good investment.

Lack of Parametric Information

One of the most serious problems in government work today is the tendency to place greater faith in completeness of numbers rather than in validity of analysis [1]. In a great deal of work that is carried out, the results show not much what is really happening as acting as proof of the biases and assumptions built into the work in the first place. A significant amount of work carried out in this country today is based on a simple cause-effect relationship that in many cases is not true; important factors are omitted. The process is self-correcting to the extent that when the conclusions are put into action, things go wrong and it becomes clear that something was overlooked. This iterative approach is, however, extremely expensive and time-consuming, and can probably be avoided in most cases with a little more care on the part of the manager.

The statistician's way of achieving accuracy is through a series of tests to eliminate bias. One of the most frequent errors arising in transportation analysis is that associated with what mathematicians call interrupted time series. This arises from the newness of transit analysis and the lack of data so patterns are not observed and serious errors made on too short an observation period. As happens in most public reporting of program effectiveness, results are often simply reported as to before and after measures, and an obvious conclusion drawn may completely misrepresent the facts.

For example, in 1955 Connecticut instituted an exceptionally severe and prolonged crackdown on speeding to save lives. In 1956 there were 284 deaths as compared with 324 in 1955. The governor issued the statement: "With a saving of 40 lives in 1956 . . . we can say this program is definitely worthwhile." Figure 8-1a represents this conclusion graphically. There are, however, many other reasons why this decrease may have occurred, and the question arises as to why one assumes, if there had been no crackdown, that nothing would have happened. It is an assumption made without realizing an assumption had been made. In comparing data taken over a broader time range, it seems that the crackdown in actuality had little effect. The exact answer depends on more complicated statistical analysis and question called "interference," but the error of simple before-and-after analysis is apparent. Add to this the injustice practiced in much transit analysis, that of taking a questionable experiment and applying it to an entirely different environment and the depth of today's planning analysis becomes compounded.

Another illustration of a similar concept is to be found in the recent rail versus bus analysis. The point of these studies has been to discover some general guideline as to when subway development might be preferable to exclusive busways. The use of buses below grade w: , not considered since such construction is considerably more expensive than rail subway

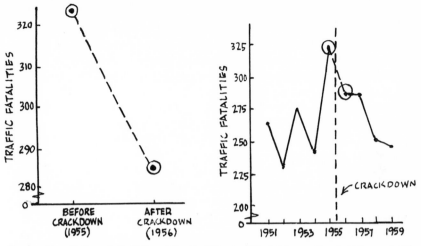

Source: Donald Campbell, "Measuring the Effects of Social Innovation by Means of a Time Series," *Statistics, A Guide to the Unknown* (San Francisco: Holden-Day, Inc., 1972). This portion of the work was supported by the National Science Foundation, Grant No. GS 1309X.

Figure 8-1. Connecticut Traffic Fatalities.

construction owing to ventilation problems. [2] Over the years, a number of analyses had been attempted and all were inconclusive. Finally a major comprehensive work was undertaken [3] that turned out to be one of the most controversial reports in the history of the Department of Transportation.

The intention was good: to leave no stone unturned in collecting the most up-to-date operating and construction information. The model chosen for analysis was then determined to be that of comparing an express bus on an exclusive right-of-way as compared with a conventional rapid transit system, assumed to be completely in subway. A complex, comprehensive computer model was created that included such detail as charging the transit patron for waiting time according to a preselected cost per hour; every kind of detail was considered that could in some sense be measured. It has resulted in an excellent collection of operating and construction information, but not much that is useful to the transportation system analyst.

The basic conclusion of this study revealed that the bus is always superior in terms of cost and service. Operators of subway systems were stunned at this conclusion, since it is well-known that buses cannot handle the peak-hour traffic demands from concentrated employment areas.[a]

---

[a] It was once humorously mentioned, when excessive repairs were needed on the CTA's Jackson Park Elevated system, that the only alternative to repairing the structure was to line up buses in the streets and let the patrons run through.

Bus volumes based on empirical information were known to be too small to replace rapid rail service. The question is, where did the analysis go wrong?

One problem, of course, is that in any extensive transportation analysis, the type of data needed just does not exist in most cases. The analyst must make do with existing information in various ways and base the analysis on a complex interweaving of assumptions. It is usually not clear what effect some assumed value or behavior will have on the outcome of the analysis. Disagreement over statistics can then cloud the basic argument.

A more important problem concerns the choice of model. One of the key characteristics of rapid transit is that the average speed, and, therefore, traffic volume is a function of the number of station stops a train makes. This has nothing to do with the maximum speed of the train [4]. It is assumed that the maximum speed of acceleration is about 3 miles per hour per second and that stops are 20 seconds in duration; then the average speed for stations 1 mile apart is 33 miles per hour. In dense business districts, stations are much closer, frequently less than 1/3 mile apart making the average speed less than 20 miles per hour.

This is one of their reasons why during rush hour, the Chicago Transit Authority uses a psuedoexpress service that essentially skips every other station by every other train so as to speed service and the number of passengers moved per unit time. (See figure 8-2.)

Thus, no matter what kind of vehicles are compared if one of them is an express service and the other a vehicle having many stops, the express vehicle will always win this contest. Consequently, the answer was rooted in the problem statement and had little to do with the complex analysis.

Such pitfalls make the task of transit management difficult and require making the best possible use of existing information. One then arrives at a crucial point: When management must decide if a project is worthwhile, that is, that plans can be carried out to a conclusion. Consequently, a competent manager must have good sources and contacts to improve the quality of decisions being made.

Operating Data

The proper interpretation of published information is one of the most serious difficulties facing transit analysts today. Some function relationships, such as the effect of station spacing on vehicle speed (discussed previously) admittedly are valid over broad areas of application, but this is more the exception than the rule. In general, public transit is a field in which similarity parameters are as yet unknown.

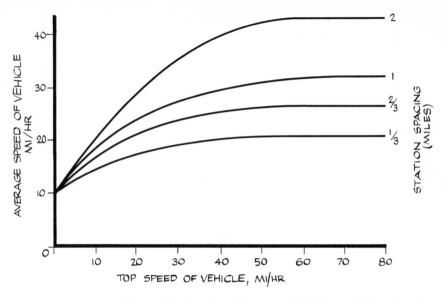

Figure 8-2. Effect of Station Spacing on Rapid Transit Speed.

This means that great care must be exercised in making use of published data, and this is especially true of aggregate values. Consider, for example, the tabulated values of the average speeds of various transit systems [9] in table 8-1.

Such information may be useful in a variety of contexts, but it must be remembered that there can be greater variation within a single system than the variation of the average of many different systems (see table 8-2).

As long as the data are used in the proper context, such information can be helpful. This example illustrates the importance of understanding—out of context—more than the bare numerical values but something of the circumstances; in this case, their averaging. This statement applies to all types of information, in addition to vehicle speed data.

There is also great variation between different rapid transit systems and within any one system regarding energy use. Larger cars carry, typically, 60 percent more people with only 25 percent increase in power [22]. This efficiency arises in part because the acceleration is less. With small cars, such as Chicago has to negotiate the tight turns of the Loop, acceleration is of the order 3.3 feet per second per hour, which is 50 percent higher than many systems and about as rapid as possible without knocking over standing passengers, the energy use [28] is considered higher than average, again the value depending on whether the cars are air-conditioned, whether the heat is on, and what the electrical and physical characteristics of the system are, as shown in figure 8-3.

Table 8-1
Average Speed of Rail Systems

City	Approximate Average Overall Speed (mph)
Toronto	
Yonge Street Subway	17.6
New York	
IRT Lexington Avenue Express	19.6
IND 8th Avenue Express	28.7
Cleveland	
Rapid Transit	28.0
Chicago	
Dan Ryan Line	30.0
Boston	
Red Line	32.0
Philadelphia	
Lindenwold Line	39.0
San Francisco	
BART	47.0

Source: Characteristics of Urban Transportation Systems: A Handbook for Transportation Planners, by De Leuw, Cather and Co., prepared for the U.S. DOT, May, 1975. (Computer print-out)

Table 8-2
Rail Speeds of the Chicago Transit Authority, 1975

Transit Line	Velocity
Skokie Swift	40.72 mph
West-South	29.33 mph
West-Northwest	27.13 mph
North-South	23.51 mph
Evanston Shuttle	22.31 mph
Evanston Express	22.21 mph
Ravenswood	19.70 mph
(Average System Speed)	26.41 mph

Source: The Chicago Transit Authority, Scheduling department 1975.

Therefore, taking system averages and making comparisons between major systems must be done with care since it is possible that larger variations occur within a single system than between systems. Some reported average values are given in table 8-3.

The operating efficiency of buses is similarly highly dependent on sys-

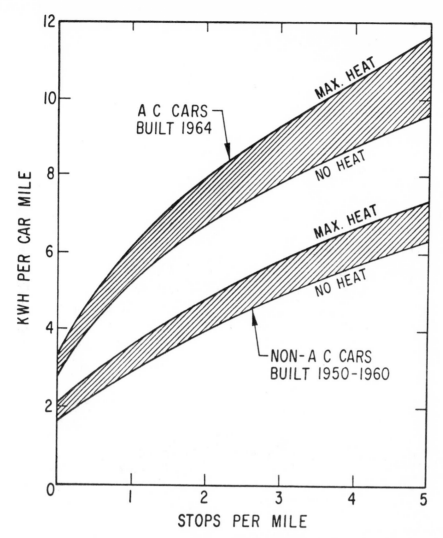

Figure 8-3. Energy Use According to Electrical and Physical Characteristics of a Rapid Transit System.

tem variables such as the number of stops, acceleration rate, and average speed, and whether the bus is air-conditioned or heated. Actual operating data for the Chicago Transit Authority is shown in figures 8-4 and 8-5 and table 8-4.

Much depends on the traffic conditions. If exclusive bus lanes can be used for express service, buses yield typically 6.4 miles per gallon [21].

Table 8-3
Operating Efficiency of Five Rapid Transit Systems

System	Power Consumption kwh/Car-Mile	Car Weight Lb.	Efficiency, kwh/Ton-Mile
Chicago	4.9	42,000	0.23
BART	5.5	57,000	0.19
New York	5.4	79,000	0.14
Cleveland	3.6	55,000	0.13
Toronto	5.2	84,000	0.12

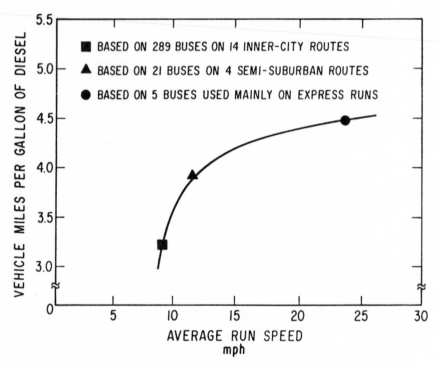

Figure 8-4. Bus Operating Efficiency: Chicago Transit Authority.

Normalizing Data

Perhaps the most important use of numerical data at the present time is not in the obvious computational application but as a means of illustrating the various elements and parameters of the problem, as well as for alerting the user to what trade-offs and alternatives are possible. The summary

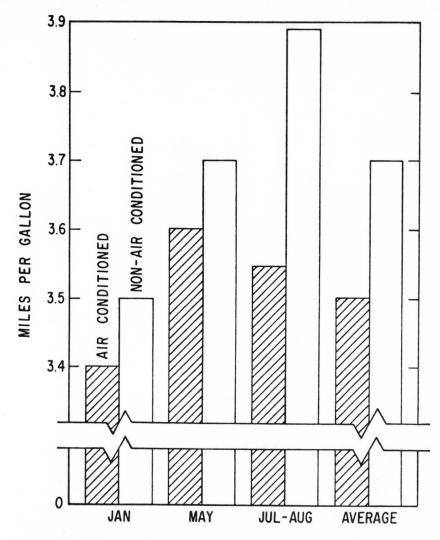

Figure 8-5. Miles per Gallon of Buses of the Chicago Transit Authority for Various Seasons of the Year.

data of a study examining, for example, relative cost advantages of a number of different transit systems probably cannot produce conclusions that are universally applicable. However, such a study can provide a good discussion of trade-offs and ways to compute them, and ideas or organizing thinking relative to meeting certain needs, and mention important considerations that might otherwise be overlooked. The fact that a table of summary information is not numerically applicable to specific system design

Table 8-4
Performance Characteristics of Eight Rapid Transit Systems

	Vehicle Length (ft./in.)	Weight (lbs.)	Acceleration (mph/sec.)	Motor Horsepower	Nominal Voltage
CTA	48'	45,000	3.2	85	600
WMATA	75'	72,000	3.0	160	650
BART	75'	56,000	3.0	150	1000
CTS	70'	65,000	2.75	100	600
MBTA/Blue	48' 10"	49,000	2.5	85	600
MBTA/Red	69' 10"	65,200	2.5	85	600
NYCTA/R46	75'	85,000	2.5	120	600
PATCO	68'	78,000	3.0	130	600

Note: The Chicago system has the highest performance characteristics in the nation with an acceleration of 3.2 miles per hour per second. Chicago cars are just 40 feet in length in order to negotiate the curves in the Loop.

does not mean that the information is not in some sense responsive to the needs under consideration. It is important to recognize this distinction in making use of available information.

Another problem in making use of different sets of published information concerns the hidden errors resulting from normalization processes. This actually occurs much more frequently, and among highly trained professionals, than might be imagined. An interesting example of this was a high-level policy statement [11] that gathered national ridership data making the point that ridership was still declining when, in fact, the decline had been stopped on a national level and ridership had actually increased. This error was a result of using older normalized data with newer data that was not normalized, so that recent ridership appeared to be lower than was actually the case.

To amplify this point, consider the bookkeeping and reporting tasks of a transit agency. Fares are counted daily and reported weekly. How does the analyst, who is looking for small changes on the order of a few percent, resolve the fact that some months have more weeks than others? There are many different bookkeeping practices in effect throughout the nation. The CTA, for example, produces 4 financial reports a year based on 4 13-week periods; every 7 years, to take care of the missed periods, the data are reported on the basis of a 53-week fiscal year. The last 53-week year was in 1972. Clearly, an analyst could make significant errors in analyzing trends for 1973 data unless the extra week in 1972 was taken into account.

On a national level, the situation is even more complicated. Major organizations such as APTA collect data from all operators and must take into account the normalizing procedures of the process involved and adjust for it.

No mention has been made of revenue data. One of the key decisions facing transit managers everywhere is estimating what effect new service will have on ridership, whether it is an entirely new system or simply added service to an existing system. Through information forecasts and surveys, a continual flow of information reaches the manager, which helps to reduce the risk such new services entail. However, as San Francisco's Mayor Joseph Alioto inferred when he said that BART was a billion dollar gamble to coax people out of their cars, all transit services do involve an element of risk. The objective is to reduce that risk through data collection and careful evaluation.

Another factor is estimating revenue from various tax sources such as sales and motor fuel, which may vary according to economic conditions, and externalities such as the Arab oil embargo that depressed gasoline sales. Both federal and state governments maintain a continual flow of information relative to tax income forecasts. Such information is available to the transportation manager on a regular basis so that adjustments and preparation can be made in advance.

The question of which strategies should be employed for allocation of tax revenue and for seeking additional revenue is a more complex issue. These are not topics covered in handbooks since such questions have to do with optimum benefits to the community and of value judgments. These points are not quantifiable in the normal sense and so comprise a different category of managerial concern.

Cost Data

Transit managers always need to know:

1. Cost of construction
2. Capacity per-unit cost
3. Operation and maintenance requirements
4. Potential for expansion

It usually is not possible to simplify this information in any general format. There are too many variables, and changing conditions not only increase unit costs but alter orders of relative costs of competing systems. In some cases, simple analytic evaluations can be made. For example, in looking at Personal Rapid Transit (PRT) systems, one study found a simple way to analyze costs and capacity (see figure 8-6).

Cost and capacity of conventional rail systems are more difficult. First, the capacity is nearly unlimited for practical purposes since extra cars can always be added. Second, the costs vary widely depending on local circumstances, as illustrated in figure 8-7.

Within a given system costs vary widely depending on whether the

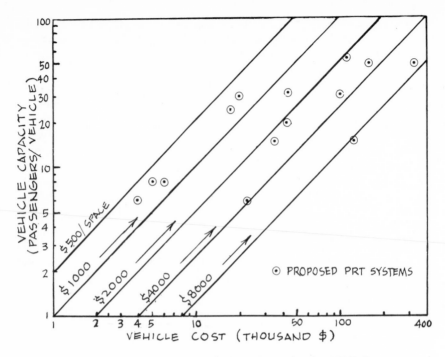

Figure 8-6. Vehicle Cost vs. Vehicle Capacity for PRT Systems.

system is in subway; whether the subway is in clay, bedrock, or loam; and whether major buildings must be underpinned or utility lines moved. These factors are reflected in table 8-5, which shows the variation in rail cost for various types of construction.

Costs of rail cars also vary widely depending on size and design (figure 8-8) as do the operating costs (table 8-6).

Wide cost variations also occur in busway construction (table 8-7). Costs of underground busways (table 8-8) are significantly higher than for rail subway because of the ventilation cost. Operation costs are typically a strong function of fleet mileage (figure 8-9) and fleet size (figure 8-10).

Until recent years, the rise in the consumer price index was reasonably uniform and predictable. The continuing inflation makes any cost estimating difficult. No doubt one of the accomplishments of transit management within the next decade will be the control of costs through mass production and standardization techniques as well as improvements in purchasing to prevent the often nonuniform overloading of suppliers corresponding to the annual congressional budgetary allotments. Cost control is the most challenging area of transit management today.

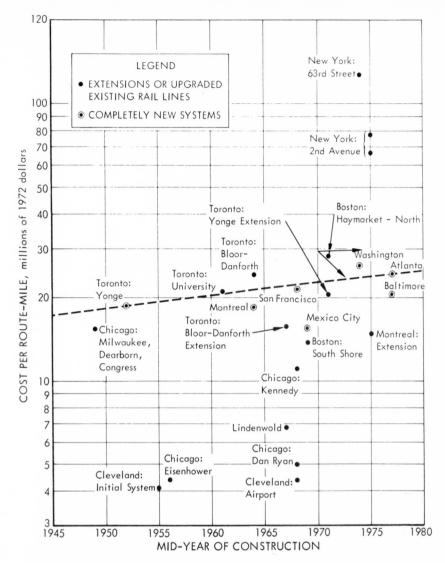

Figure 8-7. Rail Transit System Costs vs. Midyear of Construction.

Energy Arguments

Energy use in the United States has doubled within the past 20 years [33, 34, 35]. The omnipresent automobile symbolizes this use. Almost 200 million cars have been produced during these two affluent decades—the

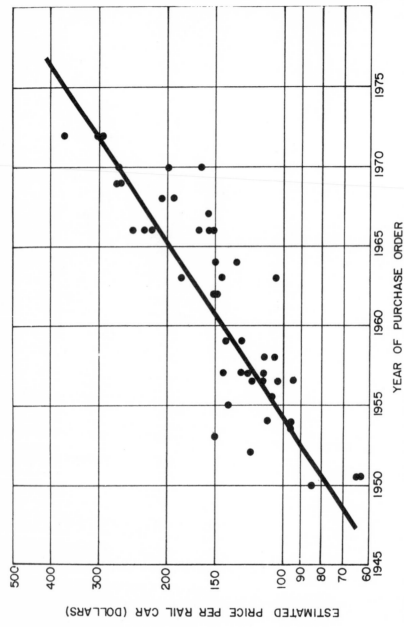

Figure 8-8. Rail Transit Car Prices vs. Year of Order.

Source: J. Boyd, N. Asher, and E. Wetzler, *Evaluation of Rail Rapid Transit and Express Bus Service in the Urban Commuter Market*, Institute for Defense Analyses, Arlington, Virginia, 1973.

Table 8-5

Typical Rapid Rail Transit Line Construction Costs *(Millions of Dollars)*

Type of Construction (Location)	Approximate Route-Miles	Cost per Route-Mile[a]
Tunnel		
Chicago-Congress-Dearborn Lines	4.0	34.6
Chicago-Kennedy Lines	1.0	34.4
Cut and Cover		
New York - 63rd Street Line	6.0	64.2
New York - 2nd Avenue Line	6.0	64.3
" - 2nd Avenue Line	3.6	71.4
At Grade		
Chicago-Eisenhower Line	9.0	7.5
Chicago-Dan Ryan Line	9.5	7.0
Chicago-Kennedy Line	4.2	7.0
Station[b]		
Central Areas	—	12.1
Fringe Areas	—	2.6

[a]Includes all line costs such as signalling, communications, lighting, power, and station costs (except where isolated in above table).

[b]Assumes station lengths of about 800 feet.

Note: Above data expressed in terms of 1973 prices. Low tunnelling costs compared with cut and cover occur because the former are constructed only in certain soil/rock formations. Route miles reflect equivalent two track miles.

Sources: K. Bhatt and M. Olsson, "Analysis of Supply and Estimates of Resource Costs," Urban Institute, Technical Reports No. 2, Washington, D.C., November, 1973; Washington Metropolitan Area Transit Authority, Washington, D.C., 1973.

"Golden Age of the Automobile." The toll on the nation's petroleum resources has been heavy [29]. Yet, astonishingly in our energy-conscious society, the very individuals most responsible for oil depletion seem unaware of their cumulative economic behavior [31, 32, 33].

Although all sectors of the economy use oil for a wide variety of purposes [36], the facts show that transportation consumes over 50 percent of the nation's oil and that the drive-alone vehicle, in the trip to and from work, burns over 50 percent of that large share of energy. Such computations do not include the energy involved in automobile production nor in road construction—both substantial [37, 38].

Perhaps one reason why this fact is so difficult to comprehend is that energy use is usually stated in terms of total energy expenditure rather than in terms of oil use. One of the most commonly quoted statistics states that, out of the nation's total energy expenditure, transportation accounts for just 25 percent [35, 39, 40, 41]. Some might draw the logical inference that, as against the oil use of heavy industry, together with all the air travel and freight movement by trucks, the passenger car thus must

Table 8-6
Total Rail Rapid Transit Operations Costs, by Property (U.S. Property Only)

Property	Operating Cost per Passenger Car-Mile (Dollars)		
Property	1960	1970	$\frac{1970}{1960}$
New York City Transit Authority	.70	1.24	
Chicago Transit Authority	.70	1.06	
Massachusetts Bay Transportation Authority	1.42	3.06	
Southeastern Pennsylvania Transportation Authority	.79	1.39	
Port Authority Trans Hudson Corporation	1.36	2.04	
Lindenwold Line	—	1.18	
Cleveland Transit System	.48	.98	
Shaker Heights Department of Transportation	.95	1.53	
Public Service Coordinated Transport, Newark	1.00	1.64	
Average	.92	1.57	1.71
Median	.87	1.39	1.60
Average (excluding Lindenwold)		1.61	1.85
Median (excluding Lindenwold)		1.46	1.67

Source: John D. Wells, et al. *Economic Characteristics of the Urban Public Transportation Industry*, Institute of Defense Analyses for U.S. Department of Transportation, February 1972 (Section VI).

represent only a small fraction of total expenditures. But this total accounts for all energy expended, even the fraction lost in forest fires. A distinction must be made between general energy souces and oil-energy uses. The importance of the automobile then comes to light.

Without question, the private auto represents the key factor in the petroleum picture. In 1970 transportation consumed 53 percent of our petroleum, and, of this, the private auto consumed well over 50 percent of the transportation expenditure [35]. Both of these figures increase each year. Between 1960 and 1970, passenger travel increased an alarming 86 percent per capita [35]. The journey to work—the most frequent auto trip—rolled up nearly half of all auto miles, mostly in single-occupant cars.

Since the auto consumes a larger share of the transportation energy budget than all other modes combined, realistic energy-conservation policy requires energy-efficient alternatives to the auto. The journey to work—nearly four out of five trips with only the driver in the car—repre-

205

Table 6-1
Existing or Proposed Busway Construction Costs

Location	Length (Miles)	Cost (Million $)	Cost per Mile	Basic Configuration	Notes
East-West Transitway Milwaukee (proposed)	8.0	$40.2	$5.0	At grade	45 foot average busway width
San Bernadino Busway Los Angeles (existing)	11.0	54.0	4.9	At grade	Partial use of Southern Pacific railroad; 54 foot average busway width
Crosstown Busway Chicago (proposed)	20.0	97.2	4.8	At grade	Slight cut and fill; 44 foot average busway width
South PATways Pittsburgh (proposed)	4.0	16.8	4.2	At grade	partial use of existing tunnel; 36 foot average busway width
North Central Busway Dallas (proposed)	10.0	32.2	3.2	Partially elevated	33 foot average busway width
East PATways Pittsburgh (proposed)	8.0	21.4	2.7	At grade	36 foot average busway width
KCI Transitway Kansas City (proposed)	19.0	29.5	1.6	At grade	36 foot average busway width
Canal Line Busway New Havel (proposed)	13.3	15.0	1.1	At grade	Use of existing ROW; 50 foot average busway width
Penn Central Busway Dayton (proposed)	7.5	4.8	0.7	At grade	Use of Existing ROW; 32-42 foot average busway width
Shirley Busway Washington, D.C. (existing)	5.0	2.8	0.7	At grade	12-28 foot average busway width

Note: The above construction costs assume a variety of cross-section dimensions.

Sources: Wilbur Smith and Associates, "Design and Analysis of Bus and Truck Roadway Systems in Urban Areas," New Haven, Connecticut, November 1973; H. Levinson, W. Hoey, D. Sanders, et al. Bus Use on Highways: State of the Art, National Cooperative Highway Research Program Report 143, Washington, D.C., 1973.

Table 8-8
Busway Construction Cost—Underground Facility
(Million $ per Mile)

	Type of Construction[a]				
	Shallow Cut and Cover		Cut and Cover With Mezzanine		Bored Tunnel
Station Frequency per mile	On-line[b]	Off-line[c]	On-line[b]	Off-line[c]	
1	27.0	27.6	33.0	33.8	46.5
2	27.8	29.0	34.0	35.0	46.6
3	28.7	30.7	35.0	36.5	47.0
4	29.5	32.5	36.0	38.2	47.3

[a]These estimates are based on a two-lane busway with no median or adjacent shoulders; approximate cross section is 24 feet. Costs include ventilation and lighting, roadway, station, and contingencies (at 15% of cost).

[b]Bus stops are along main alignment.

[c]Bus stops are off the main alignment.

Note: Expressed in terms of 1973 costs; does not include land costs. The above data reflects a smaller cross-section width than some of the preceding tables; care must be exercised in assigning an average speed to this type of facility, since buses will be operating without the advantage of shoulders and median strips.

Source: Wilbur Smith and Associates, "Design and Analysis of Bus and Truck Roadway Systems in Urban Areas," New Haven, Connecticut, November 1973.

sents a key place for conservation. So does the two-car family—especially by replacing the car in family business trips.

Interestingly enough, the 1970 census revealed that autos in two- and three-car households average more miles per vehicle annually than autos operated from one-car households [12]. The convenience factor of having the transportation available stimulates making trips. One can see this in the results of a survey to determine how households managed to cut down driving during the oil embargo of 1974. Most people (about 80 percent) said that they simply made fewer trips [13].

The two-car household—representing more than half of all autos in the country [12]—generates almost half of all trips and vehicle miles of travel [14]. Some 70 percent of households with incomes of $15,000 and over own more than one car. Consequently, the affluent suburbs should be carefully considered in any study [15].

With increased inflation, many families that previously could afford two or more cars now may find the capital expenditure and upkeep expenses more than can be handled conveniently. Such families may, therefore, be looking for a suitable alternative. They present the engineering community a significant challenge.

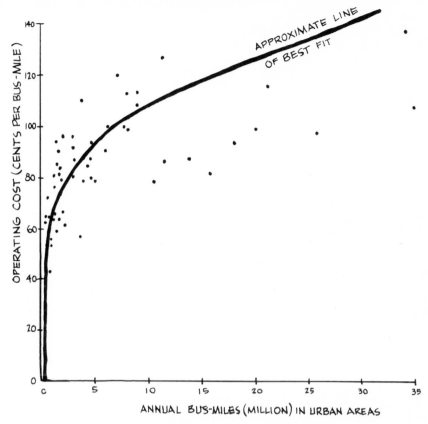

Source: American Transit Association, *Transit Operating Report*, Washington, D.C. August 1972.

Figure 8-9. Bus Fleet Operating Cost vs. Bus-Miles.

A suitable alternative need not match each trip on a one-to-one basis. We know that a household eliminating an auto drastically reduces both the total number of miles driven and number of trips. In statistical terms, 54 percent of all trips take less than 5 miles [16], yet account for only 15 percent of all vehicle miles. Some studies interpret this to mean that even shifting 50 percent of all such trips to public transportation would save only 5 percent in fuel [10]. Yet, this calculation assumes a one-to-one matching—not the real case. Clearly, offering a transportation alternative for important and necessary trips may well eliminate much of small-trip travel by car altogether.

Other types of auto travel will be difficult to replace on a broad basis. Social and recreational travel accounts for only 22 percent of trips taken

208

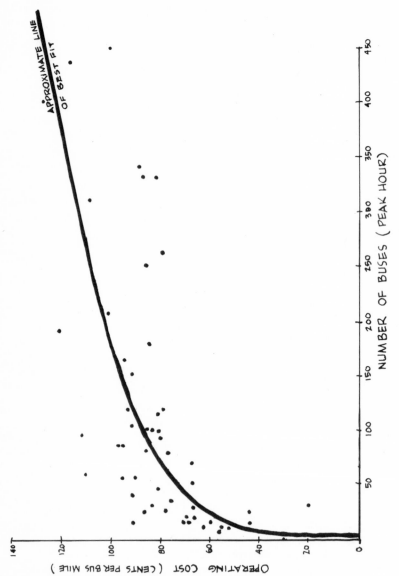

Source: American Transit Association, *Transit Operating Report*, Washington D.C., August 1972.

Figure 8-10. Operating Cost vs. Bus Fleet Size.

but for 33 percent of the mileage driven annually. Social and recreational auto travel show average loads factors higher than for other trip purposes, ranging from 3.3 per car for vacations to between 2 and 3 per car for other social trips. Moreover, census analysis shows that, since trips made purely for driving pleasure comprise only 1-2 percent of all auto travel, pleasure tends to be combined with other purposes, such as visiting friends or going to places of recreation [17]. Considering the high auto-load factors and the esthetics involved, these trips do not seem as good a source for conservation as do the journey to work and family business trips.

By placing the emphasis on auto markets having the greatest potential transfer in terms of energy conservation, optimum use can be made of public transit modes. (This differs from approaches that put special services such as "service to job centers not served by areawide transit" in the same category as "service for handicapped persons" [18].) For conservation, the planner must examine cases where high annual mileage rates made by single-occupant cars can represent a large potential in oil savings and where public transit can offer comparatively high operating efficiencies.

The varying role of the private auto and public transit in conserving energy has been projected in an array of controposing suggestions and predictions. Some planners conclude that public transit's role will be very limited [13, 19]. Others conclude the nation must have public transit development [20]. Most underestimate the potential contribution of public transit [11, 30].

Most studies of transit efficiencies examine only total, average system efficiencies [16]. It is well-known that, even including after-midnight ("Owl") and low-density services, public transportation proves several times more efficient than the private car. Typical analysis shows the bus to be 70 percent and rail service 130 percent more efficient than the car [13]. But even these figures conceal transit capability in three respects:

Certain time periods are much more efficient than others. Assuming that the total, average efficiencies account for the social aspects of transit services, much larger efficiencies can be gained by special services.

The computations assume a one-to-one trip matching basis when it is clear that offering an acceptable alternative to a second car may eliminate certain trips altogether.

The practice of computing an "oil equivalent" consumption for electric service that may in fact use no oil conceals the present ability to effect large oil savings through services that operate on hydroelectirc, coal, and nuclear energy sources. Moreover, electrical production losses are customarily charged against transit while auto fuel production losses are not computed.

It is instructive to consider the case of the bus and rapid-transit car separately and examine efficiencies at rush hour; this includes peak loading, average rush loading, and optimum loading (permitting every patron to be seated).

In the following calculations, assume that the auto carries just one occupant (true for almost three-quarters of all commuter trips) and that the auto makes 10 miles per gallon (mpg), reflecting the effects of traffic congestion (overall average of 13 mpg usually cited [35]).

Each 50-passenger bus in Chicago carries about 70 passengers at rush hour. Although it is possible to obtain loadings higher than this, complaints rise quickly when more than 70 persons occupy one bus. (An exception occurs in severe, inclement weather when buses carry over 80 passengers, but this case is rare.) At rush hour a typical bus on a Chicago street, therefore, gives about $7 \times 4 = 280$ passenger miles per gallon (pmpg) and a design performance of $50 \times 6.4 = 320$ pmpg.

Compared to the single-occupant, rush-hour auto giving 10 pmpg, the rush-hour bus carries the equivalent of 28 autos and produces design performance equivalent to 32 cars. Consequently, at rush hour, a packed bus is approximately 30 times more efficient than a single passenger automobile. During off-peak conditions, the comparative efficiency of the bus drops since loading is less and the automobile energy use higher. During the day buses carry typically less than half maximum load or about 20 passengers per bus giving $20 \times 4 = 80$ pmpg. An off-peak automobile may give typically 13 miles per gallon, with two occupants, yielding 26 pmpg. Under these conditions the bus is only about three times as efficient as the automobile.

Comparison between rapid transit, which is electric, and the gasoline consuming automobile is less straightforward. Rapid transit may use no petroleum fuel at all.

Many cities having electric transit do not use oil in electric energy production; some are completely hydroelectric; others' power are generated from coal. In such cases, the oil equivalences are infinite compared with gasoline-operated transport modes, which illustrates the lack of suitability of this method of defining efficiency. With the new restrictions from the Federal Energy Commission regarding the burning of oil for electrical production [23] and the rapid increase in electrical technology using non-petroleum fuels, that tradtional method of assigning equivalent gasoline ratings to electrically powered systems has become less meaningful. (See table 8-9).

Reviewing the methods commonly used for efficiency calculations, an engineer finds some unusual practices. For example, the conversion from kilowatt hours to Btu's with the purpose of computing an equivalent miles per gallon has already been shown to be a questionable practice when electric power does not come from burning oil. A related practice includes power-production losses, regardless of the source, as part of the energy used in transit. (See table 8-10.)

Table 8-9

Use of Oil and Gas in Producing Electrical Energy in Major Cities

Region	Regions Using Oil and Gas	Source	Remarks
Chicago	10%	Edison Company	35% nuclear
Seattle	0	City Electric	96% hydroelectric
Washington, D.C.	44	Potomac Elec. Power	No nuclear planned
Baltimore	40	Baltimore Gas & Elec.	Includes 1975 nuclear
Philadelphia	30	Phila. Electric Co.	
San Francisco			
Muni	0	City Electric	100% hydroelectric
BART	16	Pacific Gas & Electric	5% geothermal
New York City	40	Con Edison	Includes 1976 nuclear

Table 8-10

Energy Units

1 barrel	contains	42	gallons
1 metric ton	contains	7.33	barrels
1 short ton	contains	6.65	barrels

Gasoline:	125,000	btu/gallon
Naphtha jet fuel:	127,500	"
Kerosene jet fuel:	135,000	"
Distillate fuel oil:	140,000	"
Residual fuel oil:	150,000	"

Electrical power generation:

Oil:	9,000	but/kwh
Gas turbine:	14,000	"
Ideal:	3,413	"

By definition [24], 1 kilowatt hour is equivalent to about 3,413 Btu's. Yet, most computations for transit applications use a value of 10,000-13,500 Btu's—a factor of more than 3 or 4 times—which takes into account the heat lost in electrical power production. Some of this lost power regardless of how produced can be recycled, and sometimes is [25]. But transit efficiencies are usually charged with the complete loss as if it were an operating loss.

This retracing to basic energy sources does not characterize the bookkeeping on automobile gasoline consumption, although just raising the octane level consumes 12 percent of the fuel. Other gasoline energy requirements are not well-known, since much depends on the process, type of fuel used as input, and kind of by-products produced. Figures on gasoline loss in the delivery system to local dealers are also not generally available.

Aside from the fact that such accounting methods tend to reduce the computed potential for transit as an alternative in the energy crisis, these practices also conceal from the public eye the need for engineering improvements, as in the recycling of presently lost power and of more efficient methods for handling energy. As long as very cheap fuel was available, private industry felt little impetus to develop new technologies. Further, as long as industry can simply pass along increased fuel costs to the consumer, there is little need to risk company funds in improved methods unless they guarantee increased profits. Such practices also cloak the extensive need for the federal government to become involved in what might be thought to be the province of private research. To a large degree the responsibility rests with the engineering community to call attention to the savings to the nation that improved technology could bring.

Another type of energy accounting that disguises the need for technological innovation and development concerns the computing of energy consumption by commuter trains. To reduce maintenance cost, most railroads run diesel engines continuously even in the summer and on Sundays [26, 27]. Before September 1973, in Chicago the three major diesel commuter railroads followed the practice of running the main diesels 24 hours a day throughout the year. The Northwestern changed this practice and began turning off the main diesels during the nighttime and weekends owing to complaints about noise. The Burlington Northern and Milwaukee Road never turn their main diesels off, except when they are in the shop for repairs.

Newer diesels are quipped with electrical heating elements that can be plugged in, but such units require a standby facility, which most railroads do not have. Granted that such practices ensure that the cooling water does not freeze, help to prevent water leaks, avoid start-up problems, and reduce maintenance, improved engineering development could be expected to cut the problems and greatly improve oil conservation.

Railroads engage in other energy-wasteful practices usually charged against passenger energy consumption. Typically, trains include empty cars, weighing over 100,000 lbs., to avoid disconnection costs. Energy consumption could be significantly reduced by improved car design with better connectors.

Consequently, computing comparative efficiencies between automobile and rail (table 8-11) is at best a questionable practice. Any number of answers can be generated depending on the modeling. As one possible set of examples, consider a less than average efficient transit car, such as a Chicago car operating under conditions of many stops and high acceleration, requiring about 8 kwh per mile. As shown in figure 8-11, a single transit passenger may be the equivalent of only slightly more than one

213

Table 8-11
National Average Fuel Consumption for the Automobiles as Compared with Transit Buses and Rail Transit

	Passenger Miles	Passenger Miles per Gallon Fuel	Percentage Efficient Compared with Auto
Automobile	83.86%	29.7	—
Transit buses	0.72	50.0	70%
Rail transit	0.47	68.5	130%

Source: "A Report on Actions and Recommendations for Energy Conservation through Public Mass Transportation Improvements," U.S. Department of Transportation, Washington, D.C., October, 1974. Data for 1973.

automobile driver or as much as 1,200 single-passenger automobiles, where the electrical energy is produced by 10 percent use of oil fuel. Under this type of comparison, systems such as Seattle and San Francisco Muni give infinite efficiencies since transit passengers there use no oil at all as both systems are completely hydroelectric.

Clearly, in the case of oil embargoes and oil scarcity for any reason, electric rapid transit can provide transportation in the absence of oil or fuel, or by using very little.

Computer Graphics

The broad resources of the computer are believed by many to be capable of changing the course of urban transit within the next decade. One type of analysis now being initiated is the use of computer graphics for route planning.

Workable programs have been devised to map information important to transit planners. For example, the census data are stored and automatically plotted on maps to show any prescribed matter of interest. In a simple mapping, the planner might want to see first where the population lives. Usually well-known routes are at once apparent including commuter rail lines. It may be of use to know where the families having the most number of cars per household, and, therefore, presumably the least likely to use transit are located, or perhaps large families with three or more children since such families are identified as potential transit users. Again, two-car families may represent a good source of future routes if the families would like to eliminate one car in favor of using transit for a journey to work. (See figures 8-12, 8-13, and 8-14.)

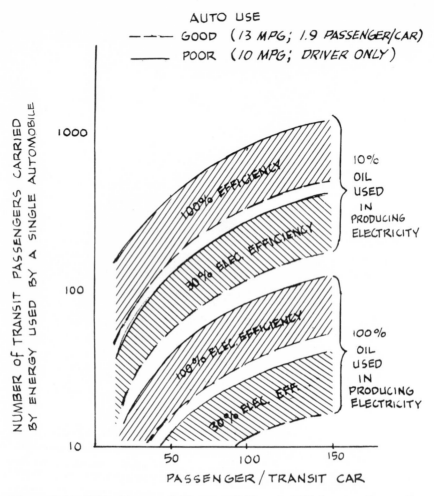

Figure 8-11. Wide Range of Computed Transit Efficiencies Depending on Assumption.

A somewhat different type of map is that of journey-to-work identification. In such maps, a one-quarter section of area is taken from the census and trips mapped for each worker. In some cases the work locations are so diffuse as not to be useful. In other cases, important traffic corridors can be identified and some found have had sufficient densities to justify new rapid transit corridors. Presumably, the time is not far off when composite maps will be possible lending much greater accuracy to transit route predictions. (See figure 8-14.)

With sophisticated tools being developed, transit planning within the next decade will change dramatically from practices known today. As

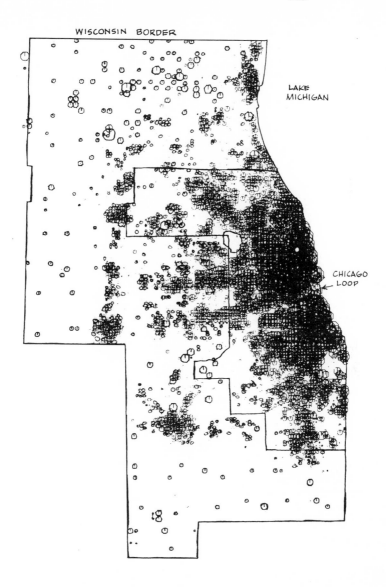

Courtesy of Ashish Sen and Siim Soot, professors, University of Illinois at Chicago Circle.

Figure 8-12. Computer Map of Population Density in Chicago Region. Portions of Chicago have densities equal to downtown To-kyo (40,000/sq.mi.) as indicated by the large symbols in the Loop area. Suburban concentrations along commuter rail lines can be traced radiating from the Loop. Small groupings of symbols indicate location of rail stations showing how transit shapes a city.

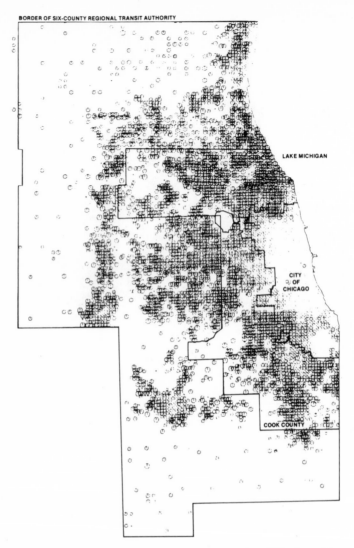

BORDER OF SIX-COUNTY REGIONAL TRANSIT AUTHORITY

LAKE MICHIGAN

CITY OF CHICAGO

COOK COUNTY

Courtesy of Ashish Sen and Siim Soot, professors, University of Illinois at Chicago Circle.

Figure 8-13. Computer Mapping of Families with Two or More Cars. The concentration of two-car families within the suburbs indicates the effectiveness of public transportation within Chicago proper. The high-density, two-car area represents the key regions for potential energy conservation. The largest symbol means 100 percent of the families own two cars for each one-quarter-section area and the smallest symbol means 10 percent of the families own two cars or more.

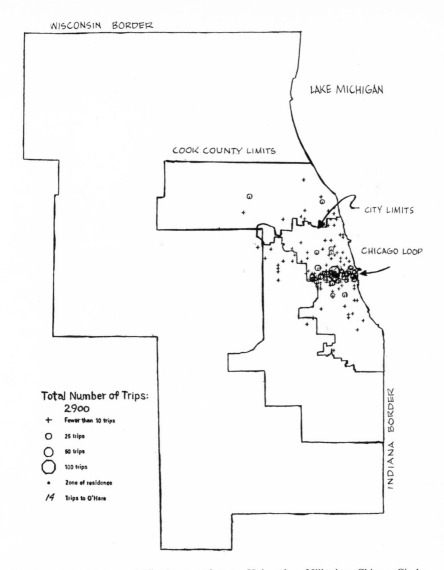

Courtesy of Ashish Sen and Siim Soot, professors, University of Illinois at Chicago Circle.

Figure 8-14. Computer Mapping of Journey-to-Work Trips. Shown here is an area of one-quarter-section from the 1970 census, namely, all of the households on Madison between Damon and Western. The work destinations are mapped. A very strong east-west corridor is found stretching across the width of the city suggesting a need for transit where little presently exists.

data and information increase and become better understood, handbooks of the type frequently used in other engineering and planning endeavors will gradually become available. Building a firm groundwork for such planning handbooks is one of the most important activities of present-day efforts.

Commentary: Problems in a Manager's Planning Handbook

Roger Bacon (1220-1292) wrote: "He who know of not mathematics shall never learn any of the other sciences; and what is more, will never recognize his own shortcomings nor discover their proper remedies." These observations were believed heretic at the time and in spite of the friendship of this Franciscan monk with Pope Clement IV, Bacon was put in prison for these and other writings. Now, 700 years later, the world has come to accept these teachings with magnificent accomplishments in many fields of human endeavor. Public transportation cannot be said to be an outstanding example, however.

9 Toward Getting Things Done

There has been an important change in the way things happen within our government within recent years. Previously, government action was ordinarily taken in accordance with visible, established procedures: first, an action would be proposed in public, perhaps disguised as to the public benefit with regard to individual gain; then, a decision to take action would be made and again not all of the hand shaking behind the scenes would be clear but the decision itself would be visible; finally, the action would be taken, whether or not all facts were known and understood.

Today, in broad areas of interest important to national life, the sequence has been drastically altered. For some reason, the vast resources of information and means of analysis have slowed and sometimes paralyzed the decision-making process. The traditional modes of bringing action about seem to have broken down, and other ways of doing things have come into being. Sometimes it is surreptitious. That is, an action is taken first, without public knowledge, and then revealed, perhaps with the assistance of the media, after which it becomes a matter of public debate as to whether the action should continue. Often confusion ensues, that is, should the French Concorde be allowed to land? Will it really cause a thinning of the life-protecting ozone layer? Lawsuits are filed, citizen action groups meet, and a host of activities go on different from what the nation has witnessed before.

One clear reason for this state of affairs has to do with the growth of the bureaucracy. This method of deciding things has the great advantage of concealing the point of origin, one of the greatest fears of a bureaucratic system, and in concealing its origin shifts the weight of inertia of the system as a whole. In a modern bureaucratic state it turns out to be much harder to stop something that is already going than to prevent something from starting in the first place. This is the critical dilemma of modern transit, for example. There are many activities, such as transit, that few people would dare initiate but many people will accept once they are happening. The problem for transit advocates everywhere then is, clearly, to get something done, one must somehow get it going. Strategies and tactics for such purposes must, therefore, be uppermost in the minds of successful transit managers.

219

The Ad Hoc Task Force

One tactic that worked well on at least one occasion was that of the ad hoc task force, wherein experts and individuals of various backgrounds and interests are brought together to gain access to channels normally closed for the purpose of initiating some action. An interesting example of such a task force occurred in the fall of 1974. At that time, most transit properties throughout the nation were in dire economic straights for operating assistance funds, then prohibited by Congress. Efforts to interest the Department of Transportation had proven fruitless. Consequently, an influence organization, the U.S. Conference of Mayors, unable to get a hearing with the secretary of transportation, formed a consortium of city mayors, transit experts, at least one automobile manufacturer, and other authorities in transportation, and gained a meeting with the President, Gerald R. Ford. At this meeting, economists pointed out that unless operating assistance was provided, the transit industry would have no recourse but to raise fares substantially. It was estimated that about $350 million would be taken out of the economy through fare increases to meet operating deficits. However, the effect of this economic drain on the consumer price index would be such that the procurement offices of the United States government would find it necessary to spend an additional $500 million for the same goods planned for purchase. Since it was actually cheaper for the federal government to give the operating subsidy rather than pay the inflated price increases, the president called together the necessary congressional leaders to bring about, within a few weeks' time, the legislation that for the first time provided federal operating subsidies.

The point, of course, is that investments in transit represent an overall savings in total benefit bookkeeping. Some say that a $1.00 transit investment saves $1.50 overall. The hope is that somehow, with the developments in technology assessment and our increased technical ability to analyze and understand complicated processes, improvements will come about both in the way things are done and the validity of the analysis.

Benefit Bookkeeping

If the true benefits of public urban transportation were known and understood, public transit would not be in the dilemma it is today. The protracted pleadings for funds, the talk of only "starter systems" and of incremental stretch-outs for systems under construction, would not be heard.

Unfortunately, such is not the case. Somehow the benefits have not been convincing. The statistical arguments seem unreasonable. To say that economists have computed that each gallon of gasoline would have to be taxed 40¢ to pay for ancillary costs of the automobile seems unreasonable. Pointing out, for example, that 40% of fire department calls nationwide are for burning cars, and that they are currently paid for by property taxes, is not of interest to the average citizen. It may be true, but the ramifications are that a better accounting system might somehow cause an individual to lose his automobile (next to a home, the second largest investment of a lifetime). Consequently, it is not likely that individuals will show marked interest in a better balancing of the books.

Progress away from extravagance comes incrementally. Gradually it is clear that many of the things the nation does as a whole are wasteful and not in our own best interests in the long run. The need for improved efficiency in transportation both from the standpoint of being one way to live within our means as a people and as a conscious way to improve urban form and life-style is coming about, albeit at a pace that is exasperating in its slowness.

Traditionally, the objectives of improved public transportation systems have included a variety of personal and social benefits. The only element of public transit that has won passengers out of their automobiles has been those cases where appreciable time savings was involved. Whether by express bus as on the Shirley Highway near Washington, D.C. or on commuter rail service, time savings is one key issue to which the public responds. Conversely, ridership is lost at a continuing, steady pace from long, cross-town bus routes, which move at a sluggish pace in congested traffic on city streets. Time savings require, however, extensive investments and these come only slowly with time.

Aside from the time-savings factor, the public has not yet responded to other personal factors in terms of a strong advocacy; increased safety, savings in personal costs in vehicle space and better land use, improved energy conservation, reduction in noise and air pollution, and equality of access for the poor, handicapped, and elderly. All of these factors have some influence as is evident from the increase in interest and support of public transportation programs in the past decade.

The broad community benefits are also known somewhere within that public consciousness, if indirectly: revitalization of the economic base, more equitable distribution of income and reduction in welfare costs, increased participation in urban opportunities, improved quality of the urban environment, and energy conservation are mentioned as important contributions of public transit. A flow chart of the so-called primary linkages [1] is shown in figure 9-1.

Analytic arguments have generally not been convincing on a sufficient level to produce strong citizen support for transit. Such arguments have only been strong enough to produce some progress. The people of San Francisco did vote by nearly 70 percent to support transit and other cities

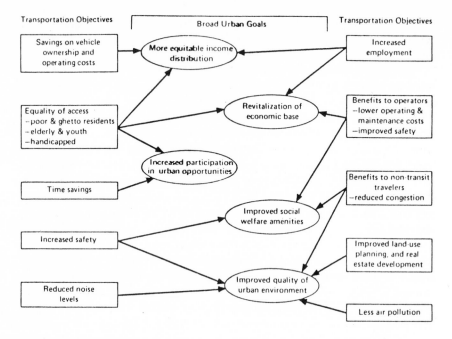

Source: Nancy Sheldon and Robert Brandwein, *The Economic and Social Impact of Investments in Public Transit* (Lexington, Mass.: Lexington Books, D.C. Heath and Co., 1973).

Figure 9-1. Broad Urban Goals and Transportation Objectives.

throughout every part of the country have approved major bond issues. The point of many transit proponents is that this support is not yet as strong as it eventually will be, or will have to be.

Part of the slowness comes from a tendency of all democracies not to act on problems until they reach a crisis stage; any government that runs on the process of citizen advocacy, as a successful democracy must, have considerable problems, therefore, in dealing with anticipatory problems, that is, problems that only a sector of concerned individuals may sense and understand. Gaining broad public support for issues that reflect complicated analysis requires an ability to communicate and project that has not yet been developed in this country.

Certainly, the facts are there for those who would see them, but few cases are so clear cut as to affect the individual in a conscious way:

1. For every 50 persons diverted to public transit, a reduction of approximately 30 cars in the traffic stream occurs. Even cities, however, with excellent transit systems seem nearly as congested as those without such systems. The overall advantages of transit in terms of total community economics are not always in evidence in personal life-style either.

2. Research shows that truckers [2] in the Los Angeles region would accrue $1.2 million in time savings if highway congestion were reduced due to operation of a rapid transit system.

3. Estimates [1] show Los Angeles could reduce its monthly welfare roles by 4,200 people if rapid transit were available to provide better access to jobs.

4. It has been estimated that only about 36 percent of the handicapped between the ages of 17 and 64 are members of the work force as compared with 71 percent of the nonhandicapped of the same age group. These handicapped used either a bus or streetcar to get to work [3]. Better transit could clearly work to reduce the handicapped unemployment. One study [4] found that for 30 percent of the handicapped seeking employment, inadequate transportation was considered the principal obstacle for finding a job.

5. Automobiles require extensive public space, land taken from tax roles that could be revenue producing, thus reducing the tax burden generally. It is computed that the average automobile requires 300 sq. ft. or storage at home, another 300 at work, 600 while traveling, another 200 for sales and service, for a total of 1,400 sq. ft. or about the size of a family living unit. One projection showed that if urban transit were not in operation, an additional 6,000 parking spaces would be required at a cost of $12 to $56 million [5]. In Miami, studies showed that unless some rapid transit were provided, an additional $30 million would be spent on parking alone not counting the lost use of space [6]. In Chicago, analysis showed that if the rapid transit were to shut down, an additional ten lanes of freeway would be needed to transport rush-hour employees.

6. Rapid transit always brings increased business investment. In Toronto [5], the Yonge Street subway resulted in an increased $50 billion in appraised land use and facilities. In Brooklyn, land values increased 10 to 12 times with the introduction of a new transit station [7]. In San Francisco, since the voters approved BART, over 500 floors of office space have been added to the San Francisco skyline on Market Street. Between 1962 and 1969, office space construction increased capacity from 16.7 million sq. ft. to 30.4 million sq. ft., an increase of 78 percent, and all within five minutes from a BART station [8].

7. Air pollution has been identified as a known hazard aside from the toll in human discomfort [9]. In 1966 the surgeon general stated [10]: "There is no doubt that air pollution is a factor which contributes to illness, disability and death from chronic respiratory diseases." Just the expenditures on house painting costs, car wash outlays, curtain cleaning, and so on were shown in a Washington, D.C. study to cost the average family more than $355 per year [11]. Smog reduces property value; a St. Louis study [11] showed that property declined an average of $245 per house for each 0.25 mg rise in sulphur trioxide.

Perhaps part of the reason that these advantages are slow to be perceived by the public is due to the fact that our society is highly interdependent. There are many reasons why any given action occurs. Most benefits discussed, although true, take place over a long period. Truckers would realize substantial advantages if congestion were reduced, but the building of a viable transit network in any region takes years, perhaps a decade to complete; by that time the trucking firm may be into another business in another area. The advantages are realized in increments too small to be realized by many businesses. The deterioration of health due to air pollution again is so slow as to be nearly imperceptible to the average person, which in itself is one reason for the seriousness of the problem. Similarly, housing values may decline for many reasons, of which smog is only one, and the owners may choose to move for completely different reasons. Thus, the cost of not having viable transit is rarely immediately perceived, and, therefore, the advantages are only marginally appreciated, in terms of personal benefit to the electorate.

What is happening, however, is that costs are rising and impinge on the next generation. One reason why so-called urban sprawl, the move to the suburbs, was so successful is that it was easy and cheap. Homes could be bought with little or nothing down. There was a wide choice. The commuting to work by automobile increased the absence of the breadwinner of the home, but by only a portion of an hour. It was affordable and practical, regardless of what the inefficiencies of total societal bookkeeping might be.

Today, most of the cheap land around cities is gone. The increase in population is now just enough to have insufficient space for the new generation, in the old land-use manner. Housing costs have also increased markedly. Consequently, major metropolitan areas already show an increase in condominium construction and grouped housing of a different type. No one has seriously suggested this has come about because of academic arguments showing planned and efficient housing is more efficient to society as a whole. It is simply becoming the only way that reasonable housing can be delivered to the newer generation based on what it can afford to pay.

However, these events did have their beginning in an earlier era during the 1960s; officials and concerned citizens began examining the true costs of the diffusion of population to the fringe areas of metropolitan areas. Reports with titles such as "Do Single Family Homes Pay Their Way?" and "Happiness is a Green Place" began appearing. In April 1974 a comprehensive study of costs and alternatives was published. Called *The Costs of Sprawl*, this work [12] prepared a detailed cost analysis of all crucial factors of land use and development.

The results were startling. It had been known for some time that low-density housing contained many hidden cost factors absorbed for the most part by other sectors of the society. What was not known, and perhaps suspected only by a few, was the degree to which "sprawl" affects the nation's total economy.

Stated in the most general form, sprawl is the most expensive form of residential development in terms of economic costs, environmental costs, natural resource consumption, and many types of personal costs.

In terms of alternatives, the study showed that better planning will reduce all types of costs, especially the total costs that local governments must absorb. These conclusions can be quantified as follows:

1. Planned development of all densities is less costly to create and operate than sprawl in terms of all costs, especially those of environmental and energy consumption. These cost differences are particularly significant in terms of costs borne by local governments. The figures show a 4 percent savings on construction, 15 percent savings in road and utility, 20 percent costs in land-use efficiency, 6 percent in public services (water and sewer), 6 percent savings in maintenance and operation, and 8 percent cost savings in local government.

2. The environmental advantages are also significant: 30 percent less air pollution from reduced automobile travel, and improved life quality factors not easily quantified such as the preservation of significant wildlife and vegetation habitats, minimized noise, less run-off and peripheral flooding, sedimentation, and water pollution.

3. Energy consumption is reduced at least 15 percent in a planned community even considering only automobile travel.

These cost savings simply assumed better planning and organization of single-family dwellings. If apartment dwellings are considered, all of these cost improvement factors are multiplied, even allowing for much larger recreation and open spaces per household. Some figures are:

1. Assuming the same living-space area, the apartment construction cost is only 57 percent of the single-family dwelling.

2. Cost of roads and utilities is reduced 80 percent.

3. Cost to local government is reduced 62 percent.

4. Public maintenance and operating costs are reduced 73 percent.

5. Energy and water use is reduced 40 percent.

6. The cost of commercial and shopping centers is reduced at least 20 percent both in terms of construction and servicing.

Given that the population is increasing and the nation's resources are being depleted, it is essential that costs of living be reduced if the quality of life is not to be reduced. In assessing likely effects between 1970 and the year 2000, it was concluded from this study that a greater urgency exists than might have been suspected based on obvious trends in daily life-style: "It is imperative that public authorities determine the nature of these differences (between unplanned and planned communities) . . . and the total amount of resources required to accommodate future growth."

The management of public transportation is clearly dependent on the type of community being addressed. Present communities have been developed only for automobile use and, because of the lack of planning, cannot easily adapt to the advantages of public transit. It is nevertheless clear that the nation will be forced, because of land and resource constraints in addition to economic considerations as to costs of government and maintenance, to pursue a different course in terms of community development. This will have a significant affect on the use of public transportation and on transit management.

As detailed studies have shown, these new and imperative changes in the physical form of the community are not accompanied by deterioration of the quality of life, but represent an improvement in almost every of human concern, whether it is access to needed services and shopping, the environment, aesthetics, or free time available for recreation and enjoyment. The pioneering spirit, which encouraged individuals to go anywhere and build anything, will now find other forms of expression.

Our situation today is said to be one of being well into a new phase of social and economic development, but without realizing it. We may not yet have found an agreed-upon direction that can be easily articulated and understood, but there is evidence that we are gaining on disorder and inefficiency and gaining in matters of consequence to the human condition in general. Transportation is very much a part of all of these factors of change, crucial part of the outcome, yet strangely tenuous in its perceived impact.

The importance of transportation in building the nation's future is not to be underestimated even though this importance may not always have been understood or appreciated by those who must eventually support it. Transportation management is, therefore, essentially in the position of progressing into a new era where needed support is not always in evidence, but where the signs and guideposts of a new era can be recognized. To respond effectively to this coming era in human progress is the crucial challenge of transportation management today.

Commentary: Toward Getting Things Done

"In dreams begin responsibility." The appealing dignity of these familiar words of the poet Yeats remind us that even in this land of freedom and abundance, our hopes for the future are tied with our willingness to assume responsibility for the results. This responsibility need not be a burden, but can be a rare opportunity. Those regions that solve their transportation problems will survive and prosper. It can mean a brighter future for ourselves, our children and our grandchildren. We must all work together so this opportunity is not lost. It is time the world sees something of what a strong, vital people can accomplish.

Appendix A
Excerpts from "A Statement of National Transportation Policy"

1. The policy statement issued by William T. Coleman, secretary of transportation, on September 17, 1975, began with this foreword:

This National Transportation Policy Statement is my initial attempt to set forth the broad policy considerations that should underlie the Federal government's response to the Nation's transportation needs.

Policy is an evolving process that reflects and builds on existing laws, precedents, programs and public perceptions. It indicates the changes that are required to move toward a better transportation system, consistent with other important national priorities.

Comprehensive policy also reveals to the public the inevitable inconsistencies in laws and programs that arise from our pluralistic political processes and changing conditions. This exposure is important because it helps us work toward a more useful definition of Federal responsibility vis-à-vis the private sector and State and local governments.

We summarize our policy direction and principles in Chapter I: Policy Overview. The subsequent text discusses those principles in more depth, relating them to programs and legislative initiatives. We have attempted to state our views directly and candidly because it is important that the public understand the reasons and thinking that underlie government decision making.

Since policy formulation is a continuing process, the positions presented here are preliminary and may be amended and refined as we learn from experience and as we listen to your views. Also, no transportation policy statement may be fully implemented unless it has the support of the Congress, Federal and State public officials, shippers, consumers, the industry and other concerned citizens. Thus, we invite and urge your criticisms and comments. In fact, your views are most necessary because a living, national transportation policy must reflect an evolving concensus of what the American people want and expect from their transportation system.

2. The first chapter of the policy statement is called "Policy Overview"; the following statements are abstracted from the original (pages 8 and 9):

Urban Transportation

Urban transportation policy must be part of a coordinated and comprehensive approach to city and suburban needs. Each urban area is unique—with different

---

The policy statement may be purchased from the Superintendent of Documents, U.S. Government Printing Office, Washington, D.C. 20402 for a price of $1.15. Reference stock number is 050-000-00103-2.

needs and different development objectives—and each should be free to choose for itself the transportation solutions that best serve its objectives. At the same time, urbanized areas across the country have many transportation problems in common.

Federal policy for urban transportation should at once respond to locally determined transportation goals and serve such national objectives as the enhancement of our cities as vital commercial and cultural centers, control of air pollution, conservation of energy, access to transportation for all citizens and particularly the disadvantaged, facilitation of full employment and more rational use of land.

Because mass transit serves all these objectives, simultaneously and well, it merits strong Federal as well as State and local support. This is now possible because of the National Mass Transportation Assistance Act of 1974 and Federal-Aid Highway Act of 1973, which provide greater local flexibility in the use of Federal financial assistance and offer new and expanded sources of funds for public transportation improvements. States and metropolitan areas must work together to update their proposals for Federal funding on the basis of changing conditions and a continuing comprehensive planning process.

Many Americans live in suburban places of lower population densities, which are well served by the private automobile, and tend to commute to work in central cities, which suffer from the adverse side effects of the automobile—congestion, pollution—and thus would benefit from public transit. An efficient metropolitan transportation system, therefore, requires a mix of modes, public and private, properly coordinated and utilizing the relative advantages of each.

The burgeoning demand for increased public services, however has put a serious strain on available public funds, making it essential that Federal resources be allocated fairly and used with maximum effectiveness. Therefore, Federal policy should:

- Require analysis of the cost-effectiveness of transportation alternatives as a condition of eligibility for Federal assistance for any major mass transportation investment;
- Require as a condition of Federal funding the development and implementation of transportation system management plans to improve the efficiency of existing facilities and transit services and conserve energy (e.g., carpools, exclusive bus lanes, higher parking fees);
- Give increased emphasis to improved service in the near term as distinguished from building new facilities to meet anticipated transportation demand over the long term;
- Regard the present types of fixed rail systems as appropriate only in a few highly populated metropolitan areas where State and local land use and development policies are explicitly committed to the generations of high densities sufficient to support these modal choices on a cost-effective basis;
- Support efforts to develop a type of rail system which is much less costly to build, operate and maintain;
- Give preference in Federal funding to localities that demonstrate consistency with broader community development goals, effective processes for resolving jurisdictional conflicts, effective cost controls and a substantial State, regional and local financial commitment;
- Encourage the planning and operation of public transit on a coordinated, metropolitan-wide basis.''

3. In chapter II, "Government and the Private Sector," under "Subsidy," pages 16-17, urban transportation again receives consideration:

Subsidy

Federal subsidies, both direct and indirect, were in many instances developed without adequate consideration of the competing interests or at a time when conditions were unlike those of today. As a consequence, there are inequities in present subsidy practice. We must, therefore, periodically examine Federal subsidies of private elements of the transportation sector for their continued validity. New requests for Federal subsidy should be given careful scrutiny.

The power of subsidy to promote national objectives is exemplified by the mail rate subsidy which fostered the development of our national and international air transportation system, now the best in the world. Conversely, the inequities that may result from such well-intentioned policies may be illustrated by the present structure of Federal programs in support of the different surface freight-carrying modes:

Water Carriers. The inland and Great Lakes water carriers do not maintain or pay taxes on the rights-of-way they use. The inland waterway system is under constant improvement by the Corps of Engineers and enjoys the benefits of services by the U.S. Coast Guard. International water carriers receive Federal construction and operating subsidies.

Motor Carriers. The extent to which motor carriers bear their share of the cost of construction and maintenance of the highways they use has not been fully established. The most recent study, which indicated underpayment, is soon to be updated. In any case, motor carriers are not required to make massive capital outlays for their use of highway rights-of-way.

Railroads. The Nation's rail freight carriers build and maintain their own rights-of-way and often pay taxes on them.

While the carriers in all of these modes are today privately owned, our national transportation policy often affects their respective cost structures and the relative competitive relationships of the modes themselves. For example, if the barge operators were to be charged for rights-of-way now constructed and maintained wholly out of public funds, parallel rail transportation would be better able to compete on price.

In the passenger area, we see similar disparities:

Urban Transportation. Most intracity bus companies and all subway systems are owned and operated by the public and require Federal, State and local government funds to supplement cash from the fare box in order to keep operating and for major capital improvements.

Rail. Some railroads continue to operate passenger trains privately without Federal assistance (e.g., the Southern Railway System). AMTRAK, on the other hand, provides Federally-subsidized rail passenger service which the private sector is unwilling or unable to provide.

Intercity Bus. Privately owned intercity bus companies receive no direct payment of public funds and make a partial if not complete payment to government at all levels for their use of the streets, roads and highways through fuel and license taxes. They receive a benefit in that they do not have to make an initial capital outlay for their right of way. They must compete, however, with subsidized AMTRAK and local service airlines.

Air. Privately owned trunk airlines receive no direct public subsidy while local service airlines receive some for the purpose of providing air service to small communities. The users of airlines pay essentially their full share of airport and airway costs through ticket and waybill taxes. In contrast, general aviation, also privately owned, pays only about one-fifth of its share of the costs, primarily through fuel taxes; the general Federal taxpayer pays the rest.

Auto. Privately owned automobiles pay to maintain our streets and highways through registration fees, tire taxes, and gasoline taxes paid at the State and local levels. The Federal gasoline tax has provided more than adequate capital funds for highway construction.

Government subsidy practices thus reflect a conflict in national concerns. On the one hand, government should provide equitable treatment to all modes because the market place is the best barometer of efficiency and consumer preference and for reasons of essential fairness. On the other hand, subsidies may be used to achieve Federal, State or local objectives or to remedy problems which differ among the modes, or the government may consciously favor a particular mode because it provides vital services consistent with other economic and social benefits such as energy efficiency, clean air and water, elimination of congestion and improved community development and land use. Consequently, differences in treatment are to be expected among modes, as well as among segments within modes. But, public policy now requires that the differences be the result of consciously made decisions and for specific reasons that are valid today other than habit, politics or historic precedent.

We are now conducting an analysis of the present structure of Federal subsidies from general revenues to the transportation sector. Since subsidies appear in a number of guises, the results of such a study depend somewhat upon what is included as a subsidy and how the amount is computed. The preliminary findings on the direct 1974 expenditures by mode indicate great contrast: The marine mode received more than one-third of the direct Federal subsidy monies, while the pipelines received virtually none. *Urban mass transit was* the second largest beneficiary followed by aviation, highways and rail. Highway subsidies were about twice as large as these of rail.''

4. In chapter III, under the subheading of "Federal Assistance to States and Local Governments," the following comments appear regarding public transportation (from pages 27 and 28):

Urban Transportation. The Federal interest in urban transportation arises, in part, from transportation laws of recent years, culminating in the National Mass Transportation Assistance Act of 1974, and from other laws responding to the problems of complex metropolitan areas and establishing new Federal priorities for the environment, community development and energy conservation. There is strong and continuing Federal interest in preserving our central cities, vital to the Nation's cultural and economic life. There is a similarly strong Federal interest in promoting rational patterns of development in our suburbs. Low density residential development create a costly and inefficient sprawl of metropolitan growth in disregard of shrinking energy, land and environmental resources.

Effective metropolitan-wide transportation planning is therefore necessary to meet Federal air quality and noise pollution standards and to satisfy Federal laws protecting historic buildings, park and recreational lands. It is also needed to assure that transportation in metropolitan areas is accessible to all citizens, including the disadvantaged, for whom mass transit may be the only transportation alternative.

Urban transportation policy must be part of a coordinated and comprehensive approach to city and suburban needs. While mass transit can effectively serve the various Federal priorities, no single mode can meet all the transportation needs of a metropolitan area. An efficient urban transportation system requires a mix of modes, public and private, working in a cooperative partnership as elements of a unified and coordinated metropolitan-wide transportation system—a system that involves not only the automobile and public transit, but also easy access to rail passenger and air service.[a] This is now possible, in part, because of the National Mass Transportation Assistance Act of 1974 and the Federal-Aid Highway Act of 1973, which provide greater local flexibility in the use of Federal financial assistance and offer new and expanded sources of funds for public transportation improvements. The Urban Transportation Program envisioned in our proposed new highway legislation would extend this flexibility to transfer funds between highways and mass transit even further. Ultimately, we would anticipate a complete merger of highway and mass transit funding authority for metropolitan areas.

A Federal-local partnership of this magnitude should be premised on the principle that each urban area is unique—with different needs and different development objectives—and each should be free to choose for itself the transportation solutions that best serve its objectives. Federal support for mass transportation must therefore be flexible, relying on local ability to assess requirements, identify and evaluate opportunities for improvement and initiate needed action.

The Federal government, however, has an essential obligation to ensure that Federal funds for mass transportation assistance are used prudently, and that there is a solid and defensible basis for local transit decisions that are premised on Federal assistance.

In assessing future Federal support for mass transit, we believe that preference should be given to communities that:

(1) Demonstrate innovative, comprehensive planning and propose cost-effective utilization of existing facilities. Under Section 5 (d) (a) of the National Mass Transportation Act of 1974, we will require each urbanized area, as a condition of Federal assistance, to submit a stage implementation plan listing the measures that will be adopted to improve the efficiency of transit services, conserve energy and improve air quality. This plan should include action such as a coordinated network of reserved transit lanes, improved transit scheduling and dispatching techniques, traffic signal preemption, and other bus preference techniques, parking restrictions, differential highway tolls and transit fares to promote off-peak travel, staggered work hours, and incentives to shift people from private cars to transit and carpools.

(2) Demonstrate how transportation planning responds to long-term metropolitan planning objectives in meeting urban problems, assuring effective processes for resolving conflicts among jurisdictions and interest groups and harmonizing with land use and community development objectives.

(3) Propose alternatives that do not involve high capital investment costs and the prospect of substantial continued operating subsidies, and that will provide

---

[a] The bicylclist and pedestrian should also have an increasingly prominent role in urban transportation planning. By improving their pathways and safety, there will be substantial benefits to the community and to the health of its citizens.

improved service in the near term. Government cannot afford indiscriminate massive open-ended construction programs. We will encourage urban areas to implement their transportation plans in a time-phased, incremental fashion so that tangible benefits can be realized from the investment in the short run. We will also emphasize the need to improve the quantity, quality and efficiency of service as a condition of continued operating assistance.

(4) Demonstrate commitment to projects proposed Federal support by the extent of their own financial participation.

Fixed rail systems are appropriate only in a few highly populated metropolitan areas where State and local land use and development policies are explicitly committed to the generation of high densities sufficient to support these modal choices on a cost-effective basis.

Additional highway construction in major urban areas, including nonessential segments of the Interstate System, should be the subject of careful review and planning in order to avoid expensive lawsuits and the needless expenditure of the taxpayer's money on the design of projects that fail to meet the many tests of Federal, State and local priorities. New urban highways are appropriate when they are part of a coordinated metropolitan transportation plan and will help to alleviate congestion, air pollution, noise and energy waste by diverting through-traffic around city centers, or from side streets. New highways are inappropriate where they induce more automobile commuters into the city center, encourage suburban sprawl, divert passengers from public transit and violate environmental standards. Since some highway planning preceded recent public concerns with the environment and energy, the State and local communities should be encouraged to review those proposals to make sure that new highways are still the best solution to their transportation problems. Where there is an acceptable and preferable transportation alternative, it should be selected; where the highway is still the appropriate solution, it should be built as soon as possible.

5. The final section of the statement, chapter VI, "Concluding Note" reflects the present concerns including those of public transportation (from pages 49 and 50):

In our democratic constitutional society, a transportation policy statement issued by the head of one Federal Department does not become the Nation's transportation policy. Even more important, a transportation policy is not a plan. Policy helps direct decision making along more rational lines toward national goals and provides the reasons for proposed changes, but it does not define the optimal infrastructure or transportation system for the future, or identify the cities in which we will build rapid transit systems or designate which railroads will become the appropriate nationwide interstate freight railroad system.

It may be useful in conclusion, however, to anticipate what the transportation system might look like if the policy set forth in this statement were first adopted and then successfully translated into programmatic action. We would see a more safe, efficient, accessible, diverse, competitive transportation system, mainly in the private sector, which would enhance the Nation's environment, economy and quality of life, by providing:

• Privately owned, financially healthy and competitive high performance national networks of marine, rail, truck, bus, pipeline and air freight and passenger service;

- A system of feeder line and links that provide access to the nationwide interstate systems and effectively meet the transportation needs of urban, suburban and rural areas, privately maintained where possible, and supported, on a fiscally responsible basis, primarily by States and local governments with Federal financial participation where necessary;
- A safer, more energy-efficient, environmentally sound automobile that will be utilized more intelligently and with greater social responsibility but which will continue to be the most pervasive form of transportation, essential to our life style and economic activity.
- A modern highway system which serves the needs of the future, consistent with our environmental and new energy concerns;
- Progress each year in safety performance, environmental protection, energy conservation and transportation crime prevention.
- Comprehensive urban transportation systems, involving efficient mass transit and a mix of modes that are consistent with broader metropolitan goals;
- Safe and modern rural transportation facilities, providing access to the Interstate network and creating an infrastructure that enhances rural living and development;
- A strong international transportation system with the participation of privately owned financially health, unsubsidized U.S. flag carriers;
- More equal competition between firms and among modes, freed from the encumberance of outmoded regulatory restraints;
- New, more cost-effective, energy-efficient and intermodal technology;
- Accessible transportation for the poor, the minority, the handicapped and the elderly;
- Opportunities for employment and advancement for all citizens, particularly women, minorities and the disadvantaged;
- An economy conducive to adequate capital formation, enabling private firms to earn a reasonable return on investment and keep facilities and equipment modern, safe and environmentally sound.

A more perfect transportation system will evolve primarily through the efforts of an innovative, competitive, and forward looking private sector. The Federal Government must support this evolution, reinforcing the strengths of our system and shoring up its weakness.

At a time when there is claimed to be an erosion of public confidence in the capacity of government to respond to public needs efficiently, it becomes imperative to define clearly and realistically the responsibility and potentiality of the Federal Government.

Only when the reality of limited Federal resources if fully recognized and expectations accordingly brought into balance with that reality, will the gap between the promise of legislation and the performance of the government is narrowed.

Only when we cease to seek narrowly focused solutions to the problems of each transportation mode and begin to plan comprehensively, will the distortions of Federal intervention yield to the efficiency of intermodal competition and cooperation.

Only when we realize that practices of the past do not necessarily provide the best transportation systems needed today, will we have the courage to terminate programs that have fulfilled or failed to attain their original purposes, and seek new solutions to the needs of tomorrow.

Only when the level of government closest to the problems has the necessary financial resources program flexibility and management authority, will we succeed in blending transportation systems with broader national and community development goals.

Although there are old habits and ways of thinking, and strong forces, of politics, precedent and program inertia at work, we must now seek new, more efficient ways of responding to the Nation's transportation needs. This document is an initial attempt to do so. It may well contain inconsistencies, omissions and policies that the public will not accept. It is hoped, however, that it will stimulate discussion of the issues so that there will be progress and ultimately consensus on a policy which will all work implement.

References

Chapter 1
Introduction

1. *Public Policy Development*, by R.F. Baker, R.M. Michaels, and E.S. Preston, New York: John Wiley & Sons, 1975.
2. "Reshaping the American Dream," by Thomas Griffith, *Fortune*, April 1975.
3. *The Urban Transportation Problem*, by J.R. Meyer, J.F. Kain, and M. Wohl, Cambridge; Harvard University Press, 1965.

Chapter 2
Urgent Issues in Public Transportation

1. National Transportation Report of 1974, U.S. Department of Transportation, Washington, D.C., 1975. (Subtitled: "Current and Future Prospects").
2. "Improvements of Mass Transit Security in Chicago," by the Transportation Research Institute and Urban Systems Institute of Carnegie Mellon Institute, Pittsburgh, June 30, 1973.
3. "Chicago Transportation Planning and Development," by Milton Pikarsky, presented before the National Academy of Engineering, Washington D.C., October 12, 1972.

Chapter 3
Regionalism

1. "Metropolitan Area Definition," by Brian Berry, U.S. Bureau of the Census Working Paper 28, Washington, D.C., 1969.
2. "Journey to Work," Subject Reports, U.S. Bureau of the Census, Washington, D.C., June 1973.
3. "The Concept of Community Development," Iowa State University, March 1961.
4. "The Regional Factors in National Planning," National Resources Committee, Washington, D.C.: U.S. Government Printing Office. 1935.
5. "Crisis and Solution: Public Transportation in Northeastern Illinois," Governor's Task Force, Chicago, January 1973.

6. "An Assessment of Community Planning for Mass Transit," by the Office of Technology Assessment, United States Congress, Washington, D.C., March 1976.

7. "Toward More Balanced Transportation," Report A-49; by the Advisory Commission on Intergovernmental Relations, Washington, D.C., 1975.

Chapter 4
The Evolution of National Transportation Policy

1. "Reshaping the American Dream," by Thomas Griffith, *Fortune Magazine*, April 1975.

2. *Improving National Transportation Policy*, by John H. Frederick, American Enterprise Institute, Washington D.C., 1959.

3. *National Transportation Policy*, by Charles L. Dearing and Wilfred Owen, The Brookings Institution, Washington, D.C., 1949.

4. "What the President Is Proposing," *Business Week*, January 22, 1966, p. 160.

5. "Congress Fears Creation of a Czar in Transportation Department Legislation," by George C. Wilson, *Aviation Week*, Vol. 84, No. 15, April 11, 1966.

6. "Hearings Will Open on Proposal for New Department," *Congressional Quarterly Weekly Report*, Vol. 24, No. 12, March 25, 1966, p. 614.

7. Editorial, *Life Magazine*, Vol. 60, No. 11, March 18, 1966.

8. "They All Want to Call the Shots," *Business Week*, May 28, 1966, p. 78.

9. "Toying with Transportation," *Wall Street Journal*, June 1, 1968.

10. "First Annual Report," U.S. Department of Transportation, Washington, D.C., 1972.

11. "National Transportation Report—Current Performance and Future Prospects," U.S. Department of Transportation, Washington, D.C., December 1974.

12. "A Review of Urban Mass Transportation Administration Guidelines for Evaluation of Urban Transportation Alternatives," National Research Council, Transportation Research Board, Washington, D.C., February 1975.

13. "Federal Aid Highway Act of 1975," President Ford's Message to Congress, July 7, 1975.

14. *Federal-Metropolitan Politics and Commuter Crisis*, by Michael N. Danielson, New York: Columbia University Press, 1964, pp. 125-26.

15. *Highway Revenue and Expenditure Policy*, by Phillip H. Burch, Jr., New Brunswick: Rutgers University Press, 1962, p. 243.

16. "How the Interstate Changed the Face of the Nation," by Juan Cameron (quoting Daniel P. Moynihan, Harvard professor and presidential advisor), *Fortune Magazine*, July 1971, pp. 78ff.

17. "The Legislation of Balance," by Milton Pikarsky, American Society of Civil Engineers, Preprint 1773, New York, July 1972.

18. *Superhighway-Super Hoax*, by Helen Leavit, New York: Doubleday, 1970.

19. "National Transportation Policy—A Proposal," *Transit Journal* (APTA), Vol. 1, No. 1, February 1975.

20. "Troubled Urban Interstates," *Nation's Cities*, December 1970, p. 8.

21. "Highway Fund Challenged—Hit as Distorted," by Charles E. Flinner, *The Herald*, April 8, 1965.

22. *National Municipal Policy*, chapter 5, "Transportation," National League of Cities, Washington, D.C., 1975.

23. "Urban Transportation Policy: Time for Reorientation," by V.R. Vuchic, presented at the National Conference of Democratic Mayors, New Orleans, March 1975.

24. "The Politics of Technological Choice: Some Lessons from the San Francisco Bay Area Rapid Transit District (Bart)," by Stephen Zwerling, *Bulletin of the Institute of Governmental Studies*, Vol. 4, No. 3, June 1973.

25. "A Study of Technology Assessment," by the Committee on Public Engineering Society, National Academy of Engineering, for the Committee on Science & Astronautics, U.S. House of Representatives, Washington, D.C., July 1969.

26. "Statement Before the House Appropriations Subcommittee on Transportation," by Claude S. Brinegar, secretary of transportation, Washington, D.C., March 5, 1974.

27. "Comments on the Statement Before the House Appropriations Subcommittee on Transportation, 5 March 1974," by Vulkan Vuchic, Department of Civil Engineering, University of Pennsylvania, Philadelphia; see also "National Transportation Policy: The Basic Requirements for Progress," a statement presented at the House Transportation Appropriations Subcommittee, Washington, D.C., 6 March 1974.

28. "Urban Transportation or Dilemma at a Time of Decision," Staff Report, Subcommittee on Investigation and Review to the Committee of Public Works, House of Representatives, Washington, D.C., April 1973.

29. "Toward a New Economic Policy," Monograph No. 26, by Michael Boretsky, U.S. Department of Commerce, presented at the Smith-

sonian Institute in Washington, D.C., 1974. See also *U.S. Technology: Trends and Policy Issue*, Monograph No. 17, The George Washington University, Washington, D.C., October 1973.

30. *Attitudes, Innovation and Public Policy*, Harriet Nathan, Editor, Institute of Governmental Studies, University of California at Berkeley, 1972.

31. "Tomorrow's Transportation—New Systems for the Urban Future," U.S. Department of Housing and Urban Development, Office of Metropolitan Development, Washington, D.C., 1968.

32. "The Transportation System of Our Nation," Message from the President of the United States, House of Representatives, Document No. 384, 87th Congress, 2nd Session, Washington, D.C., April 5, 1962.

33. "A Study of Urban Mass Transportation Needs and Financing," U.S. Department of Transportation, Washington, D.C., July 1974.

34. "A Study of Revenue Mechanisms for Financing Urban Mass Transportation," U.S. Department of Transportation, Washington, D.C., February 1974.

35. "F.T.C. Chief Calls Role of Agencies Inflationary," *New York Times*, October 8, 1974.

36. "A Report on the Actions and Recommendations for Energy Conservation through Public Mass Transportation Improvements," U.S. Department of Transportation, Washington, D.C., October 1974.

37. "Getting at the Big Facts in Transportation," by D. Christensen and M. Pikarsky, *Aeronautic/Astronautics*, September, 1975.

Chapter 5
The Capital Grant Program

1. *Urban Mass Transportation Assistance Act of 1970*, Report No. 91-1264, House of Representatives, 91st Congress, 2nd Session, Washington, D.C., 1970.

2. "Transit's Need for Assured Federal Aid," by Michael Cafferty, presented at the ASCE National Transportation Engineering Meeting, Milwaukee, Wisconsin, July 17-21, 1972.

3. *Capital Grants for Urban Mass Transportation, Information for Applicants*, Urban Mass Transit Administration, U.S. Department of Transportation, Washington, D.C., June 1972.

4. *The Urban Mass Transportation Assistance Program, Federal Transit Subsidies*, by George W. Hilton, American Enterprise Institute for Public Policy Research, Washington, D.C., 1974.

5. *Mass Transportation Capital Improvement Grants, Information*

for Applicants, Office of Mass Transportation, Illinois Department of Mass Transportation, Chicago, November, 1972.

6. "Capital and Operating Assistance Formula Grants: Interim Guidelines and Procedures, Advanced Notice of Proposed Rulemaking," *Federal Register*, Monday, January 13, 1975.

7. "UMTA Proposed Guidelines," *Federal Register*, Friday, August 1, 1975.

8. "Step-by-Step Mass Transit Proposed," *Washington Post*, August 9, 1975.

9. "The Local Role in Programming," by Milton Pikarsky, presented at the Conference on Transportation Programming Process, Orlando, Florida, March 24, 1975.

10. "Federal Aid to Municipal Transportation: Salvation or Pandora's Box?" by Richard A. Abend, *The Federal Bar Journal*, pp. 277-78.

11. *Report by the Governor's Commission on Organization*, Illinois Department of Transportation, Springfield, January 1972.

Chapter 7
Financing and Marketing Structure

1. "Federal Transit Subsidies," by George W. Hilton, American Enterprise Institute for Public Policy Research, Washington, D.C. 1974.

2. "Toward a Policy for the Automobile," address by Kenneth Orski, associate administrator for policy and program development, UMTA, Washington, D.C., April 21, 1975.

3. "A Study of Revenue Mechanisms for Financing Urban Mass Transportation," U.S. Department of Transportation, Washington, D.C., February 1974.

4. "A Study of Urban Mass Transportation Needs and Financing," U.S. Department of Transportation, Washington, D.C., July 1974.

5. "A Proposal for a National Transportation Policy," American Public Transit Association, Washington, D.C., 1975.

6. "Future of the Highway Trust Fund at Issue," *Transportation and Communications*, August 23, 1975, pp. 1850.

7. "The Need for a Transportation Trust Fund and a Transportation Energy Allocation Proposal," Testimony presented by Milton Pikarsky before the Committee on Public Works' Subcommittee on Transportation, U.S. Senate, Washington, D.C., July 18, 1975.

8. *The Urban Transportation Problem*, by J.R. Meyer, J.F. Kain, and M. Wohl, Cambridge: Harvard University Press, 1965.

9. "The Economic Rationale for Transportation Planning," by Jo-

seph S. DeSalvo, University of Wisconsin, as published in *Perspectives on Regional Transportation Planning*, Lexington, Mass.: Lexington Books, D.C. Heath and Co., 1973.

10. "A Critique of Governmental Intervention in Transport," by James C. Nelson, Washington State University, as published in *Perspectives on Regional Transportation Planning*, Lexington, Mass.: Lexington Books, D.C. Heath and Co., 1973.

11. "Urban Travel Demand," Special Report 143, proceedings of a conference at Williamsburg, Virginia, Highway Research Board, December 3-7, 1972.

12. Summaries of DOT Projects on Travel Demand," Department of Transportation, Washington, D.C., December 1974.

13. "Energy, The Economy and Mass Transit," Office of Technology Assessment, U.S. Congress, Washington, D.C., June 1975.

14. "The Patronage Effects of Free-Fare Transit," by James I. Scheiner, *Traffic Quarterly*, January 1975.

15. *Some Evidence of Transit Demand Elasticities*, by Michael A. Kemp, Working Paper 708-52, Washington, D.C." Urban Institute, November 1971.

16. "The Effect of Fare Reduction on Transit Ridership," *Summary Report 1, Analysis of Transit Passenger Data*, Metropolitan Atlanta Transit Authority, Atlanta, Georgia, 1973.

17. "Energy, The Economy and Mass Transit," Office of Technology Assessment, United States Congress, Washington, D.C., June 1975.

18. *Stochastic Choice of Mode in Urban Travel: A Study Binary Choice*, by S.L. Warner, Evanston: Northwestern University Press, 1962.

19. *Socio-Economic and Level of Service Variables, Their Effect on Demand for Public Transit*, by D.P. Consantino, Syracuse: Syracuse University Press, 1973.

20. "Supply Functions for Public Transport: Initial Concepts and Models," by E.K. Morlock, Manuscript, 1975.

21. "Measuring the Influence of Soft Variables on Travel Behavior," by Richard B. Ross, *Traffic Quarterly*, July 1975.

Chapter 8
Problems in a Manager's Planning Handbook

1. "Measuring the Effects of Social Innovation by Means of a Time Series," by Donald Campbell, Northwestern University, from *Statistics, A Guide to the Unknown*, San Francisco: Holden-Day, Inc., 1972.

2. "Characteristics of Urban Transportation Systems: A Handbook for Transportation Planners," Report URD DCCO. 74. 1. 4. DFOT-UT-T0019, by DeLeuw Cather and Company, Washington, D.C., May 1974.

3. "Evaluation of Rail Rapid Transit and Express Bus Service," Report DOT. P-6520-1, Institute for Defense Analysis (IDA), Virginia, October 1973.

4. "Systems Analysis in Urban Transportation," *Scientific American*, July 1969.

5. "Economic Characteristics of the Urban Public Transportation Industry, Institute for Defense Analysis, Virginia, February 1972.

6. *Transit Fact Book*, an annual publication of the American Public Transit Association, Washington, D.C. 20036; see also *Transportation Facts and Trends*, annual publication of the Transportation Association of America, Washington, D.C.

7. "Nationwide Personal Transportation Study," a series of eleven reports, by Federal Highway Administration, U.S. Department of Transportation, Washington, D.C., 1972-74, see also "Public Transportation in the Chicago Region," The Transportation Center, Northwestern University, Chicago, February 23, 1973.

8. "Journey to Work," *1970 Census of Population*, by the Bureau of Census; Washington, D.C., June 1973; see also "Where Workers Work," prepared by Department of Labor, state of Illinois, Springfield, 1974. (Also known as the Postal Zone Study.)

9. *The Urban Transportation Problem*, by J.R. Meyer, J.F. Kain, and M. Wohl, Cambridge: Harvard University Press, 1972.

10. "Summary Data for Selected New Urban Transportation Systems," Report No. DOT-TSC-OST-72-35, by Robert F. Casey, Department of Transportation, Washington, D.C., November 1972.

11. "A Report on Actions and Recommendations for Energy Conservation Through Public Mass Transportation Improvements," Department of Transportation, Washington, D.C., October 1974.

12. "Annual Miles of Automobile Travel," Report No. 2, Nationwide Personal Transportation Study, Department of Transportation, Washington, D.C., April 1972.

13. "A Report on Actions and Recommendations for Energy Conservation Through Public Mass Transportation Improvements," Department of Transportation, Washington, D.C., October 1974.

14. "Purposes of Automobile Trips and Travel," Report No. 10, Nationwide Personal Transportation Study, Department of Transportation, Washington, D.C., May 1974.

15. "Automobile Ownership," Report No. 11, Nationwide Personal Transportation Study, Department of Transportation, Washington, D.C., December 1974.

16. "The Potential for Energy Conservation," by the Office of Emergency Preparedness, Executive Office of the President, Washington, D.C., October 1972.

17. "Household Travel in the United States," Report No. 7, Nationwide Personal Transportation Study, Department of Transportation, Washington, D.C., December 1972.

18. "Guidelines to Reduce Energy Consumption Through Transportation Actions," prepared by Alan M. Voohees & Associates for Department of Transportation, Washington, D.C., May 1974.

19. "Mass Transit and Energy Conservation," by Mayo S. Stuntz, Federal Energy Administration, Washington, D.C., March 5, 1975.

20. "National Transportation Policy," *APTA Transit Journal*, February 1975.

21. "Evaluation of Rail Rapid Transit and Express Bus Service in the Urban Commuter Market," Report DOT P 6520-1, prepared by the Institute for Defense Analyses; Washington, D.C., October 1973.

22. "Energy Conservation and Transportation," by E.L. Tennyson, *Mass Transit*, February 1975.

23. Speech before the American Mining Conference, by Frank G. Zarb, Federal Energy Administrator, Washington, D.C., May 5, 1975.

24. *Handbook of Chemistry and Physics*, Cleveland: The Chemical Rubber Co., pp. F-226.

25. *Chicago Public Works: A History*, by R.J. Daley, and M. Pikarsky, Skokie, Ill.: Rand McNally, 1973, pp. 152.

26. "A Perspective of Transportation Fuel Economy," by R.D. Nutter, The Mitre Corporation, Washington, D.C., April 1974.

27. "Per Passenger-Mile Energy Consumption and Costs for Suburban Commuter Service Diesel Trains," by E.W. Walbridge, University of Illinois, Chicago Circle, August 1974.

28. "Energy Conservation in Urban Transit Systems," by M.J. Bernard and Sarah LaBelle, Regional Transportation Authority of Northeastern Illinois Report TR-75-06, Chicago, December, 1975.

29. "Highway Fund Challenged—Hit as Distorted Funding for Transportation," by Charles E. Flinner, *The Herald*, April 8, 1975.

30. "A Summary of Opportunities to Conserve Transportation Energy," by J. Pollard, D. Hiatt, and D. Rubin, Final Report, Department of Transportation, No. TSC-OST-75-22, Washington, D.C., June 1975.

31. "A Reporter at Large: The Energy Bazaar," by Elizabeth Drew, *The New Yorker*, July 21, 1975.

32. "The Need for a Transportation Trust Fund and a Transportation

Energy Allocation Proposal," Testimony by Milton Pikarsky, before the U.S. Senate Subcommittee on Transportation, Washington, D.C., July 18, 1975.

33. "Getting at the Big Facts in Transportation," by D. Christensen and M. Pikarsky, *Aeronautics/Astronautics*, September 1975.

34. "U.S. Energy Use at New High in 1971," News Release, U.S. Bureau of Mines, Washington, D.C., March 31, 1972.

35. "Transportation Energy Conservation: Opportunities and Policy Issues," by Eric Hirst, *Transportation Journal*, Spring 1974.

36. "Patterns of Energy Consumption in the United States," Stanford Research Institute, prepared for the Office of Science and Technology, Washington, D.C., January 1972.

37. "Taxing Gasoline," Editorial, *New York Times*, February 3, 1975.

38. "Energy, Manpower and the Highway Trust Fund," by R. Bezdek, and B. Hannon, *Science*, August 23, 1974.

39. "Energy and Environmental Aspects of U.S. Transportation," The Mitre Corporation, Washington, D.C., February 1974.

40. "Transportation Energy Conservation Options," Report No. DP-SP-11, by D. Rubin, et al., Department of Transportation, Washington, D.C., October 1973.

41. "Home-to-Work Trips and Travel," DOT Report No. 8, Nationwide Personal Transportation Study, Department of Transportation, Washington, D.C., August 1973.

Chapter 9
Toward Getting Things Done

1. *The Economic and Social Impact of Investments in Public Transit*, by Nancy Sheldon and Robert Brandwein, Lexington, Mass.: Lexington Books, D.C. Heath and Company, 1973.

2. *Benefit/Cost Analysis of the Five-Corridor Rapid Transit System for Los Angeles, California*, Palo Alto, California, Stanford Research Institute, 1968.

3. "Latent Demand for Urban Transportation," Carnegie-Mellon University, Pittsburgh, May 1968, p. 57.

4. *Travel Barriers: Transportation Needs of the Handicapped*, Cambridge: Abt Associates, p. 2, August 1969.

5. *St. Louis Metropolitan Area: Rapid Transit Feasibility Study, Long-Range Program*, PB 204-060, St. Louis: Parson, Brinckerhoff, Tudor, Bechtel, Sverdup & Parcel, August 1971, pp. 79-80. See also *A Tran-*

sit Improvement Program for the Utah Transit Authority, McLean, Virginia: Alan M. Voorhees & Associates, Inc., March 1971, p. 53.

6. *Public Transit Master Plan*, Philadelphia: Simpson and Curtin, 1969, p. 88.

7. "The Economic, Effect of Rapid Transit on Real Estate Development," by G. Warren Heenan, *The Appraisal Journal*, April 1968.

8. "The Impact of Transit: The Central Business District," by Terrell W. Hill, *Transportation: Lifeline of an Urban Society*, Pittsburgh Urban Transit Council, Fourth International Conference on Urban Transportation, Official Proceedings, pp. 140-46, 1969.

9. "Fundamental Air Pollution Considerations for Urban and Transportation Planners," by Edwin W. Hauser, Leonard B. West, Jr., and A. Richard Schleicher, *Traffic Quarterly*, January 1972, pp. 73-74.

10. *Concepts for Evaluating Center City Transportation Programs and Projects*, by M.J. Kamrass, J. Crane, P. Hughes, and E. Parker, Virginia: Institute for Defense Analysis, December, 1969, p. 38.

11. *Joint Development: An Economic Input*, by David W. Rasmussen, Tallahassee, Florida: Florida State University, June 1970, p. 20 ff.

12. "The Costs of Sprawl: Environmental and Economic Costs of Alternative Residential Development Patterns at the Urban Fringe," by Real Estate Research Corporation, prepared for the Council on Environmental Quality, Office of Policy Development and Research, Department of Housing and Urban Development, and the Office of Planning Management, Environmental Protection Agency, Washington, D.C., April 1974.

Bibliography

Chapter 3
Regionalism

The following documents are of interest in connection with research on the Regional Transportation Authority of Northeastern Illinois (RTA):

Legal History of Mass Transit Operations in Northeastern Illinois, Task force on a Public Transportation System for Northeastern Illinois, state of Illinois, December 1, 1972.

A summary of the legal history of 70 years of mass transportation in Northeastern Illinois from 1900 to 1970, the chronology covers both proposed and implemented legislation, and documents the roles of the state and local government, as well as regulatory agencies in dealing with mass transportation in Northeastern Illinois.

Crisis and Solution, Public Transportation in Northeastern Illinois, Task force on a Public Transportation System for Northeastern Illinois, Chicago, January 1973.

This work details recommendations that shaped the final RTA legislation. The report summarizes the mass transit problems facing Northeastern Illinois as well as the transportation facilities in existence and those needed. Included in the recommendations is a discussion of fundamental transportation issues as well as alternative solutions.

Legislative Analysis, Regional Transportation Agency Statutes and Proposals, Governor's Task Force on Public Transportation in Northeastern Illinois, Chicago, January 1973.

Considered one of the few documents of its kind in existence, this document compares in matrix form all the major regional transportation authorities in the United States and Canada. There are six major areas of comparison with several subdivisions in each. They include: responsibilities and powers of a transportation agency; form and structure of governing bodies; form and structure of management and operations; fiscal requirement and capabilities; relationship with existing governmental and transportation entities; and a "catch-all" category.

Public Transportation in the Chicago Metropolitan Region, a Benefit Statement, Development Research Associates, Chicago, 1973.

This document considers the "costs" and "benefits" of three approaches to the transportation problems of Northeastern Illinois: (1) status quo, (2) stabilization, (3) investment and expansion. Although the methods and results can be argued, this is one attempt to systematically analyze the benefits of a RTA (and P.T.) in relationship to the investment costs. Benefits considered include access time, pollution, fare structure, and service levels.

"Special Report, the RTA," *Planning in Northeastern Illinois*, Northeastern Illinois Planning Commission, Chicago, Vol. 16, No. 2, 1974.

This is an analysis of the RTA in the context of total regional planning and the dramatically increased regional accessibility through coordination of existing transportation facilities.

"The Critical Need for the Regional Transportation Authority," by Milton Pikarsky, Chicago Transit Authority, Chicago, 1974.

This text forms the basis of many speeches given in support of the RTA. It outlines specific benefits to the region and advocates that public transportation be viewed as a public service, much like a hospital or police force.

Perspectives on Regional Transportation Planning, by Joseph S. De-Salvo, Santa Monica, California, Rand Corporation, 1973.

This work is one of the first books to address regional transportation planning and administration. As such, it is a collection of major papers on various aspects of regional transportation that have been published elsewhere. Of particular interest are the papers dealing with definition of a transportation region and a critical review of existing regional planning experience in the United States.

Intergovernmental Responsibilities for Mass Transportation Facilities and Services in Metropolitan Areas, The Advisory Commission on Intergovernmental Relations, Washington, D.C., April 1961.

This work is useful in outlining the fundamental problems underlying urban mass transportation in all metro areas. In addition, the report reviews the creation of the first RTAs and discusses the problems and prospect of regional government.

Regional Transportation in Northeastern Illinois, by Joseph A. Tecson, manuscript submitted to the *Chicago Bar Record*.

This is a well-researched summary of the evolution of the RTA. Of particular value are the sections on the RTA legislation referendum and RTA's first year, because they are written from the point of view of an "insider"—an RTA board member who represents a suburban constituency.

"RTA Today," *CTA Quarterly*, Vol. 1, No. 2, Reviews the first year of RTA, including charts of the first RTA grant schedule and the first RTA budget.

Improved Accessibility, by John E. Hirten, an American Society of Planning Officials, Policy Report, Chicago, March 1, 1975.

The report is divided into four sections: (1) Role and Impact of Transportation, (2) Evolution of National Urban Transportation Policy, (3) Recent Policies, (4) Elements of a Proposed Urban Transportation Policy. Section three is extremely valuable as an annotated list of all recent federal legislation affecting urban mass transportation.

"The Regional Transportation Authority," by Ronald C. Johnson, *Chicago Public Works*, Vol. 3, No. 4, 1974.

A promotional piece for RTA, this article summaries the composition, financing, and administrative approach of RTA. Particularly useful is a glossary of "RTA isms" and a table of intraregional access times using pleasing transport facilities.

Illinois Department of Transportation, Report by the Governor's Commission on Organization of the Illinois Department of Transportation, Springfield, January 1972.

Valuable in understanding the structure and administrative orientation of IDOT, this report contains numerous charts showing how IDOT relates to other transportation groups in the planning and funding of transportation projects.

Urban Mass Transportation, A Dozen Years of Federal Policy, by George M. Smerk, Bloomington: Indiana University Press, 1974.

In this book, Smerk has examined the creation and evolution of urban transportation from several points of view. Beginning with a historical chronology of legislation, he examines the transportation institutions, railroads, commuter railroads, and trends in financing and ridership behavior, as well as the results of various grants and demonstration projects on these institutions.

Chapter 5
The Capital Grant Program

"The Capital Grants as a Subsidy Device," by William B. Tye, *The Economics of the Federal Subsidy Program*, A Compendium of Papers, Department of Transportation, Washington, D.C., 1973.

"Elderly and Handicapped Transportation Services," Codification of Requirements, *Federal Register*, February 26, 1975, pp. 8314-19.

"Evaluation of Federal Effort in Mass Transportation," by George M. Smerk, *Traffic Quarterly*, October 1972.

A Guide to the 1972 National Transportation Needs Study, Department of Transportation, Washington, D.C., 1971.

"The Legislation of Balance," by Milton Pikarsky, presented at the ASCE National Transportation Engineering Meeting, Milwaukee, Wisconsin, July 17-21, 1972, preprint 1773.

Mass Transportation Capital Improvement Grants, Procedural Guide for Grantees, Office of Mass Transportation, Illinois Department of Transportation, Chicago, September 1973.

Mass Transportation Capital Improvement Grants, Information for Applicants, Office of Mass Transportation, Illinois Department of Transportation, Chicago, November 1972.

National Transportation Planning Manual (1970-1990), General Instruction, U.S. Department of Transportation, Washington, D.C., July 1970.

A Review of Urban Mass Transportation Administration Guidelines for Evaluation of Urban Transportation Alternatives, Transportation Research Board, National Research Council, Washington, D.C., 1975.

Chapter 6
The Cities and UMTA

The major sources of information for this chapter were from annual reports published by the various operating authorities, special brochures and news releases. Two useful books were *The Urban Transportation Factbook*, parts 1 and 2, published by the American Institute of Planners, 1776 Massachusetts Avenue, N.W., Washington, D.C. 20036. A set of reports published by the Office of Technology Assessment under the general title "An Assessment of Community Planning for Mass Transit," U.S. Congress, 1976, is for sale by the U.S. Government Printing Office, Washington, D.C. 20402, under stock number 052-003-00149-7. Twelve volumes are to be published during 1976 at a price of $1.15 each. These volumes do not include Baltimore, Cleveland, or New York, but do include St. Paul-Minneapolis, which was not presented in the present chapter.

Index

Ogilvie, Richard B., 50, 53, 56
Operating Assistance: action, 173, 220; first
    use, 13; funding of, 153, 154; legisla-
    tion, 98, 107; need for, 66, 73; objec-
    tions to, 13, 22

Paris: rapid transit hours, 25; rapid transit
    size, 33
Patricelli, Robert E., 23
Personal Rapid Transit (PRT): cost vs. ca-
    pacity, 200; system design, 29
Pettibone, Hollman D., 13
Philadelphia: electrical production, 211;
    funding, 136; highway transfer, 137;
    operating assistance, 154, 194; oper-
    ating data (PATCO), 198, 204; rapid
    transit ridership, 29; SEPTA (region),
    46, 47
Planning, 58ff; agencies, 58-65; conferences,
    66, 73; review processes, 67-69, 71
Planning Agencies. See Cities (history)
Policy, 75ff; character of, 76-83; compre-
    hensive, 85-90; crisis oriented, 83-85;
    DOT statement, 100ff (appendix A,
    229); federal influence, 94ff; manage-
    ment of, 90ff
Political Influence, 12-14, 49
Profits, 6, 8

Rapid Transit: cities having, 133; countries
    having, 162; effect on auto owner-
    ship, 134, 135; effect on station spac-
    ing, 193; fares, 26; major cities
    (hours), 25; necessary density, 29;
    operating costs, 204; operating data,
    194-198; rail versus bus issue, 191,
    192
Regional Transit Authority of Northeastern
    Illinois, 45-47, 49-58, 65
Regionalism: Amtrak, 44; Chicago, 49-58;
    criteria for, 42; general, 39ff; transit
    regions, 46-51; types, general, 18, 40;
    UMTA, 41
Revenues, 4, 27-29
Ridership: by city, 33; by year, 36; demand
    analysis, 168ff, 175; demographic,
    174; fare effects, 168ff
Roche, James, 12

San Francisco: area and density, 137, 138;
    BART, 22, 48, 49, 155ff; construction
    costs, 201; electrical production, 211;
    funding, 136; highway transfers, 137;

history, 155-157; investment growth,
    223; operating assistance, 154; oper-
    ating data, 198; SMSA rank, 152;
    transit energy use, 196
Saturday Review, 8
Scheduling: general, 175ff; implementation,
    178, 179
Seattle: area and density, 137, 138; electrical
    production, 211; funding, 136; histo-
    ry, 157-159; operating assistance,
    154; SMSA rank, 152
Sen, Ashish, 216
Stevensen, James, 8
Subways. *See* Rapid Transit

Tokyo, 25, 33
Toronto: construction cost, 201; energy
    consumption, 196; investment
    growth, 223; operating data, 194
Traffic fatalities, 191
Transportation, general: full employment
    policy, 10; Gallatin's report—1808,
    76; historical, 3ff; objectives, 222;
    percent G.N.P., 7; percent total em-
    ployment, 7; rising costs, 21; union
    influence, 11

Ullman, A., 8
U.S. Conference of Mayors, 220
U.S. Department of Transportation: need
    for, 86; organization, 91
Urban area, 39, 40
Urban goals, 222
Urban Mass Transportation Administration
    (UMTA): cities, 133ff; formation of,
    97-99; funding, 136, 137; grants, 109-
    131; in DOT, 91; legislation table,
    103-107; New York assistance, 153;
    operating assistance, 154; regions, 41
Urban Sprawl, 224-226

Volpe, John, 97
Voting data, 56, 97, 98, 140, 150, 156, 158,
    159

Weiner, Edward, 66
Washington, D.C.: area and density, 137,
    138; construction costs, 201; electri-
    cal production, 211; funding, 136;
    highway transfers, 137; history, 159-
    162; Metro, 22; operating assistance,
    154; operating data, 198

About the Authors

Milton Pikarsky is Chairman of the Board of the Regional Transportation Authority of Northeastern Illinois, a six county area of Illinois including Chicago. He earlier chaired the Board of the Chicago Transit Authority and was for ten years Chicago's public works commissioner. A professional registered engineer, he received a bachelor's degree in civil engineering from City College of New York before entering the U.S. Navy during World War II, and a master's degree in civil engineering from the Illinois Institute of Technology. He is the recipient of many awards and honors and is a member of the National Academy of Engineering.

Daphne Christensen is the Science Advisor for the Chicago Transit Authority and was Director of Environmental and Community Affairs for Chicago Public Works. Her undergraduate work was in physics and engineering at the University of Washington with graduate work at the University of Southern California and the California Institute of Technology where she was a Ford Foundation Fellow. Dr. Christensen received a Ph.D. in engineering science from Nebraska. She has headed up research groups in the aerospace industry in southern California and received a certificate in Urban Sciences from the University of California at Berkeley. She worked as a consultant for the U.S. Conference of Mayors in Washington, D.C. before going to Chicago in 1971.